Survival in the Classroom

# Survival in the Classroom

*Negotiating with Kids, Colleagues, and Bosses*

**Ernest R. House**

*University of Illinois*

**Stephen D. Lapan**

*Northeastern Illinois University*

Allyn and Bacon, Inc.          Boston London Sydney

*Second printing . . . September, 1978*

**Library of Congress Cataloging in Publication Data**

House, Ernest R
   Survival in the classroom.

   Bibliography: p. 275
   Includes index.
   1.  Classroom management.  2.  Teacher
participation in administration.  3.  Teacher—Student
relationships.
I.  Lapan, Stephen D., joint author.  II.  Title.
LB3013.H672   371.1′04   77-25247
ISBN 0-205-06093-5

*For* DONNA, *unfailing in her support and acceptance of those she loves, in recognition of her unvoiced thoughts.*

ERNEST R. HOUSE

*To* GLADYS *for all the books you didn't get to write.*

STEPHEN D. LAPAN

# Contents

*Preface*

*Survival in the Classroom* is intended as a message to the teacher. In unabashed terms it describes some of the most pressing concerns of the teacher's professional life—concerns such as discipline, testing, salary negotiations, tenure, principals, parents, teacher organizations, even getting a job. The book's suggestions on how to deal with all of these are offered in a straight-forward, often anecdotal style that we hope teachers will find enjoyable as well as informative.

The book is organized so that it can be read all the way through, but more likely it will be read section by section as particular problems make certain parts relevant. The book can be used by teachers in both preservice and in-service training courses, as well as passed from hand to hand within the schools.

The theme of the book is that the teacher faces an overwhelming set of demands from a wide range of groups: kids, colleagues, administrators, parents, school boards, interest groups, etc. Some demands are legitimate and some not, but in total they are overwhelming in number and often contradictory in substance. Demands from parents to teach their children to read, demands from children to love them, demands from the principal to control the class at all costs—all pull the teacher apart. The teacher has only so much time, limited resources, and—like all of us—limited ability and emotions. Tied to these demands, and hence greatly intensifying them, are all the vital parts of the teacher's career: his salary, his promotions, his mental well-being, his job itself, and his self-respect. What to do? There are various resolutions: some teachers try to meet all demands, working themselves to the bone and never "catching up," some play to one audience and burrow forward with the head down, many quit, and so on through a range of different responses.

Our solution is a different one, however. For someone who finds himself with overwhelming demands and limited power to affect the circumstances of his professional life, we think there is one most reasonable answer to the situation: he negotiates. Informally and formally, individually and collectively, one balances the demands of one group against those of others, always keeping in mind one's own goals, priorities, and self-interest, of course. Negotiation is not capitulation. One has certain powers and can muster considerably more, depending on the issues involved. We contend that negotiation is not only the rational and effective solution, it is the democratic one.

On the issue of salary, one negotiates formally with one's colleagues against the board; on the issue of innovation, one negotiates informally for resources as the head of a small group against the administrator; in classroom discipline one negotiates as an individual against the class. Of course, in order to negotiate successfully one must understand how the board thinks, how the principal thinks, and how the students think, as well as have a realistic appraisal of one's situation and an understanding of the negotiation process itself. Negotiating for survival as a teacher is what this book is about.

Since we hope each section can stand by itself as the teacher encounters a problem with a particular group, we have tried not to over-organize the book. It is divided into four parts. The first part describes the general circumstances of the teacher's job as we see it. It then presents our solution to these conflicting demands and ideas about how a teacher might move to implement this solution.

The next three parts are organized loosely according to the settings in which concrete events transpire. The most familiar is that of the classroom, and the major reference group there is the student. The second part describes what students expect of the teacher and suggest how the teacher might manage his or her class successfully by negotiating out the differences between what he or she wants and what the students want. The result, we think, is the type of classroom discipline and control that both teacher and students can live with. Specific, concrete suggestions are offered on how to achieve this.

Part three deals with the school setting as a whole: the teacher's colleagues, principal, central office staff, and superintendent. This part details the different perspectives each of these groups has, how they communicate with each other, and the intrigues one can expect to swirl around these groups. The final section tells how to start and maintain new programs—a very tricky business, but often necessary to promotion. There is a regular course of events of which one must be aware.

Part four describes teaching as a profession—from how to get a job and get on tenure to what to expect from teacher evaluation. Formal teacher organizations and legal teacher and student rights are discussed in the last sections. These have an important role in defining and expanding the limits within which the individual teacher works.

**E. R. House**
**S. D. Lapan**

# part one

# The Teacher

.

# 1

## Survival through Understanding and Negotiation: An Interview with the Authors

INTERVIEWER   Come on. Why are you guys writing another book for teachers? Don't you think there are too many floating around already?

AUTHORS   Well, there are a lot. But most of them aren't too good.

INTERVIEWER   Too good. You mean a lot of them are a bunch of bull.

AUTHORS   You said that. We didn't.

INTERVIEWER   What makes you think you can do any better? Chances are you're going to add to the drivel.

AUTHORS   The thought has occurred to us. But we finally decided we'd try anyway. We confess it may not work. But we thought we'd try.

INTERVIEWER   Why?

AUTHORS   Well, we thought we knew some things that might be helpful to teachers. Not to tell them how to do their job. Nobody can do that in a book. Or perhaps any other way. But to share some information that might be helpful. That's a modest aspiration, isn't it?

INTERVIEWER   What makes you think *you* know something useful? A lot of other people think the same thing and the result is usually disappointing.

AUTHORS   Well, for one thing we're trying to take the teachers' point of view. To see things from their perspective.

3

INTERVIEWER    Hah!

AUTHORS    No, really. We're trying to see what the problems look like from their perspective and provide some information that might be helpful.

INTERVIEWER    They already know what it looks like from their perspective. They don't need someone to tell them that, do they?

AUTHORS    No, of course not. But if we understand some of the problems from the teachers' perspective, maybe, just maybe, we could muster some information that might bear on those problems.

INTERVIEWER    You have information other people don't have?

AUTHORS    Not exactly. We do have a unique perspective of our own. We have been teachers ourselves—

INTERVIEWER    I was just about to ask that.

AUTHORS    —and we have been involved with the schools in teacher training and evaluation and research on teaching.

INTERVIEWER    Oh, boy. Just what we need, more research.

AUTHORS    It's true that most research is not relevant to teaching. Most of it is not even comprehensible to anyone outside the research field.

INTERVIEWER    You can say that again.

AUTHORS    Actually, there is a lot of stuff that *is* relevant to teachers and that they can make good use of.

INTERVIEWER    Like what?

AUTHORS    Like politics, for instance. The politics of the school and how it functions. The political scene in the office. A lot is known about this that never gets to the teacher.

INTERVIEWER    Hmmm. I haven't seen much along that line. Teaching is getting to be more and more a political game. Often called "Get the teacher."

AUTHORS    Right. The school has always been political. It's just more obvious and more intense now.

INTERVIEWER    You mean like who's brown-nosing the boss and who's on the teacher's back?

AUTHORS    Right. And where the boss is coming from and how to handle him and the kids and other teachers.

INTERVIEWER    Things *are* getting a little pressurized around here. Teaching is getting tougher all the time.

AUTHORS    That's right. You might even say that understanding and being able to analyze the classroom and school environment is necessary for survival for the teacher.

INTERVIEWER    Hey! *Survival in the Classroom.* I got sucked into that one.

AUTHORS    We're saying that the teacher needs to know how to deal with the other people in his environment, to understand where they're coming from and to have strategies for dealing with them. Strategies for surviving. Strategies for personal advancement, if that's the teacher's bag.

INTERVIEWER   And you guys were teachers once, right?

AUTHORS   One of us taught in a small rural district and in a large suburban district, and the other taught in an urban area. Both of us taught long enough to be experienced and fairly successful teachers.

INTERVIEWER   Congratulations.

AUTHORS   Then we both went into teacher training for a few years. Separately, of course. We found that the most effective teacher training was to work with teachers on things in their classrooms.

INTERVIEWER   Like what?

AUTHORS   Well, we might take the teachers' tests and help them analyze the questions on them. Or teach the teachers a way of analyzing their classes and help them to analyze their own classes. We found out that it always worked better if the teachers analyzed their own classes rather than analyzing someone else's or having us look at theirs for them. It was more meaningful if they did it.

INTERVIEWER   Okay, okay. We get the message. What next?

AUTHORS   Well, after a few years of that we got into evaluation and worked together on evaluation of a large-scale state program—one of the first big evaluations in the country. After that House stayed in evaluation and research, doing studies and articles and research books. He's especially noted for his political analysis of evaluation and innovation in education, of how fundamentally political these things are. Among other honors, in 1976 he was chairperson of the 12,000-member American Educational Research Association convention.

INTERVIEWER   Whoopee. Sure glad he took time to talk to us simple folk.

AUTHORS   Meantime, Lapan has gone back into teacher training. He has been working with teacher trainees in the classroom and in teacher centers. Students seek him out as someone who can really help with their teaching.

INTERVIEWER   Listen, I'm really impressed. You guys are so good you don't *have* to write another book.

AUTHORS   Well, we just wanted to let you know where we are coming from and what we're doing.

INTERVIEWER   So now you're both professors.

AUTHORS   Right. We still teach but being professors gives us time to study the problems and situations we're talking about. That's what the average teacher doesn't have that we have—time to study and reflect on things.

INTERVIEWER   At least you're right on one thing.

AUTHORS   We think we've had the time to read and collect information on significant issues, to pull things together, and to relate it to the experiences we've had ourselves. So our book is a combination of experience, research, and reflection on issues and problems teachers have.

INTERVIEWER   I notice that you've also put issues into the form of dialogues and plays and such. You've put in things that at least you guys think are funny.

AUTHORS   Well, we've tried not to be too cute. But we have tried to jazz things up a bit. Reading in education tends to be a little dull, don't you think?

INTERVIEWER   That's two things we agree on.

AUTHORS   And pompous.

INTERVIEWER   That should be a challenge for you.

AUTHORS   And not realistic.

INTERVIEWER   Bingo.

AUTHORS   We've had to avoid those things as best we can. I'm sure we haven't always succeeded.

INTERVIEWER   Don't lay this false modesty on us at this stage. You've just told us that you've written a book full of brand new ideas that will change our lives, and that the book is written in a dazzling style. I think you had better take off the sackcloth.

AUTHORS   Maybe we've oversold it a little bit. Nothing can tell teachers how to do their job. It's too complex. The very most one can hope for is to be helpful. That's all.

INTERVIEWER   O.K. So much for the fanfare. Do you really have something to say? Or is it all fanfare?

AUTHORS   I guess the main message is that teachers are beset on all sides by groups telling them to raise test scores, to humanize and not damage the children's personality, to be accountable, to be professional, and a dozen other things.

INTERVIEWER   Two dozen.

AUTHORS   A lot of these demands are conflicting. The teacher couldn't fulfill them all even if she wanted to and knew how.

INTERVIEWER   And a lot of the demands aren't even legitimate.

AUTHORS   Right. The teacher is subject to a lot of conflicting demands. Our advice is first to understand where these people are coming from. Why are they pushing for certain things? What's in it for them? For example, once you understand how ambitious superintendents are and how they want to move on to higher status and a higher paying job, you're well on your way to understanding and even anticipating their behavior.

INTERVIEWER   Now we're getting some place.

AUTHORS   The same thing is true of principals, the central office administrators, parents, the kids, and even other teachers. Each has his own perspective.

INTERVIEWER   Teachers, too?

AUTHORS   Sure. You have to understand your fellow teachers to be able to work with them, to survive day by day, to get them to do things, not to transgress their boundaries.

INTERVIEWER   Is there anything more powerful than understanding? That seems a little too passive to me.

AUTHORS   Understandably. Our second step in the plan for survival is to negotiate with those various forces. If the principal's main concern is not to have anyone rock the boat, you can negotiate with him on that.

INTERVIEWER   The teachers have some influence on that.

AUTHORS   Definitely. The teachers can make his life miserable if they want. One of the things the principal fears most is a few bad words about him floating back to the central office.

INTERVIEWER   The principal can also make life miserable for the teacher in a lot of ways.

AUTHORS   That's true. That's where the negotiating comes in. Each has the power to affect the other.

INTERVIEWER   Are you talking about the teacher by himself vis-à-vis the principal or as a member of an organized group like a teachers' union?

AUTHORS   Both. This is where it gets complex. The negotiation is not the simple two-sided negotiation of collective bargaining, although that might be part of it. The negotiations involve the superintendent, central office staff, principal, parents, and students simultaneously. The teacher sometimes faces these people as an individual and sometimes as a member of a group of colleagues.

INTERVIEWER   Like in collective bargaining.

AUTHORS   Right. But there are a lot of other small groups in which the teacher is active. For example, a small informal group trying to start a new program. Or a department trying to add a new staff member.

INTERVIEWER   All these involve a political role for the teacher.

AUTHORS   Yes. Teachers often think of themselves simply as individuals who teach groups of kids. Actually, they are members of groups and coalitions within the school system that push for quite a variety of things. We are suggesting that the teacher assume an aggressive, active role in these essential matters. That the teacher be a leader in this regard.

INTERVIEWER   A politician. A negotiator. An organizer. An instructional leader. Even an administrator at times.

AUTHORS   Yes. Of course the teacher is essentially and always a teacher. But even here the teacher must negotiate with her kids and arrive at agreements that work. Especially in areas like discipline.

INTERVIEWER   Negotiate with the kids?

AUTHORS   Why not? Isn't that what the teacher does anyhow, whether she calls it that or not?

INTERVIEWER   What if the kids want one thing and the parents another?

AUTHORS   That's precisely where the negotiation comes in. But you're leaving out an important person here—the teacher herself. The teacher is a real person and a highly skilled professional. What is it she wants? That also counts.

INTERVIEWER   I'm glad to hear someone recognize the needs of the teacher for a change.

AUTHORS   Absolutely. The teacher is a person with both individual and collective needs that are legitimate. To pretend otherwise is to be less than authentic. The teacher also has a right to pursue those needs.

INTERVIEWER   Negotiation is a way of doing that.

AUTHORS   Informally and formally, individually and collectively, the teacher balances the demands of one group against the others, always keeping in mind her own goals, priorities, and interests. That's the key to survival, both as a person and as a professional. And that's what this book is about.

INTERVIEWER   I must say I'm impressed with the idea. But aren't you getting a little preachy.

AUTHORS   Perhaps so. We tend to get a little righteous sometimes. It's just that we think self-sacrifice is admirable—up to a point. Then it becomes counterproductive, even in the job. Self-interest should be recognized as a legitimate concern. It can be dealt with better that way.

INTERVIEWER   Now, I notice you've divided the book into four main parts.

AUTHORS   Yes. The first part deals with the "authentic teacher"—some of the things we've been talking about here. We talk about what teachers and teaching are really like. To help teachers get a better understanding of themselves and their colleagues.

INTERVIEWER   Don't teachers already know what their colleagues are like?

AUTHORS   Yes, certainly. But it's also helpful to get a little distance from the job and to see it as others might describe it—the way it's always interesting to hear what a foreigner says about the United States. Also, we talk about some aspects of the job that teachers don't often talk about among themselves—the loneliness, the exhaustion, the guilt of not living up to highly idealized standards.

INTERVIEWER   The guilt?

AUTHORS   Yes. We contend that teachers have internalized an extremely idealistic set of goals that they can't possibly accomplish. "Developing every child to his fullest potential" is a wonderful ideal but there isn't anyone who could possibly do that, is there?

INTERVIEWER   This leads to guilt and exhaustion?

AUTHORS   In some people. And to other things in others. All that—the discipline problems the first year, the subjective experience of what it's like to be a teacher—is discussed in the first part of the book.

INTERVIEWER   The second part is about the classroom itself.

AUTHORS   Right. The teacher is the focus of the first part. Then we move in to the teacher operating in the classroom environment in the second part. This includes chapters about discipline problems and how to handle them, and on how to be credible with the kids—which we feel is a key element in effective teaching—and suggestions on how to plan teaching activities and get feedback on those activities.

INTERVIEWER    Do you really think these chapters are helpful?

AUTHORS    We hope they are helpful. They certainly are not "pie-in-the-sky" kinds of suggestions.

INTERVIEWER    They aren't going to solve all the teacher's problems.

AUTHORS    We said helpful, not magical. By the way, the book isn't really meant to be read all the way through at one sitting. There are common themes that run through the book and there is a logical progression from beginning to end. But we feel that teachers will want to read the chapters that they are particularly interested in. For example, if they are having discipline problems, they might want to read the chapter on discipline. If they are interested in starting a new program, they could read that chapter. If they are preservice students concerned about getting a job, they could read that one.

INTERVIEWER    If they are preservice students, they may even read the chapter on what teaching is like to see whether they went to be teachers.

AUTHORS    Right. Although there is no substitute for actual experience. So the book is meant to be read a chapter at a time. We have written each chapter in a different style. Some chapters are essays, some are dialogues, some are even plays. Some are light and funny, some are heavy.

INTERVIEWER    You wanted to make it not quite so dull.

AUTHORS    Right. When the teacher wants to read another chapter, she may be surprised and entertained by the novel mode of presentation. We intentionally varied the book's style.

INTERVIEWER    How can you present ideas in play form?

AUTHORS    Well, the teacher who is being evaluated or wants to read up on the tenure process may pick up the book and read the chapter on teacher evaluation. She will find a three-act play involving a teacher and a principal.

INTERVIEWER    We were talking about the contents of Part II.

AUTHORS    The last two chapters on the classroom deal with how to raise test scores and how to communicate what's going on in the classroom to parents. There seems to be a great deal of pressure on teachers over test scores. We think this pressure is ill-advised and that test scores are misunderstood by the public. Nonetheless, it is a pressing issue for teachers, and we offer advice on how to raise such scores both legitimately and illegitimately. The last chapter is on the critical problem of how to communicate to parents.

INTERVIEWER    The third part of the book is about the school.

AUTHORS    We move from a focus on the classroom to a focus on the school as a whole.

INTERVIEWER    This is where the administrators enter the picture.

AUTHORS    Yes, the first chapter in this section is about dealing with bosses. It presents an in-depth picture of how superintendents, principals, and central office staffers operate. The next chapter, on teacher evaluation, shows how teachers and administrators interact on tricky issues like teacher evaluation, particularly for purposes of tenure.

INTERVIEWER    That chapter's in the form of a play.

AUTHORS    Yes, and so are some of the others. "Starting New Programs and Getting Promoted" deals with the intricacies of these interrelated processes. In the last chapter, which is on office politics, we describe how to build a power base within a faculty.

INTERVIEWER    That's the one that has the interview with Machiavelli on school politics.

AUTHORS    Yes.

INTERVIEWER    The last part of the book deals with the profession itself.

AUTHORS    Yes. Of course getting a job is the first concern of anyone who aspires to be a teacher. We do not guarantee that anyone who reads our chapter about getting a job will be able to do so. But we do offer some helpful hints, based on experience, about how to go about it in the most effective manner.

INTERVIEWER    The chapter on teacher and student rights has to do with what is legally possible.

AUTHORS    Primarily legal. It's very difficult for teachers to keep up with all the rulings, regulations, and guidelines that define legally what teachers and students are able to do. We try to summarize those here.

INTERVIEWER    And that's the end of the book.

AUTHORS    Yes.

INTERVIEWER    Well, you really cover a lot of topics and material. If the book is half as good as you have made it out to be, it might be worth reading.

AUTHORS    Thanks.

INTERVIEWER    Now tell us the truth. In spite of all this rhetoric, didn't you really write this book in order to become famous and get rich?

AUTHORS    It's true that when people start to write books they are thinking of fame and fortune. By the time they get into them, however, all they really want to do is to get done.

INTERVIEWER    You did manage to finish it, at least.

AUTHORS    Having finished it, we have reduced our expectations considerably. We would be happy now if we become either rich *or* famous.

INTERVIEWER    Watch it. I'm in charge of this interview. I might be asked to review this book for a journal, you know. Thanks for your time. Now let's see if you can write as good a book as you talk.

# 2

## What Are Teachers Really Like?

### A DAY IN THE TEACHERS' LOUNGE

The memory, after all these years, is apt to play tricks. One may remember what did not happen and forget what did. Nonetheless, I can remember very clearly my first day of teaching and my first entry into the teachers' lounge. It is a strange world to stand in front of a class of students for the first time—the confusion, the fright, the panic. Afterward, one repairs with relief to the refuge of the teachers' lounge. It is a haven from the firing line. But the solace one receives there is limited. Companionship, yes, but not much help. Though teachers are surrounded by people, teaching is one of the loneliest professions around.

The mainstay of any teachers' lounge is the coffee pot. There one can always find a few convivial souls—or many depending on the time of day—seated around the urn like crusty New Englanders around a pot-bellied stove, patiently waiting for someone with a good story or a new bit of gossip. Judging from the dozens I've been in, teachers' lounges are all remarkably the same.

The conversation among the men (for the men and women teachers usually sit at different tables) dwells on athletics, and sometimes drifts to politics or to current events. Scandals involving the students are popular topics. The women often talk about their families or the social life of various students. Both men and women trade gossip as to what is happening in the school and who is doing what to whom.

There is plenty of talk among teachers, but it is not normally talk that might help one do his job better or that might help solve professional

11

problems. Eventually, the beginning teacher realizes that each teacher is on his own as a teacher, in spite of the friendliness of fellow teachers. One rises or falls on what one does by oneself behind the closed door of the classroom.

Recently I visited a classroom where the teacher was having a horrendous time with her students. The best students had been drained off for another teacher with more seniority, who consequently had quite a good class. The beginning teacher was caught with a class of the poorest students. Even the most experienced teacher would have had trouble managing the class and doing something educationally useful. For the inexperienced first-year teacher, it was a nightmare.

She admitted she was not doing well. I asked her if the other teachers and the consultants in the school were helpful to her. Yes, they helped supply materials. Had they been helpful in teaching the class? Oh, no! It was *her* class and *she* was responsible for it. It was no one else's duty to help her in any way with her teaching, as she understood it. Help was not offered and help was not asked for. Among teachers it is understood that one manages one's class by oneself. Sink or swim. Many sink.

It is not that there is not a close communication pattern among teachers within a school. In schools of about this size—about thirty teachers—news of a certain sort travels quite rapidly and freely throughout the school. The faculty contact structure is highly integrated. But apparently only certain kinds of information are transmitted. This is among the reasons why teaching is an isolated occupation.

The loneliness of the teacher on the job has historical roots. Schools started as single classrooms. The growth was cellular: more classrooms were simply added. It was not required that teachers come into contact with one another or cooperate in teaching, for there was only one teacher. Even in modern attempts at team teaching, teachers usually divide up the work by having one teacher teach one day and another the next.

The financial support of teaching was tied to the local property tax so that raising monies became a problem. With the resulting low pay, teaching was seen as a suitable career for a woman, and salaries were adjusted to what people thought an unmarried woman would need. An unmarried woman living at home could supplement her family's income quite nicely with a relatively low salary. Two or three unmarried daughters at home meant affluence.

To supply enough people for such a low-paying, high-turnover profession, entry into teaching was made relatively easy. People could enter the profession with little training and few requirements. An alternative manner of recruitment might have been the way in which modern doctors are recruited: through very high salaries and high social prestige. Entry into modern medicine is long and arduous but the rewards are great once one has attained the position.

Teaching, on the other hand, has remained a profession relatively easy to get into. In college one can decide at the last minute, as I did, to go into teaching. The idea of someone deciding suddenly to start practicing medicine is of course ludicrous—a reflection of the difference in entry standards. As the demand for universal education has increased, the supply of teachers has been maintained by building easy-access teachers' colleges, which are cheap and easy to get into and do not disqualify one for other types of employment.

The result of these policies is that people go into teaching because it is easy to get into (Lortie, 1975). Those who enter the profession are not necessarily the people most committed to teaching, and, as they are not required to endure a long, arduous training period in which the uncommitted are weeded out and the others made even more committed by the arduousness of the training, many teachers are not dedicated to teaching in the way that other professionals are to their occupations.

There are, of course, some teachers who are extremely dedicated. The ones who really want to be teachers also find it easy to get into the profession. The most common motivations for them are wanting contact with the kids and wanting to do something socially useful.

Teaching has also traditionally served as a step up the social ladder for people from blue-collar working-class families. This is more true of men than women. In fact, as a group women teachers come from higher-status homes than do men teachers. Women tend to decide to become teachers in high school, whereas men tend to decide when in college.

Although teaching is not a particularly high-paying occupation, it is a secure one—at least until recently. Also, teachers' colleges have traditionally been much cheaper than other universities. For women, the material advantages of going into teaching have been good pay combined with a job highly compatible with family demands—short office hours, summers off, and opportunities for moving out and back in.

There is no overall teacher personality—as indeed there could hardly be in a group as large as two million people. Teachers tend to be somewhat more socially conscious than other groups. They also appear to be relatively conservative in their attitude towards their job. People unhappy with their educational experiences are not the ones who tend to go into teaching. Those who identify positively with teachers and teaching are more inclined to enter the profession.

It is partially the conservative orientation to the job that is reflected in the lack of business talk in teachers' lounges. Teachers generally are not burning to change their profession, so they do not spend a great deal of their free time plotting how to do so. This is partially a function of the recruiting patterns of the profession. But the conservatism, the loneliness, and the nature of the conversation in the teachers' lounge are largely the result of the way the profession is structured. The teachers' lounge talk is often a catharsis from intense personal stress.

## ENTRY WITHOUT A HEAT SHIELD

Entry into the first teaching job is like a space satellite entering the earth's atmosphere—except the beginning teacher doesn't have a heat shield for protection. The heat becomes progressively more intense until many novices simply burn up.

The first shock is the extreme abruptness with which one assumes the full responsibilities of the job. One day one is a student oneself; the next day one is a teacher with five classes of thirty students. The transition is traumatic. It is true that one has been in classes observing teachers all one's life. One may try to do what one remembers other teachers did (another source of conservatism, of doing the same thing).

But a lifetime of exposure to teaching is dangerously deceptive. First, watching someone do something is not the same as *knowing* how they do it. As an observer one is likely to miss the most critical factors. One can ride as a passenger in a car with someone else driving to an unknown destination and still not be able to find it by oneself. One may be able to picture in one's mind a pole vaulter doing his or her thing—running down the runway faster and faster, the jump off, the flex of the pole, driving the hips upward, the release, the clearance, the fall—and still not be able to vault five feet.

Much of the knowledge involved in performing a complex task—which teaching certainly is—is *tacit* knowing. Tacit knowledge is acquired by doing, by experience, but it is not easily expressed or transferred to others. This is part of the difficulty the novice has in learning how to teach from the more experienced teachers. Teaching doesn't lend itself to easy rules. So the student in the classroom can see the kind of role the teacher performs, but observing doesn't really enhance the student's teaching techniques very much.

The teacher has also had a number of college courses in education but these too are inadequate in helping students learn how to teach. They are universally derided by teachers as too theoretical and too "mickey-mouse." Education courses are usually either background courses on subjects like the history of education or methods courses, which deal with formulations about how to teach.

Tacit knowing doesn't result from either of these approaches. Courses on the history of education, although perhaps worthwhile for other purposes, will no more help someone to teach than will medical history courses help a surgeon learn his trade. The principles and slogans taught in methods courses may be of some use but are inadequate in the same way a book on how to pole vault would be. Tacit knowing involves practicing an activity and having someone coach you as you do it, as a coach would help an atRlete to improve his or her pole vaulting.

The closest teachers come to this training is perhaps student teaching, if they are lucky. And of all their educational experiences, teachers say that practice teaching prepares them best for the job. Unfortunately, all too often the practice teaching consists of being put in a classroom and left alone. The experienced cooperating teacher goes to the teachers' lounge, leaving the student teacher to flounder. The supervisor from the university shows up only once.

Another sad version is that the cooperating teacher is not a good coach or tries to make the student teacher over in the other teacher's image. In teaching as in athletics a good practitioner is not necessarily a good coach. The student teacher is too often left with the class—the equivalent in pole vaulting of the coach handing a novice pole vaulter a pole and saving, "See you later." Of course the student teacher may be able to learn something even under these conditions.

Meanwhile, some professors in college classes are too likely to shout inspiring slogans about the nobility of the profession, the importance of the mission, the goal of serving every individual child. This may actually make things worse because they offer no way of *achieving* these goals.

In addition, the last example of teaching the new teacher has been exposed to as a model is the teaching in the four years of his or her college preparation. College teaching is far removed from the demands of teaching in the public schools. The students are different, the interests are different, the motivation is different, and the time scheduling is different. So the beginning teacher often arrives at his or her first job woefully unprepared and headed for disaster. What makes it bearable is that the teacher is usually ignorant of this.

Plunging into the fiery furnace of public school teaching is one of my most unpleasant memories. Like many people I had not really intended to teach. I was more interested in things like Renaissance poetry than in teaching adolescents. After wandering around the university library for a few years and finding dusty books of scholarship that had not been opened for fifty years, I decided that a retreat into antiquity was not for me.

I gave up a promising trek into that domain and began to look for something socially useful. After much circuitous wandering I arrived at public school teaching. I had had only a few education courses, and needless to say I was not prepared for the shock of the classroom.

First, I had a problem with stage fright. How could I stand up in front of thirty people and think of something to say for fifty minutes, let alone for five periods a day? As the first day of school approached I became increasingly anxious. In fact, even after all these years of teaching and speaking to large groups, I am still nervous about meeting a class for the first time, and frequently for the first several classes until I become better acquainted with the group.

The entertainment problem also weighed heavily, particularly after I achieved some minimal control over my stage fright. How could I fill five hours of time five days a week? Tap dance? Tell jokes? Send them to the library? Give them busy work? I never entirely resolved this one either. After many years of teaching in a university for only a few hours a week, I still marvel at how I was able to fill time in the public schools.

But by far my worst problem was discipline. My original idea was to run very relaxed, informal classes that were more like discussions in graduate seminars. ("Open classroom" had not yet come into the popular vocabulary.) I would teach lyric poetry in such a way that it would become personally meaningful to the young students and they would thus see its value. It would change their lives. Instead of the dried-up rigidities of much of the teaching to which I had been exposed, I would bring real life and emotions into the classroom. Such were my aspirations.

Of course, what happened was that I was almost driven from the classroom. My classes were chaos. The noise was so loud that teachers down the hall complained to the principal (never to me) in hopes he would do something about it. Instead of reading John Donne's sonnets to the students in a hushed, contemplative tone, I spent my days yelling at them to shut up. Every day that I got up to go to work was sheer misery.

The kids, whose parents worked at oil refineries and steel mills (much like my own background), were not interested in poetry or in anything academic that I could discover. My own handling of the classroom varied erratically from day to day. On days when I felt good and they seemed to be reasonably well behaved, I let them go. Within a few days the classes would be wild and I would be screaming and yelling to try to regain control. This pattern occurred over and over again.

Life was miserable. At a party the students talked me into before Christmas break, a window of my classroom was accidently broken. By this time I had become stoical; I merely shrugged my shoulders. The seventeenth century began to look better and better.

## LONELY AMONG ALL THESE PEOPLE

The other striking feature of my first year of teaching, besides the strong feelings of my own failure and despair, was that I was entirely alone. There was no senior partner in the firm from whom I could solicit advice on my first case. There was no fellow doctor to whom I could talk about what new treatments to try out since what I was doing wasn't working. There was no older professor who would coauthor an article with me and help me get started publishing.

Professionally I was alone. It was sink or swim by myself. There were some people who *might* have helped. I was teaching in a combined junior and senior high school so both the principals theoretically were supervisors of instruction—at least so goes the flaccid rhetoric of texts in school administration. Of course this is far removed from the truth.

The high-school principal was a very nice man who was remarkable for saying absolutely nothing about anything. The maxim among the teachers was never to send discipline problems to the principal because they would come back worse than they went. The junior-high principal, a very personable man and a favorite of the superintendent, talked all the time. His contribution was limited to one thing: helping teachers scale down their idealistic expectations so they could survive—and so he could survive himself. He was an expert in survival and wanted the least trouble possible. Like professors, many supervisors spend their time exhorting teachers to capture new heights. So this principal's slant, if narrow, was a distinct contribution.

The person who really knew what she was doing in teaching was the head of the English department. She had invested her entire life in teaching and was already past retirement age. Crusty, erratic, determined, she was a superb teacher of the old style—discipline them and drill them. For the most part the students liked her manner—it hurt so bad they knew it must be good for them.

She was a natural source of knowledge from whom I might learn something. For the first year or two, however, she was not of much help, except to confirm that I wasn't doing as well as I should be. From her perspective offering help to someone required that the other person admit the superiority of her way of doing things. She was not about to bend herself to the style of freshly minted graduates. Also she had no experience in supervising others in spite of her years. Like most teachers she had focused entirely on her own classroom.

For my part, her old style put me off; indeed, I could not have managed it if I had tried. It did not fit me. Only later did I figure out how to learn from her and incorporate her knowledge into my own style. Actually, since we never saw each other teach, I really didn't know exactly *what* she was doing. Also, being twenty-two, I was not inclined to admit that I needed help. No help was asked for, and none offered. Later she was to prove helpful.

Help from sources where one might have expected it—from the common culture of teachers, from discussions in the teachers' lounge, from talks with a few colleagues—was almost totally absent. One could try to pry out of a colleague what one wanted. But it was prying. This is not to say that teachers are unsociable. Quite the contrary, the informal communication network of a medium-sized school of twenty or thirty teachers is rather close. Everyone in the school can be reached through a sequence of about two people. However, the information so transferred tends to be more personal than professional. The beginning teacher is pretty much limited to this informal network. But unless he is lucky he will not find out much that is professionally useful.

One of the communications difficulties is a lack of a technical vocabulary and technical culture among teachers (Lortie, 1975). There is no common way of attacking and analyzing problems. Two doctors may discuss a patient by describing symptoms, the treatments that have been tried, and possible reasons why the treatments have not worked. Each will be able to relate this to his or her own experience and perhaps offer advice. This is based on a common approach, which is relected in a technical language that persons without the training and experience of doctors cannot understand.

All this is pretty much lacking in teaching. Two teachers talking about a student can usually be understood by a layman. In fact, the lack of a technical language often leads laymen to believe they know as much about teaching as teachers do. The root of the problem is that there is no common study of education among teachers, no pooling and sharing of information out of which a technical culture might have grown. The traditional isolation in the classroom has prevented this. The lack of a technical culture makes teachers less able to respond to demands from outside groups and less able to assist each other themselves and display the knowledge they do possess. This knowledge is the knowledge of the individual, though, not the knowledge embedded in a cultural tradition.

This lack of a culture is the result of, and further increases, communication difficulties. The individual teacher is forced to fall back upon himself. His own background and idiosyncratic experience are what he has to bring to bear on the adjustment period. This individualistic approach to teaching stays with him always. From now on if he hears of new ideas, he will adjust them to his own style or not use them at all. He will be the judge of what is usable in the classroom. New practices will have to be tried out in the classroom, and their value depends on the context in which the teacher is embedded.

The advantage of this pragmatic and personal approach is that each teacher can make his own adjustment as he sees fit. The disadvantages are that not much help can be offered to novices since experience is not shared, and practice becomes rather conservative. Without the sharing, there is also a tendency to develop strong guilt feelings about one's own inability to achieve certain things. Guilt in teaching is personal and heavy, perhaps more so than in medicine, which has a cultural way of dealing with it.

Without resources, techniques, and advice to draw upon, one falls back upon one's own background in order to cope. In my own case I decided I could not emotionally survive another year. The everyday stress was too intense. During the summer between my first and second year of teaching I decided it was them or me. I became a disciplinarian. At the beginning of my second year I faced each class with a set of tough rules: no talking, no getting out of seats, no fooling around in any way. I enforced these rules to the letter, with no exceptions and no seesawing back and forth. I was grimly consistent. I felt that if this didn't work I would have to get out of teaching.

By the second week I had absolute control of my classes. Nobody said anything. Nobody did anything. Whether anybody learned anything or not I didn't care. Everything was quiet. Life was at least bearable. Even at midyear I could leave the classroom for several minutes and the class would remain absolutely quiet. It was grim but I was surviving. I became renowned among students and faculty for my discipline. The reputation enhanced my control even more.

By the third year I let up a little, still gaining control over the classes in the first two weeks but relaxing somewhat later. I found that you could ease discipline in a class without problems but that trying to regain it after you had completely given up control was nearly impossible. I discovered that consistency during the first few weeks of school was the key. One did not have to shout or threaten severe punishment. After consistent enforcement of fairly strict rules during the first few weeks, the class seemed to grow into a pattern. One could relax and worry about teaching something. No more shouting, no more yelling. By my fourth year I had relaxed enough to become a pretty good teacher. It did not come naturally. Meeting it head-on with force was my own solution. Others were not so fortunate.

One of the toughest problems that all teachers must face is the choice between being fair to kids and at the same time responding to them as individuals. One must inevitably create some system of rules and live by them. That's what I did. Responding entirely to the children often leads to complete lack of control. Yet rules are constraining and damaging to children as individuals. Who knows how much damage I did to those in the classroom who felt constrained by such an atmosphere? Responding to individual kids is also where most teachers find the joy in teaching, so one must continually balance off one against the other.

## GUILT BY UNCERTAINTY

During the first few months of teaching an incident occurred from which I learned something. I had in my class one of the local toughs from the wrong side of the tracks. His bravado gave me plenty of discipline problems. During one of my recurrent crackdowns, I found him out of his seat. I told him to sit down. He said no. I commanded him to sit down. He ignored me. By this time everybody in the class was watching and it was clear one of us was going to lose face.

I moved down the aisle towards him until I came up directly in front of him. "I said, 'sit down!' " He only came about to my shoulder but he was quite a burly guy, and I wondered how tough it was going to be if I had to struggle with him. He looked me in the eye for what seemed like a long time. Finally he sat down.

A few weeks later I parked my car outside the school for an evening function. With the great extravagance derived from my first teaching job, I had bought a brand new MGA, which cost me almost a year's salary (I had a lot to learn there too). The next day, a Saturday, I found an eight-inch slash in the canvas top of my car. I realized immediately that my burly friend Joe had done it. I was furious of course. Fortunately it was a weekend and there was nothing I could do about it.

After I cooled off I understood the position I had put him in. In forcing him to back down I had robbed him of one of the few claims to self-respect he had—and I'd done it in front of his friends. He had retaliated the only way he knew how. I realized that the episode had been my fault as much as his, and I vowed never to put a kid in such a situation again. I would always give them a face-saving way out. What internal damage Joe suffered I'll never know.

It is such questions about long-term intangible effects that make the teacher wonder if he ever does any good at all. Like the parent, the teacher touches the entire life of the kid. The teacher either does great good or great damage, and she rarely knows which effect she had. This uncertainty reinforces the loneliness and sometimes the feeling of worthlessness (Lortie, 1975). To monitor effects of her teaching, the teacher can look at test scores, but these measure only a very small portion of what is significant, probably not even the most important part.

The teacher can also observe the student's behavior in class, and she relies heavily on this method of feedback. Perhaps what the teacher values most is the stories told by those long since graduated. The opinions of those still in school are not quite trustworthy. Yet only the most positive students are likely to give such testimony. Clearly, the teacher has no sure way of knowing whether she is having a positive effect at all.

On the one hand, the teacher is exhorted by professors and bosses to the effect that she is responsible for the whole fragile development of the child. On the other hand, there is no good way of determining one's effect. This conflict is likely to lead to feelings of self-doubt, worthlessness, and particularly guilt. Parents, administrators, and critics hold no higher standards for the teacher than she holds for herself. Every child must be developed to the fullest. Yet the teacher has no technique for assessing this nor even a method for measuring progress in the right direction.

This uncertainty produces a phenomenon unique to education. At the end of every school year teachers stagger from the building totally exhausted and feeling as if they could not possibly go on any longer. In fact, on a smaller scale the same thing happens on a Friday afternoon. The exhaustion is not so much physical as it is emotional. The teachers are drained by the guilt produced by the uncertainty over the value of what they are doing.

The internalization of the high ideal of helping every child become fulfilled and the uncertainty of never knowing whether one is succeeding leads to high anxiety and a heavy burden of guilt. The anxiety leads to intense activity. After all, how much is enough? When can one quit? Having thirty or more pupils in the class, each of whom must achieve fulfillment, makes teachers feel tremendously overburdened. For this reason, at the end of the day, the end of the week, and the end of the year, they stagger from the classroom emotionally spent—but often with no feeling of a job well done.

Such emotional exhaustion is characteristic of people operating under conditions of high duress and uncertainty, such as air-traffic controllers and students in examinations. High goals and uncertainty are prime factors in each case. After a summer or a week off, the teachers replenish themselves psychologically. The soothing hand of time restores them. By fall or Monday morning they are ready to make another charge across the zone of uncertainty—still pursuing their high ideals.

In the job I now have—writing, teaching a few classes a week, serving on committees—I actually work more hours per week than I did teaching. But I am not nearly as exhausted at the end. Even after fifteen years I still wonder how much damage I did to burly Joe and many others. As a professor, I can recall no graduate student about whom I felt guilty.

The criteria for success as a professor are much clearer to me. I am judged by the quality of my ideas and the number of my publications. I get direct comments about my performance from my colleagues and, less important, from my students. I administer questionnaires to my classes every semester and get helpful comments about the deficiencies of my teaching. I feel the students as adults are good judges of how well I am doing for them. I have no fear of damaging their personalities in the long run. I am not responsible for their total development; my responsibility is limited.

Public school teachers have none of these assurances going for them. Part of the price of not having a "technical" culture that provides help on these problems is that the teacher has no evaluative criteria by which to judge the success of his performance and thus relieve some of the anxiety and uncertainty.

There are a few recognized criteria for performance. The teacher must be in charge of the class. He must have control. In addition he must elicit work from the students. And he must sustain the students' interest. But he has few techniques for achieving these goals. His situation is greatly exacerbated by the fact that he has a captive audience which is not necessarily committed to school goals, and he must work with students as a group rather than as individuals. Almost no other professional has such working constraints. In order to control the class, the teacher, unlike the professor, may have to institute repressive procedures that work against his other goals.

Contrast this to the situation of doctors, who are often able to handle life-and-death situations without accruing a great deal of personal guilt. A few years ago my neighbor, who is a neurosurgeon, and I were pushing our kids in our swing set. I asked him if it were depressing to have so many patients who were in such dire straits that a large percentage would not survive.

"Oh, no!" he said enthusiastically. "I've been here four years and have done about one hundred and fifty operations and only one person has died."

"Incredible!" I said, astonished.

"Yes," he said, "my surgical rate is the talk of the hospital."

"That's really unbelievable!" I said. "I always thought that many neurosurgical patients died."

"Oh, most die *eventually*," he said. "A week later, a month, within a year. But we just count deaths if they occur in surgery and within twenty-four hours after surgery."

I was so astonished that there was little I could say. "Now that's an evaluation criterion one can live with," I thought to myself. Few people blame a doctor if his patients die. The standards are such that the doctor is expected to do the best job he can with the techniques at his disposal but no more. These standards of performance are set by the doctor's colleagues and by medical culture. They enable him to do his job and survive with a minimum of guilt in the face of great uncertainty.

Meanwhile teachers operate as best they can in isolation. In fact the very issue of teacher performance tends to block communication and impede solidarity among teachers. Few know how well they are doing, so why expose their problems to their colleagues? Much of the teachers' lounge talk is a catharsis of guilt and intensity of feeling, but it is usually not talk that instrumentally improves performance. It is emotional unwinding.

The peer culture does help in some ways but not always in the best fashion. In any faculty one can always find small informal groups of teachers who tell each other that this kid or the students from that part of town are impossible. In doing so they alleviate their own guilt over being unable to succeed with particular children. Among themselves they sustain a belief counter to the general liberal educational credo that all students are educable.

Meanwhile other teachers take this message to heart, pledge themselves to individual children, drive themselves relentlessly, and feel guilty about the outcome. Each in the isolation of his own classroom makes his own compromises, for the task of total development is of course impossible to fulfill.

There is something worse than guilt: shame. In assuming full responsibility for the cognitive and intellectual development of each child, the teacher uses herself as an instrument, suppressing her own feelings and anger. There is little opportunity to vent these frustrations. Occasionally, however, these feelings boil to the surface—and not only in the teachers' lounge.

When the teacher vents her hostility and anger upon the student, she sometimes feels ashamed, as does the parent who loses self-control with a child. Teachers are not prepared by temperament or training for the inevitable interpersonal clashes that are bound to occur in the classroom. They have seldom explored or even admitted these hostile feelings.

Whereas guilt is derived from violating or not accomplishing a group standard that one has internalized, shame is much more basic. Shame strikes at one's self-esteem. Teachers feel guilty about the uncertainty of achieving the idealistic goals; they feel *ashamed* when they violate their responsibility to students or damage their relationship to students (Lortie, 1975).

The relationship to the student is the very core of the job as perceived by teachers, and insofar as one's job is associated with one's self-esteem (which is the case for the majority of people), violation of this relationship is a blow to one's self-esteem. One feels shame. One does not talk about the encounters like the one I had with Joe. One suffers these self-inflicted blows in silence and they exact their emotional toll.

Teachers as a group suffer from a low self-esteem; for example, they rate the prestige of their occupation lower than other people do. The teacher's lack of self-esteem is derived not only from societal evaluations of occupational status but also from the isolation, organization, and conduct of the job itself. It is exacerbated by the career pattern.

## Career Patterns

The sources of self-esteem are many for doctors. The entry to training in the profession is highly selective. The potential doctor undergoes training so rigorous that it seems an ordeal. In later life this shared ordeal is an important source of self-esteem and comradeship among those who survived such training.

In his career ascent the doctor passes through the stages of intern, resident, and staff doctor. After practicing for a few years, he passes his "board" examinations—a new recognized status. Whether he goes into private practice or works for a clinic or hospital, he can expect very large salary increases along the line.

The teacher's career is in sharp contrast to the physician's. The preparation required is predicated upon the idea of recruiting a large number into the profession rather than developing attitudes and skills for the practice of teaching. It is relatively easy to get into teaching, both in terms of the schools one may go to and the courses one takes. There is no sense of a shared ordeal to bolster self-steem and comradeship. For the most part the courses are perceived as being too easy.

The pay scale, too, has been developed to recruit new teachers rather than to reward experienced ones (Lortie, 1975). The ratio of beginning pay to top-level pay is about one to two, much lower than in other professions. Reliance on the property tax as a base has held overall salaries down. Teachers earn $5,000 to $7,000 less per year than do other college graduates. Even though they have made sharp gains over the past decades as a result of collective bargaining, teacher salaries compared to those of other professionals remain relatively unchanged.

In a sense the teacher's career is what the sociologist Lortie calls "unstaged." There is little chance for upward mobility. One is stuck at a salary schedule that progresses gradually according to education and years experience. No more tangible public recognition is available. The alternatives are to move to a higher paying school district, go into administration, or escape to another profession.

The lack of "staging" in the teacher career does not stimulate effort and ambition to achieve more now in hope of future reward and recognition. Rather, the lack of staging results in an orientation towards seeking gratification in the present. It also results in a sense of relative deprivation for many people in teaching. Older teachers often feel deprived and undervalued.

In any teachers' lounge one will find a group of embittered men who are friends. These are men who have been passed over for promotion to the administration and who now have no significant advancement to look forward to in the rest of their careers. In an achieving society this is a severe sentence—and it shows in their bitterness. The men are most upset in their thirties. By their fifties they have become more resigned to their fate. Fully seventy percent of the men teachers see teaching as only a means to an end and expect to go into administration or some other career eventually—and they are disappointed when they don't. I used to worry about these men and their effects upon students. I still do. Generally, women tend to see teaching as an end in itself.

Overall, the teaching career system emphasizes recruitment, even to the point of oversupply, rather than enhancement of those already in the field. It depreciates the status of teaching as a profession. It fosters private rather than shared understandings. There is no group of senior professionals to guide and shape the beginners in the profession. The career pattern does not facilitate internal collegial control.

Since both extrinsic rewards, such as status and money, and intrinsic rewards such as collegial approval are limited, teachers rely heavily on private psychic rewards. Job satisfaction is strongly related to classroom experiences. Life revolves around the daily routine activities of the classroom. The basic satisfactions of teaching must be derived from "reaching the students" or they are not derived at all.

In decision making as in other things, the career pattern fosters a private rather than a shared orientation. Teachers have not tried to challenge the hierarchy of the administration and school board governing them. They have only pressed to limit the power of other people to interfere in the classroom. Traditionally they have not pushed for the right to govern their own affairs. They have been willing to attend to their own classroom and leave educational governance to others. This attitude may be changing now, as teachers push the scope of collective bargaining beyond salary issues.

## The Good Days—The Joy of Connecting

Without opportunity for public recognition or the rewards of close comradeship, teachers derive their satisfaction mainly from interacting with the students. This emphasis on psychic reward causes them to focus on their classroom to the exclusion of all else. Individual personal satisfaction from particular students is the payoff. This can be seen in teachers' fondness for telling about their spectacular cases of success (Lortie, 1975).

After several years of teaching and learning what it was all about, I sometimes received some of the tougher cases, as well as the better classes, to teach. Such was the case with a class of high-school juniors which was loaded with jocks from the athletic teams. They had recently received much public recognition for their athletic exploits and were in the first stages of overblown self-importance. They could not recognize how small their little world really was.

The leader of this group was a boy named Jim, who was outstanding as a catcher on the baseball team. Local rumor had it that he was major league material and some professional scouts were interested in him. The second day of class Jim came in with a toothpick sticking out between his teeth. It was obviously a premeditated act meant to provoke me. The members of his gang in the class were tittering and glancing back and forth between him and me.

On the first day I had seen that I had a rebellious clique of jocks on my hands—about five boys—so I had decided to take the precaution of seating them alphabetically. Ordinarily a toothpick would not have bothered me. In this case Jim was contending for supremacy in the class. At first I ignored him, pretending I didn't notice. He persisted.

As I seated him in his assigned place, I said mildly, "Jim, would you mind getting rid of the toothpick?" I went on assigning seats, giving Jim time to think about it. When I finished, Jim still had the toothpick sticking from his mouth, even more defiantly than before. "Jim," I said, "I asked you to remove the toothpick. Would you please?" This time I was a little more insistent.

"I don't have to," said Jim. His buddies were laughing openly now.

"Yes, you do have to," I said, "if you want to stay in this class." No rancor, no anger. My tone was mild but firm. No personal hostility directed at Jim himself.

"I'm going to keep it," said Jim.

"O.K.," I said. "You can keep it. But you'll have to go to the principal's office and sit there. When you decide to get rid of it, you can come back."

Jim rose very slowly and ambled out the door, grinning at his friends in class. I showed no overt signs of being perturbed. All in a day's business. The whole episode made Jim's best friend sitting right in front of my desk indignant. He was a big, powerfully built boy named Keith. He and his twin brother were the star tackles of the football team. Both had developed a reputation among the faculty for being troublemakers. Keith was really mad.

"If he's going to the office," Keith said, "I'm going too!"

"Help yourself," I said. "You can certainly join him if you want to. Come back when you are ready." Keith left.

I turned to the rest of the class and said blandly, "Does anyone else want to go?" For all I knew the whole class might get up and walk away. But there were no more takers. Dead silence in the class. I began the lesson of the day.

Jim and Keith sat in the principal's office for four days—with toothpicks. The principal asked them why they were there and who sent them but little else. He wisely let them sit. He said nothing to me about it. For a while it was all a big joke for Jim and Keith. They were the heroes of the day. Everyone going into the office could see them sitting there. After a while, though, this excitement played out. Things got dull. They began to think about what they were doing.

After four days they came back to class—without toothpicks. I didn't rub their noses in it. I said simply, "Glad to have you back," and pretended they had never been gone. The rest of the year I treated them as if the incident had never happened. At first they were rather cool towards me, but they did their assignments. Towards the end of the year Jim got particularly interested in one unit and even became a little enthusiastic. I never had any more trouble with either of them again. In fact, the whole class was one of the easiest to control I ever had. Inadvertently, I had handled the natural leader, and the rest of the group fell into line.

I did not think any more of the incident beyond congratulating myself for getting through the ordeal without getting my car top slashed again. Four years later I had left the classroom and was serving as a state consultant and teacher trainer on a large curriculum project at the state university. On one of my business trips to my old area, I visited the leading local nightclub, a place with which I had acquired considerable familiarity during my teaching years.

As I was standing in the crowd observing the dance floor, I suddenly saw Jim. "Oh, oh," I said to myself. I pretended not to see him and thought about easing out the door quietly. A few moments later when I looked again, he had spotted me and had begun making his way through the crowd towards me. No exit.

Just as he reached me and I was fully tensed up, a heavy hand crashed down on my shoulder from behind me, absolutely startling me. I looked around. It was Keith, the football player! I hadn't seen him at all! "This is it," I thought to myself with a sinking feeling. My chances didn't look too good. Jim and Keith were now on either side of me. Keith lifted his arm—and threw it around my shoulders! "Ernie!" He yelled the name I was called among the kids. Jim grabbed my right arm and began to shake it warmly and vigorously. I had trouble keeping my balance under the affectionate embraces of these two bozos. I was truly so astonished I didn't know what to say other than hi.

After a few more minutes of greeting, Keith said, "Let me buy you a beer." As he went to the bar and I puzzled through my memory vainly trying to remember what magnificent deeds I had ever done to deserve such good fortune, Jim said, "Boy, I don't know how you ever stood us in class. If I had been you, I would have kicked our asses."

"Oh, you weren't so bad," I said. It was easy to be generous under the circumstances.

"No. We were terrible," he said. "But you handled us just right. Just right!"

Keith came back with some beers, and over the loud dance band I found out that they were enrolled as sophomores in the state teacher's college, no less, where they were involved in athletics. I was a little surprised, since they had never been very good students in high school. They attributed a significant portion of their success to how I treated them in class. I was really puzzled by this. As best I could figure, I did not humiliate them or victimize them, even though they felt they deserved such treatment. They had no reason for revenge or rancor. I had treated them firmly but fairly in their own best interest, as they now saw it.

The true point of this anecdote, however, is that every teacher has a similar story of spectacular success. The story usually involves one student whose fortunes look very dismal at the beginning. Through persisting and overcoming many obstacles, the teacher helps achieve a happy ending in which the student succeeds somehow or other. These stories are the gold medals of the teaching Olympics.

Focusing on the psychic reward in the classroom, fairly well cut off from public recognition and professional peer acclaim, uncertain as to whether their efforts are having any effect on the kids at all, teachers can be enormously exhilerated by these episodes because of the visibility of the impact of their teaching. What they're doing does make a difference! Their efforts are appreciated! By analogy teachers can well imagine other episodes in which their efforts have had similar good impact. The episode is an indicator of other invisible things that may also have paid off. An incident like that with Jim and Keith is particularly sweet to a teacher because the testimonial comes from a graduate who has little reason to flatter the teacher. The teacher does not quite believe the statements of current students. They have too much to gain. So testimony from a former student who has the maturity to recognize his own welfare and the distance and motivation to tell the truth is the most credible and satisfying source of information.

Such payoffs are rare, however, and cherished all the more for that. The more common form of personal gratification for teachers consists of "having a good day." On such a day everything seems to go right for them. They start off in an ebullient mood and find when they get to school that kids are in a similar mood. They manage to get their lesson across and the kids seem particularly responsive. There are no serious discipline problems. The class even manages to get through all the work the teacher has planned for.

Having a good day is not something one can force. Sometimes it happens and sometimes it doesn't. Much depends on the moods of both the teacher and the students. Perhaps the weather has something to do with it. In any case significant elements seem outside the teacher's direct control. One may also have a bad day in which everything goes wrong. The teacher expects the day-to-day work mood to vary erratically.

The teacher defines a good day entirely in relation to events occurring in the classroom (Lortie, 1975). The relationship between the teacher and kids on that day is the critical focus. Anything from outside the class that interferes with that continuously developing and private relationship is bad.

But the good days are sweet indeed—laughter in the classroom, jokes with colleagues, affection and respect from the students, high spirits, the satisfaction of work well done, the feeling of shaping and touching the future itself.

The good days are written in the faces of the former students themselves when they are forty or fifty or sixty years old and come back to the school to touch gently the old books, the carved desks, the yellowed maps. Tears in their eyes, they stand in quiet reverence before the teacher's empty desk, remembering their ancient days more clearly than events of the last few years. In her foreknowledge the teacher tries to taste the evanescence of these moments day by day as they actually occur. The bad days—well, the bad days are forgotten.

### The Paradox of Being Both Fair and Personal with the Kids

Read again the iron rule of American education: "Every child should be educated to his full potential." The corollaries of this uncompromising principle are that every child is indeed educable and that the development will be personal, emotional, and physical, as well as cognitive. These are heavy demands indeed and impossible to fulfill totally.

On the other hand, the teacher's real reward comes from personal interactions with students. Relationships with different students vary tremendously in satisfaction for the teacher. The teacher is more inclined towards those she enjoys than those she does not. The problem is greatly intensified by the group nature of the work and by the large number of students. Can the teacher treat all equally? Any slight deviation or favoritism can be observed by the other students. "Playing favorites" and "teacher's pet" are common enough terms to indicate the frequency of this favoritism.

When I was teaching, I had several favorites of course. One was a beautiful blond girl who not only looked like an angel but also wrote like one. I must confess that I spent considerably more time grading her essays than I did many others. It is very difficult not to have favorites.

I remember one class in which I had a boy I didn't like at all. I thought he was cheating on assignments whenever he got the chance. One day I had the class write an impromptu theme. I graded his essay, didn't like it, and gave him a D. He didn't like the grade, but he was always protesting that I wasn't fair to him—a real crybaby, I figured.

This time he brought up the paper of a friend he had sat next to while writing the exam. The two papers were the same almost word for word. But I had given his friend a respectable B on his identical paper. I was hardly in a moral position to castigate him for cheating. I gave him a B for his paper too, and every grading period after that I applied a little multiplier to raise his grade somewhat, realizing I had probably discounted his work. Of course, I still didn't like him.

Some students seem to *need* more attention. My daughter works much better, whether in math or reading or piano, when an adult works with her and pays full attention to her. She thrives on the one-to-one personal interaction and becomes passive in a large group. The perfect learning situation for her is a personal tutor. Yet is it fair for the teacher to spend time with her and correspondingly neglect the other kids in class? Is it right for me as a parent to insist on such attention?

After listening to parents complain about the school, I have come to the conclusion as a parent that what parents really want for their children is special attention. If the child is gifted, the teachers don't stimulate him or her enough to maintain his or her interest. If he or she has learning disabilities, they should spend more time with him. The overall demand is to give *my* child special attention. Taken as a total group, the demands of parents are obviously impossible to fulfill, and teachers often respond to the most vociferous ones.

Minority parents complain that they simply want their children to be treated *equally* to the others, not better. They point to poor educational outcomes such as test scores and years of schooling completed as indicating that their children are not receiving their fair shares. This raises the critical problem of how fairness is to be defined.

Does equal and fair treatment mean that the teacher must invest enough effort to bring everyone up to the same level? Does it mean the teacher must spend the same total amount of time with everyone? Does everyone get the same amount of affection? Does everyone get just what he or she *needs,* even if it's less or more than average? There are no easy answers to these questions. The definition for formal justice is that everyone be treated the same, but what does sameness mean? The teacher decides many times a day by his or her behavior what being fair means.

One reason I particularly like my story about Jim and Keith is that the success was achieved by treating them fairly without special favors. The treatment was fair as well as personally responsive. The more usual case is that in which a teacher recognizes a special feature of the child and sensitively capitalizes on it to help the child.

One of the best examples of teaching that I know occurred the year we went to Britain for several months. My eight-year-old daughter was very shy, and she was not at all happy with the idea of leaving her friends and classmates, flying across the Atlantic Ocean, and entering a new school. In fact, once we arrived she kept her watch set to American time for two weeks, refusing to reset it.

Her last day in class her teacher gave her two sealed letters, one to be opened on the plane halfway across the Atlantic and the other to be opened the first day in the new school in Britain. The letters said the class was thinking about her, she must be excited by all the new things she was seeing, and so on. Was this fair? I don't know, but it certainly was meaningful for my daughter. I call this superbly sensitive teaching. Teachers must continuously balance off what their efforts mean for one child against what they mean for others. Teachers always want more time and smaller classes so they can do more for everybody.

Equity versus personalism is a constant battle. It is more gratifying for the teacher to work closely with a few students than to work superficially with many. The results are more tangible and satisfying. Even the college professor totally absorbed in his or her own discipline finds teaching large groups of students frustrating. He or she would much rather work closely with a few graduate students. Such tendencies lead to the elitist outcome of helping the few at the expense of the many. In spite of the iron rule, there is often widespread uncertainty about getting all students to learn.

## The Classroom Is My Kingdom, I Shall Not Want

The teacher's perspective, then, is one of focusing entirely on the classroom. The teacher sees herself (and is seen by others) as *the* essential agent for student learning. Learning in a classroom setting is synonomous with the teacher's directing activities from the center. This is also how she derives her major satisfactions—from her relationships with individual children (Lortie, 1975).

She expects and tries to attain a virtual monopoly over student attention. The idea is to have an uninterrupted, productive exchange with the students. Anything that interferes with this is bad, which means that almost all outside influences are bad. This is *her* classroom. These are *her* kids. A strong possessiveness hangs over the teacher's classroom.

The critical element is time. The teacher considers the time engaged in direct learning activities productive. Time spent on other activities is not. More time is what she needs to interact more fully with every child. More time maximizes the child's learning and the teacher's satisfactions. The things that most irritate the teacher are clerical chores, extra duties, interruptions, and school activities that interfere with her productive time. Time is by far the most important resource.

This exclusive focus on classroom activities means that everything outside—parents, bosses, even colleagues—is extraneous, except insofar as it might be able to help occasionally in the main task. Parents can cause trouble by interfering in classroom affairs. Generally the teacher would like to deal with parents when the teacher requests that they help the classroom situation by straightening out a child in trouble, providing a car for a field trip, and so on. Of course, parents continually interfere anyhow.

The superintendent has very little direct effect upon classroom practice. The principal is much closer to the teacher. He can help with parents, mainly by keeping them off the teacher's back. He is expected to be firm with parents and also straighten out wayward children. The principal is judged by how well he provides emotional and material support for the central activity of teaching.

The principal is expected to be fair and to play no favorites, just as a teacher is. If there are extra duties to be doled out, the principal must see to it that every teacher does her share. Favorites should not receive extra materials or special advantages. Neither is the good principal expected to supervise the teaching closely. He is not perceived by teachers as an expert in teaching, and he is not expected to act like one. The principal ordinarily respects the boundaries of the teacher's sphere of influence. Exceptionally authoritarian principals who do interfere in various ways are not well liked.

The one exception to maintaining the respectful distance is in teacher evaluation. By tradition and often by contract, the principal is usually required to make several visits to the classes of untenured teachers in preparation for making an eventual recommendation on retaining them. Neither the teachers nor the principal see the principal as competent to do this. It is a trauma for both of them, as will be seen in the chapter on teacher evaluation. It is perceived by the teacher as a transgression of the boundaries of her classroom.

Those boundaries are maintained even with colleagues who work with the same students. Teachers have very little control over their fellow teachers. Contact with other teachers is very limited, and contact with each other is the classroom is miniscule. Each teacher is on her own.

Teachers judge other teachers mainly by the way in which they handle students (Lortie, 1975). Elementary teachers are expected to elicit respect and love from their students and secondary teachers are expected to elicit respect and esteem. Both are expected to maintain control of the class and to generate enthusiasm and respect in the students without relaxing learning demands or pandering to them.

The outstanding teacher as seen by other teachers is one who induces learning, a love of learning, affection, and great effort while at the same time maintaining discipline. Both what the students learn and the means by which they learn it are important. Not just any method goes. The outstanding teacher effects learning by maintaining discipline, getting students to work, and simultaneously generating respect and admiration in them.

In working for student affection and admiration, there is a taste of competition among teachers. But recognition as a superior teacher comes only if the teacher uses "fair" means. She cannot win student affection by lowering demands or being "palsy" with the students. Such behavior is held in disdain by other teachers.

But in spite of this awareness, the teacher-student relationship, not the admiration of peers and bosses, is the real source of teacher pride and accomplishment. The isolation of the teacher in the classroom means that the main rewards come from students. Each teacher tries to negotiate the best balance she can to obtain her own psychic rewards. The school is a collection of individual teachers rather than a collective of teachers.

The principal's authority in the school has not really been challenged, even in recent years. Each teacher confronts the principal as an individual and tries to negotiate the best classroom support she can muster. Each differs in the deal he or she makes, but the individualistic orientation of teachers does not challenge the power of the principal to run the whole school. In a recent study of written negotiated contracts, it was found that in only two of thirteen traditional areas of principal authority has the principal's role been affected. In teacher evaluation and in assigning regular teachers to substitute, the principal's power has been moderately limited (Parker, 1976).

Generally teachers have not challenged the traditional governing hierarchy of the school despite collective bargaining (Lortie, 1975). Collective bargaining has primarily revolved around salary and fringe benefits so far. Where teachers have tried to exert influence, it has been to restrict administrative authority rather than to expand teacher control of the school or curriculum. Reducing administrative authority keeps administrators from interfering in the classroom and fits with teachers' individualistic orientation.

Striving for positive control of the schools would require much more of a collectivist orientation. The structure of teaching has not generated much commitment to comradeship or to the occupation as an entity. Whether events will force a change in this perspective remains to be seen.

The highly individualistic orientation has long impeded efforts to get teachers to approach problems from a collective perspective. When I first tried organizing teachers into a teacher organization many years ago, I was stunned by their lack of a collective identity. For most teachers that's not where the rewards are. The organizer can talk himself blue without a glimmer of recognition on the part of many teachers. A common approach to problems simply is beyond their ken.

Over the past fifteen years this attitude has changed remarkably but by no means completely. At least on some issues, teachers have decided to improve themselves collectively. They much more easily make common cause on welfare issues than before. However, on curriculum and teaching matters, the reward system and the individualistic orientation still prevail without question. Teachers are not sure they want to exert control over these matters.

Overall, there is no more noble or idealistic profession around. The degree of dedication is incredible. The chief difficulties are the lack of control over teaching circumstances in the school and the lack of reflectivity about those circumstances. The highly individualistic orientation that puts each teacher on his or her own prevents teachers from forming strong bargaining coalitions which could fight more successfully for the things each teacher sees as being important.

Being so strongly oriented to obtaining psychic rewards from interaction with the kids inhibits the teacher's interaction with colleagues. This leads to a conservatism in practice that stresses doing what one can with the belief that all that is needed for success is more time. One doesn't have time to think about teaching because one is too busy teaching.

Paradoxically, I think being a little less keyed to the kids and a little more attuned to one's colleagues would enhance reflection on practice. It forces one to justify what one is doing. It promotes a collegial basis for practice rather than complete reliance on one's personal convictions. A more collegial approach to teaching would make it an even more noble, satisfying, and effective profession than it is.

## BOOKS TO READ

Lortie, Dan C. *School Teacher*. Chicago: University of Chicago Press, 1975.
   Without question this is the finest sociological study of teaching as an occupation in the last twenty years. Many of the ideas in this chapter were stimulated by this book (as well as from actual experience). It is not easy for someone who is not a sociologist to read, but the insights one will gain are well worth the effort. Most highly recommended.

*part two*

# The Classroom

# Discipline and Control in the Classroom

## Recalling the "Not So Good" Old Days

When I first started teaching in a public school more than a decade ago, a rather salty and seasoned principal took me aside to explain the facts of life—school life, that is. I did not take his warnings and admonitions lightly, since I was not yet twenty-one years old and as green as any first-year teacher off the college assembly line.

"When you get in that classroom, son," the principal warned, "just remember that those kids are going to check you out. They'll test you, find out what you'll let them get away with, and generally keep you busy with questions about 'do's and don'ts' until they've decided what kind of teacher you're gonna be. So, just remember this," he continued with deadly seriousness, "don't make hasty decisions, keep your cool, and if in doubt just say, 'We'll decide that later, we have some other things to work on first.'"

That was *good* advice, although I really didn't know it at the time. As a matter of record, I was so damned nervous that I didn't really piece together what he had told me until some weeks later. But the advice was sound because, after all, what he was actually trying to get me to understand was: relax, get your wits about you, learn the lay of the land, get a feel for the classroom, get yourself organized, decide what you want the classroom to be like, and then—only then—are you ready to establish

---

* I wish to thank the teachers who have provided many of the ideas for this chapter, with a special thank-you to Ms. Pat Arbogast, Ms. Jo Friedman, Ms. Linda Friedman, Ms. Pat Hays-Lapan, and Ms. Julie Leach for their important contributions.

how the class will operate and the limits within which you will expect the students to behave. It's a matter of carefully developing things the way you want them and *not* creating new rules for each crisis, rules that you may be sorry about later.

Yes, this was good advice, but I was too jumpy to understand enough of it even to put it together in my mind, and certainly I had no notion of how to apply it. I remember that first day, facing those kids for the first time—oh, do I remember that first day! Student teaching was one thing, but this was *my* class and it was all up to me now. I was afraid, and so damned lonely that images of digging ditches and running a gas station flashed through my mind as secure, positive alternatives to this sea of unfamiliar faces and these strange surroundings. I was faced with attendance to be taken, lunch money to be collected and counted, student questions I couldn't answer, and of course my own plans for the day, which were by now partially forgotten and totally illogical in the face of the reality that surrounded me.

Many memories of my first days and years of teaching are lodged securely in my mind, perhaps temporarily forgotten but always available when jogged by the slightest suggestion regarding the "good old days." There are good recollections of course, but what I remember most were the problems I encountered related to perhaps the most important issue facing any classroom teacher: student discipline and classroom control. Those were *not* "good old days" for me; and for some experienced teachers I know, when it comes to discipline the new days aren't so very good either.

Certainly, any experienced teacher will jump at the chance to explain how important good classroom control is to one's own survival. And this survival does not just mean keeping one's job: it is a case of psychological survival as well. There have been many teachers who have quit the profession because they simply couldn't take it anymore. The pressure can be overwhelming. The question of what to do if a kid tells you to go to hell, or won't do his work, or starts a fight, or engages in the infinite number of other possible unexpected student actions must concern every teacher when he steps inside that classroom door. I specifically recall that it didn't concern me enough during the tender, neophyte months of my first year of teaching. And why should it? After all, I had skills, concepts, facts, ideas—all of which I planned to lay on the students with the expectation that they would leap high in the air cheering at the thought of gaining all of this newly discovered knowledge. Ah, knowledge, I thought, the key to happiness and success!

To my sorrowful surprise, at least half of the students didn't appear to be interested at all. No leaping, no cheering, no nothing. Perhaps a few had said, "Oh, I see now," but many more had said, "Do we have to?"

Now, I'm sure that all of you experienced teachers are already thinking, "I could have told you that was going to happen." But this was nonetheless a shock to me, even though I had been warned by more experienced colleagues about such realities of the classroom. I had been warned, too, by a principal who was willing to stand behind me if I needed him. But no one said it was going to be like this (or if they did, I wasn't listening). What I had learned—rather abruptly—from this experience was that working with kids in a classroom is not a case of scattering crucial pieces of information and skills into waiting, grasping minds. I learned instead that the first order of business was understanding and planning for the very special situation called the classroom. My mind was beginning to discover new insights about the real circumstances behind such timeworn phrases as "motivating students to learn," "demonstrating that you are in charge of the class," and "planning with the kids in mind." While these and other issues were discussed in my college courses, this was a different ballgame altogether.

What do experienced and successful teachers do to meet the challenge of surviving in the real-world classroom? What does some of the down-to-earth research say that can provide us with important answers? Are there set solutions and simple recipes, or does one have to be a natural teacher? What does it take? Well, there are no simple remedies—we know that for sure. But organizing some of the ideas that teachers and research can provide will certainly help us along the way.

Let's look in on a group of teachers who have been given the rather ominous task of tackling the sticky question of discipline and control in the classroom. I think you'll find their ideas interesting.

# Greener Pastures School District—
# The Teachers' Committee on Discipline:

## A Three-Act Play

### The Players

Ms. BERNICE ENERGY, *A second-year teacher who is now working on her master's degree. She has had a few discipline problems in her own classroom, but feels she can solve most of them. She appears tireless in her teaching and can't understand why so many of her colleagues appear so worn out at the end of a teaching day. Ms. Energy teaches at the Kenneth Kinetic Elementary School.*

Ms. PATRICIA STROKUM, *She is a teacher with ten years' experience, six of them in the Greener Pastures district. Ms. Strokum had earned her masters' degree plus many additional hours, mainly in counselor education. She feels that the term discipline should not even be used in relation to working with students, and emphasizes a very personal approach to teaching. She teaches at Henry Humanist Junior High School.*

MR. BILLY JACK TIRANT (ALSO KNOWN AS B.J.), *He is a teacher with fifteen years' experience and some administrative experience, all in the Greener Pastures system. Mr. Tirant is well known in the district as a strict disciplinarian, and he takes some pride in this reputation. He is just about to complete his master's work in administration and hopes to become a principal some day. Mr. Tirant teaches at Barry Wright Wing High School.*

MS. EVELYN UNEVEN, *Although somewhat experienced in teaching, Ms. Uneven is probably the committee member who is least sure about her classroom control. She has taught in Greener Pastures for her four years in the profession, and she has a reputation for being somewhat flighty or at least undecided in her behavior. Her classes are not usually completely out of control, but she does have some problems. Ms. Uneven teaches at the Samuel Splinter Elementary School.*

**The Scene**

Since the Greener Pastures school district had been fraught with increasing problems of discipline and control in its classes for the past few years, the district administrators decided in collaboration with the teachers' council that a committee of teachers should be formed to attack this vexing issue. As the play begins, we find the teachers' committee on discipline opening their first meeting, which is being held at the administration building. School is out and the members of the committee are being paid to work on the discipline problem for four weeks during the summer.

**Stage Directions**

*(As the curtain rises we find the four committee members sitting around a conference table in a serious discussion regarding what is expected of them during the four weeks.)*

**Act I**

MR. TIRANT   Well, I don't know. . . . Maybe we're supposed to develop a set of rules for the students to follow. That'd be the way I'd do it.
MS. STROKUM   Oh, don't you think the kids have enough rules to follow

already? If I were going to set up rules, it'd be for the teachers, not the kids.

MS. ENERGY    This is difficult, but I'm not sure about setting up rules. I mean, well, solving discipline problems is not like baking a cake. I wish there were recipes for it, but we all know there are none, really.

MR. TIRANT    Yes, but you can have guidelines or a set of principles. I have tricks and gimmicks I use, like flipping the lights on and off and stopping my lecture when things seem to get noisy . . . you know . . . I just kind of stare at 'em. They know I mean business.

MS. UNEVEN    I thought we would have something prepared for us, like ideas or guidelines for us to follow on this committee. Does anyone here really know what we are supposed to be doing?

MS. STROKUM    Look, I think we have to work that out for ourselves. That's what we are being paid to do, I think. Don't you? I'll volunteer to take minutes so that we can have a record of what we decide upon. I don't think we need a chairperson, do we?
        (*Everyone nods in agreement.*)

MS. ENERGY    Well, I just want to say again that there are no easy remedies. I think it depends on the individual child or situation, and sometimes it depends on what the whole class is like that day.

MR. TIRANT    Maybe so, but that doesn't get us anywhere. That doesn't tell a teacher how to solve problems when they happen, does it?

MS. STROKUM    I think that's a valid point, Mr. Tirant. Why don't we think of some ideas that could help teachers solve problems? One thing that occurs to me right away is that if you can, you should stop and think before you do something—I mean . . . when I just react when some student has misbehaved, I'm usually sorry for it later. And I think that can undermine your relationship with that student and maybe with the whole class.

MS. UNEVEN    (*Excited*)    Oh, that's so true. Be sure to write that down, Pat. I think, too, that what you do with discipline depends on your personality. You have to kind of go with who you are.

MR. TIRANT    (*Frowning*)    I'm not sure I agree with that. Your personality may change from day to day and that would just confuse the students. I'm for setting up rules and sticking to them!

MS. UNEVEN    I just meant that everybody can't be the same way. We all have different ways of coping.

MS. ENERGY    (*Calmly*)    I think we can write down all of the ideas for now. Later on, we can decide what to keep. I think the personality connection is a good one, but we'll probably have to be more specific. Actually, I think what we're shooting for here is a set of hints or guides that will just make being in the classroom more hassle-free.

MS. STROKUM    (*Interested*)    I like that term, Bernice. That's what it's really all about, kind of like "We're all in this together . . . you and the kids . . . hassle-free" is what we all want. I would much rather we focus on that rather than discipline. It sounds so . . . so military.

MR. TIRANT   Oh, come on! Discipline is necessary and I think we have to face that fact.

(*Short argument ensues with everyone talking at once.*)

MS. STROKUM (*Looking serious*)   O.K. O.K. I think we can just continue to list our ideas, then perhaps we can just go from there. Another thought I had is that when a kid gets out of line, it is really important that you take the time to talk with him or her. It's really important that you find out if something is bothering them. Or, if it's just a matter of them cutting up, then they know that you really don't want them to do that—not that you just want order for its own sake.

MS. UNEVEN   Also, I think a teacher should always be programmed to expect the unexpected. If you don't, it can really throw you off. You just can't be surprised at anything that might happen.

MS. STROKUM   You know, it just occurred to me that we could be thinking up things that the teachers already know. We'll have to do better than that if we expect to earn our money.

MS. UNEVEN   You may have a point there, Pat. Of course, we have to think this through and put it down on paper, whereas the other teachers really wouldn't go that far with it.

MS. STROKUM   Well, just the same, I think we had better decide how we're really going to make a contribution here. It would seem pretty silly and embarrassing to me if we told the teachers to flick light switches and stare at children. Not that we don't do these things, but somehow we have to be more helpful.

MR. TIRANT (*Tongue-in-cheek*)   So, you pick out a couple of my ideas and go after them right away, uh, Pat? Seriously though, we'll have to do some homework on this. For example, somebody is going to have to read up on what studies say about discipline and control.

MS. UNEVEN   I think I'd like to do that.

MS. STROKUM   Hey, I think we're onto something here. Something else we could do is interview any teachers that we can find around this summer—get their ideas on what seems to work best for them.

MS. ENERGY   Just one problem, though. We still haven't decided on what we're going to come up with. I thought your point was a good one, Pat. We have to come up with a format or a goal we're shooting for here. Maybe we should talk some more about ideas we have. What have we thought of so far, Pat?

MS. STROKUM   Well, I've just been jotting these things down as we went. Here's what I have so far.

(*She shows everyone these notes.*)

*Discipline Committee Notes*

A set of rules for the students?
A set of rules for the teachers?
Tricks or gimmicks that we use?

There are no easy remedies.
Depends on individual and situation.
Must think of specific ways to solve problems.
Don't overreact—think it through.
Way you discipline depends on your personality.
Should be consistent.
Goal is a hassle-free environment.
Talk with individuals who are misbehaving.
Should always expect the unexpected.
Evelyn Uneven would like to read studies.


MR. TIRANT  Well, we haven't done as badly as I thought. Another thing to put on that list is how important it is to be organized. You can actually help the students get confused on what they are doing by being disorganized, you can lose a whole room in about five minutes. Also, I think you have to define what you expect of the students. They have to know what you consider acceptable and unacceptable.

MS. STROKUM  I think, too, that you should never stay in one place very long in the classroom. I always circulate—keep physical closeness with the students. It helps them to keep on task or to ask questions if they're stuck. Otherwise, there is a temptation to goof off.

MS. UNEVEN  Oh, my gosh, look at the time. I've got to go.

MS. STROKUM  Well, listen, before we break up today, let's get our work laid out here so that we can show some progress for next time. Evelyn, you said you wanted to read some of the studies. Does anyone else want to work on that with Evelyn? (Mr. Tirant nods his head.) OK, B.J. And Bernice, how about if you and I get together to interview any of the teachers we can find?

MS. ENERGY  Fine. That sounds like it might be fun. I guess we'll know a little more about what we'll end up with after we have done our homework, as B.J. put it.

MR. TIRANT  I think it looks like we'll probably come up with maybe a general list of principles or guides to follow, along with some other findings to give some direction for the teachers. We can even provide some sources for teachers to read if they're really interested.

MS. STROKUM  Well, I think that tells us where we are. Is it all right with everyone if we meet at this same time two weeks from today for a kind of progress report? I think then we can wrap it up with the two weeks we'll have left.

(*Everyone agrees and leaves talking with one another*. Curtain Falls.)

## Act II

SCENE ONE

(*As the curtain rises, we see Evelyn Uneven and B.J. Tirant studiously reading books and other materials, taking notes from time to time.*)

MR. TIRANT   Hmmm. That's really interesting.

MS. UNEVEN   What's that, B.J.?

MR. TIRANT   I was just reading this study by somebody named DeFlaminis. What he's saying about teachers' ways of solving discipline problems is really a new way of looking at it. Instead of deciding just what works best for you, he explains how it's important to know in what ways the students will respond depending on what you do.

MS. UNEVEN   I'm not sure I get your drift.

MR. TIRANT   Well, of course, you'd have to read the whole study a few times to really get everything he's talking about. But basically he's saying that if as a teacher you use authority or coercion to get students to behave, the students are usually unwilling to stop mis-behaving. Oh, they may shape up, but they don't like it. On the other hand, if you use what he calls persuasion, situational contracting, or relational contracting as a teacher, the students are usually *willing* to change toward a more desired behavior. Also . . .

MS. UNEVEN   Whoa! Just a minute! I think I understand persuasion—that's like convincing with logic or just making good sense. But I'm not at all sure I understand the contracting business.

MR. TIRANT   Well, I'm not exactly sure I understand myself. I think the situational contract is when you negotiate with the students on the spot—you give them something and they stop goofing off in return. And the relational contract is like you have developed a personal relationship with the kid, so when he goofs off you say something like, "I thought we had an understanding."

MS. UNEVEN   That helps a little. What else does he say?

MR. TIRANT   Oh, a lot of stuff. The other way you can respond to mis-behavior as a teacher is by manipulating the student, and in this case, DeFlaminis says that the student is *unwitting*. You know—he doesn't even know it's happening to him. Here, I've got a little chart I put together after reading this study. Maybe it will help you understand.

(*B.J. hands chart to Evelyn.*)

MS. UNEVEN   Well, this certainly is interesting, but I'm still not sure how this will help the teacher solve discipline problems. I mean, some-times you have to use authority whether you like it or not, don't you?

MR. TIRANT   Yes, of course. But what this study tells you is what the consequences might be if you use it. Here, take a look at my notes on this. If you understand the chart and then read what DeFlaminis said other studies have found, I think you'll get the picture.

## Notes*

I. Studies that focused on student responses to teachers: "Unwilling" student responses, "willing" student responses, and "unwitting" student responses.

A. When teachers use authority or coercion they get unwilling student responses.

B. When teachers use persuasion, situational contracting, or relational contracting they get willing student responses.

C. When teachers use manipulation they get unwitting student responses.

### TEACHER RESPONSES TO MISBEHAVIOR*

| Students | Teachers | Definitions |
| --- | --- | --- |
| are unwilling when | use authority | Teacher uses authority of greater status or implicit threat of coercion. |
| | use coercion | Teacher uses force or student accepts as lesser of two evils. |
| are willing when | use persuasion | Student understands as logically more desirable than own judgment. |
| | use situational contract | Teacher bestows upon student some benefit in exchange for acceptable behavior. |
| | use relational contract | Accomplished by virtue of long-standing, reciprocal arrangement where teacher has bestowed benefit in advance of misbehavior. |
| are unwitting when | use manipulation | Unwitting substitution by student of teacher's judgment for his own—accomplished when student only sees elements of environment that teacher wants him to see. |

* Adapted from DeFlaminis (1976)

* Taken from DeFlaminis (1976)

II. What other studies have shown regarding these influences by teachers.

   A. Seventy-five percent of the approaches used by teachers were either authority or coercion and they were getting unwilling student responses.

   B. These unwilling methods were counterproductive, showing an increase in student disruption.

   C. Unwilling methods were also shown to reduce student self-esteem and made it difficult for students to develop independence. Teacher coercion in particular was found to cause problems to persist and had a negative effect on learning.

   D. Persuasion by the teachers was found to be more likely to lead to student self-control and produced the largest lasting attitude change in the students.

   E. Contracting showed the next largest lasting change in student attitude, and both the teachers and students found contracting a satisfying approach because each had the opportunity to influence the other.

   F. Contracting was also seen to support providing students with opportunities to learn decision making and the necessity for self-control.

   G. Manipulation was found in most studies to have neither a positive nor a negative effect on student growth and development.

MS. UNEVEN   I get it now. Say that's pretty good stuff to know.

MR. TIRANT   DeFlaminis also conducted his own study to see if these past findings were still true. I decided to put together a little quiz to see if teachers could guess what his findings were. You should be warned that the number of teachers involved in his study was small enough (eighty-five teachers) that another study with different teachers might show different results. Here's the quiz.

**Teacher Response to Misbehavior\***
**Quiz on Study Findings**

1. What category of likely student response did teachers elicit most?

   **a.** unwilling                **b.** willing

   **c.** unwitting                **d.** none of these

2. What particular teacher response did teachers use most?

   **a.** coercion                 **b.** persuasion

   **c.** manipulation             **d.** authority

\* After DeFlaminis (1976)

3. What particular teacher response did teachers like the least?
   a. contract                    b. authority
   c. coercion                    d. manipulation

4. What particular responses did teachers like best (choose two)?
   a. manipulation                b. contract
   c. coercion                    d. authority
   e. persuasion

5. What did teachers say were the weak points of using willing methods?
   a. considered it bribery
   b. considered it too much loss of power
   c. considered it took too long
   d. none of the above
   e. all of the above

6. What three methods were most often used at the time of the misbehavior?
   a. contracting, persuasion, authority
   b. authority, coercion, manipulation
   c. persuasion, manipulation, situational contracting
   d. all methods were used often

7. Who was found to use the most authority and coercion?
   a. high-school teachers
   b. junior-high-school teachers
   c. elementary teachers
   d. all about the same

8. When schools were found to differ in their patterns of response to misbehavior, it was normally due to:
   a. the kind of undergraduate training the teachers had received
   b. the kind of personalities the teachers were found to have
   c. the kind of leadership found in the school
   d. no one reason was found as the main cause

9. Overall, the study found that teachers tended to use authority and/or coercion about:
   a. 25% of the time
   b. 50% of the time
   c. 75% of the time
   d. nearly all of the time

10. What special group of teachers tended to use authority and/or coercion the least?
   a. the most experienced teachers
   b. the least experienced teachers
   c. the most educated teachers
   d. the least educated teachers

*Answers*

| | | |
|---|---|---|
| 1. a | 4. d, e | 7. b |
| 2. d | 5. e | 8. d |
| 3. a | 6. b | 9. c |
| | | 10. d |

MS. UNEVEN    That was an interesting quiz. Some of those results really
surprised me. While we're on the subject of interesting findings, I
read a report by Tjosvold (1976) that I think is helpful. One of
the things that he reported had to do with power in the classroom
and who had it. For example, he found that when the teacher held
more power or control of things than the students, the students
would respond differently than if the power was equal or if the
students had more than the teacher.

MR. TIRANT    What do you mean by power?

MS. UNEVEN    I think it is like control over things—like when a student
misbehaves and the teacher is the one that always decides what the
punishment will be. Or maybe just that the teacher seldom gives
the students a chance to make decisions about anything that goes
on in the class.

MR. TIRANT    I shouldn't think it would be any other way. After all, you've
got to keep control.

MS. UNEVEN    Now wait. The thing is, Tjosvold is just reporting what is
likely to occur if the teacher has too much power or if that power
is distributed in another way. For example, when the teacher has
considerably more power than the students, the students are very
likely going to either try to avoid the teacher or try to control the
teacher in return. But when the power is not so one-sided, it doesn't
work that way. Here, read this quote I copied from the study.

> If teachers and students have nearly equal power, they may have
> more incentives to take each other's position seriously and to be
> less suspicious and fearful; they then may find it easier to resolve
> their conflicts so that both of them benefit. (Tjosvold, 1976, p. 26)

MR. TIRANT    Well, it's logical, but I'm still not sure I buy it.

MS. UNEVEN    Another thing, if the teacher has too much power, Tjosvold
says that the students sometimes respond by overvaluing their
freedom (Brehm, 1966, in Tjosvold, p. 14). I really find that
interesting. I think I have felt that way at times myself. You know,
if someone orders you around, you become much more concerned
about your rights. If they aren't treating you that way, you may not
even be thinking about your rights or your freedom.

MR. TIRANT    I think I see what you're saying. It's kind of like the more
pressure you get, the more you value what it was like when the
pressure wasn't there.

MS. UNEVEN    That's an example, I think. You know, Tjosvold also
reported on some other ways students acted when the teacher uses
too much control or power. Mainly, it was that students have very
subtle or indirect ways of counteracting the teacher's control. One
way is to develop a kind of subculture which has a set of rules that
deny the importance of anything the teacher says or thinks is
important (Willower, 1965, in Tjosvold, p. 15). If the teacher

demonstrates that grades, good work on assignments, or behaving in class are to be positively valued, then the students might respond by demonstrating the opposite values.

MR. TIRANT   So, in other words, if you use too much control, the students will strike back by misbehaving and not doing well in their school work. You know, I think there is some truth in that.

MS. UNEVEN   But what really got me was another set of studies on this power thing that Tjosvold was reporting. He pointed out that some students, responding to the teacher's excess control, would simply resign themselves to the lower power status and in many cases do most anything to please the teacher. They would compile good grades instead of growing and developing in a way that would make them more independent. It said that many studies have shown that students have been found to believe implicitly that bluff and personality are more useful in getting ahead in school than are learning or the ability to think (Rhea, 1968, in Tjosvold, p. 15). Now, that's really something to think about!

MR. TIRANT   I guess a teacher who uses too much power could really be messing up kids, couldn't he?

MS. UNEVEN   That's what occurred to me. Well, we'd better get back to our reading.

(Scene Changes)


SCENE TWO

(*On another part of the stage we find Ms. Energy and Ms. Strokum talking excitedly about their interviews.*)

MS. ENERGY   . . . and then he said, "Oh, I just tell 'em if they don't do as I say, I'll have 'em expelled from school."

MS. STROKUM   Oh, my God! Was he serious?

MS. ENERGY   He couldn't have been more serious. How have your interviews been going?

MS. STROKUM   Well, I got lucky, I think. I happened onto a good question to ask that really produced some interesting ideas from the teachers I talked to. I was thinking that no one can really tell someone a step-by-step procedure for how to handle discipline in the classroom, but there may be some things you definitely should *not* do. So . . . my question was this: "If you were going to set out to deliberately cause discipline and control problems for yourself, what are some things you would do?"

MS. ENERGY   Hey, that *is* a good one.

MS. STROKUM   Ya, I was very lucky. I got stuff like:

- be unprepared for class
- have no sense of humor
- sit with a few kids and just chat for awhile
- sit at your desk all the time, never moving around

- look at and teach to just a few of the students
- lack enthusiasm and don't show any emotion
- do everything the same, never varying lessons or types of work to be done
- yell a lot, jumping down kids' throats and accusing them all the time
- never trust the kids and make sure they know it
- never admit you're wrong

MS. ENERGY    You did get a lot of ideas with that question. Never admit you're wrong. . . . I know from first-hand experience that will get you into trouble. I was really afraid when I just started teaching, so I would never admit to not knowing something. All that happened was the kids started trying to find things that I wouldn't know. They were much busier doing that than anything else. I finally decided that I got myself in that hole, so I would just have to admit to not knowing some things. But of course you have to be prepared for the subject—never knowing an answer is just as bad as not admitting it when you don't.

MS. STROKUM    Oh, yes. That was another thing I ran across in talking with Grace Verdict from Lincoln School. She not only mentioned about how important it was to know your subject, but also brought up something else of great importance, I think. I remembered it when you said something about getting yourself into that hole—what Grace said was that in many cases teachers really caused their own discipline problems either by things they did or things they did not do. Yours was a good example of really causing your own problem. I think, too, that sometimes teachers will make a big thing out of something that was not that important. But suddenly it has become an important issue because the teacher has blown it out of proportion. One of the elementary teachers said that for some reason her third-graders had been falling off their chairs a lot—accidentally, in most cases. It upset her more than it should have. So instead of either laughing it off or ignoring it (as long as the kid wasn't hurt), she gave a little lecture on proper posture and the right way to behave in class. One of the many things that she said happened following that bad move on her part was that everytime the kids wanted attention or wanted her to get off the subject, off the chair they'd go. She said point-blank, "Now there is a control problem that I brought on myself."

MS. ENERGY    Well, we want to be sure to remember that. It is important to me anyway. I wish I had known something about it before I started teaching. It would have been much easier. By the way, I did get some good information from Rick Landman* from the Viking School. He's been working on what he calls preventative approaches

* My thanks to Mr. Richard Landman for the contributions here.

to class management and he's fairly satisfied with it so far. He has been using values clarification, discussion groups, and several special approaches he has learned about apparently from one book called *Values Clarification: A Handbook of Practical Strategies for Teachers and Students,* by Simon, Howe, and Kirschenbaum (1972). Also, he's been using some of the Glasser (1969) reality therapy ideas. Naturally, it's too involved to cover all of it, but he has discussions with the kids on things they value and they also talk about how the classroom can be a better place.

MS. STROKUM    Oh, yes. I do some of that too, but I've never used the values stuff. How does he set this up?

MS. ENERGY    He calls the parents before school starts and visits their home to talk with them and the child about the discussions they will be having in the fall. He said that even if the discussions themselves didn't pay off, those home visits sure did. Getting the parents' support was the best thing he ever did. Another teacher told me that parent support was the most important thing for her as well. She said that if the parents "talk you down" at home, you don't have a chance of classroom control at school. I think that is really an important point, don't you?

MS. STROKUM    I sure do. We probably should recommend some kind of communication with parents or parent participation related to classroom management. I'm interested in hearing more about what Rick Landman does with this program.

MS. ENERGY    Well, the main goal is to set up a situation where you and the student try to work out problems together. Sometimes he'll have those group discussions while at other times he will work with individual students. In a way it's kind of like active listening that Gordon (1975) talks about in his book: *Teacher Effectiveness Training.* You help the student clarify the problems and try to get him to solve it instead of telling him what to do. It's supposed to help students become more independent and able to solve their own problems instead of causing problems in the class.

MS. STROKUM    That sounds good, but it sounds like it would take an awful lot of time, too.

MS. ENERGY    Maybe so, but Rick claims that the time you use in the beginning is gained many times over toward the end, because much fewer control problems arise. I guess it would take some training and some reading to really get an understanding of how to use the program he's talking about, but it's one possible alternative.

MS. STROKUM    Well, all we can do with information like that is make it available to the teachers.

MS. ENERGY    Oh! I almost forgot. I was talking with Jo Friedman and she gave me many interesting ideas, too. Mainly, she was talking about the same type of thing that Rick was mentioning, but she seemed to emphasize the Glasser idea more. She said she uses a

"Time Out" area in the room where a student can go to work out a problem he or she is having. I think she uses an old refrigerator carton. . . . So, if this kid is in trouble or causing a disturbance, she asks him or her to go to the "Time Out" area and try to work it out.

MS. STROKUM    I think that would work for younger kids, anyway. I'm not sure about seventh- and eighth-graders though.

MS. ENERGY    You may be right. Those eighth-graders could cook up some interesting ideas in a refrigerator box. One other idea that Jo mentioned was mirroring student behavior so that they could see what they are actually doing. One way to do this is describe (without judgment) to the student exactly what the behavior was and see what the student thinks of it. Also, I read somewhere that a teacher had a group of students who constantly got out of hand. So . . . what she did was not say a word and just start writing the student behaviors on the chalkboard as they occurred. Apparently, the students were amazed at finding out what they were doing and improved their behavior almost instantly. Of course, I could see that not always working either.

MS. STROKUM    You know, I'm kind of looking forward to our meeting next Friday, now. I have to admit I was a bit apprehensive before, but I think we're coming along okay on this. If B.J. and Evelyn are getting good information, we might pull this together after all.

MS. ENERGY    I'm glad to hear you say that, Pat. Frankly, I've been a little worried too.

(*Ms. Energy and Ms. Strokum stroll off stage exchanging comments as they exit.*)

(*Curtain Falls*)


# Act III

SCENE ONE

(*As the curtain rises, we see that the second meeting of the Teachers' Committee on Discipline is already well under way. Most of the ideas exchanged between the two members of each team have now been exchanged with the other members of the committee. They are seated around a conference table.*)

MR. TIRANT    So what you're saying is that all the teachers in the district should go to the home of each student before school starts. Why, that's absurd! I have over a hundred and fifty students!

MS. ENERGY    Oh, no. Of course not. All I'm saying is that it's one idea. Even *you* could do it with maybe a particularly troublesome class. The whole point is to find some way to let the parents know that you're concerned and think their child is important.

MS. STROKUM  Well, we've shared most of the ideas we have come up with so far. I think what we need now is some way of organizing this so that it will be helpful to the teachers.

MS. UNEVEN  That's what has been worrying me all along. Now I'm even more worried. Look at this mound of stuff we have here. How can we possibly put this all together without making a book out of it?

MR. TIRANT  You know, it's been my conviction all along that we can't turn out reams of information for the teachers.

MS. ENERGY  Well, we were able to go through and find out all of this information. I don't see why the other teachers can't at least read what we have put together for them.

MS. STROKUM  There are very few with your stamina, Bernice. Anyway, I think we have to be realistic about this. Besides, we have been given time out of school with pay to do this work and I don't think we can expect teachers to find the time once school starts to go through pages of ideas and findings. As a matter of fact, once school starts, I don't think I would have the time either.

MS. UNEVEN  What are we going to do then, just be the school district experts and wait for teachers to ask us?

MR. TIRANT  Actually, that's not a bad idea. Not that we are experts, but we could recommend that we serve as consultants for building committees. I don't think we can solve the problems of every teacher in all the schools anyway. What we can do is provide maybe ten or fifteen general guideposts or suggestions backed up with suggested references plus the notes we have from our investigation. And we should recommend to the district that more building-by-building work could be done on the issue.

MS. ENERGY  That sounds acceptable to me. Maybe we could have a section set aside here at the administration building for materials we have collected or anything anyone wants to add to it. As a matter of fact . . .

MS. UNEVEN  I'm sorry to interrupt, Bernice, but I didn't want to forget to let you know about this book I found. It's called *Survival Kit for Teachers (and Parents)* by Collins and Collins (1975). I found it to be really practical and specific. We might want to make it available for the teachers.

MS. STROKUM  It would be a good one to reference in the guide we give to the teachers.

MS. UNEVEN  You should see it. It has ideas on what to do for nearly every situation you could think of. They deal with absenteeism, crying, grades, even jealousy. It's really practical.

MR. TIRANT  While we're on the subject of ideas. I ran across this list of things teachers could do to solve problems in the classroom. I got it out of a book edited by Long, Morse, and Newman called *Conflict in the Classroom* (1965). There are other ideas in there

too, like "what punishment will do to kids" in a chapter written by
Redl called "The Concept of Punishment."

   (*Mr. Tirant hands out his list of managing classroom
problems.*)


## Methods of Managing Classroom Problems*

1. **Planned ignoring:** Essentially what it says. Instead of responding to acting-out behavior, ignore it for a few days hoping that this non-reinforcement will curtail the behavior.
2. **Signal interference:** Includes eye contact, hand gestures, clearing your throat—all used in order to stop behavior and get child back to what is going on.
3. **Proximity control:** Touching or standing near child, letting her or him know that you are concerned, but not upset.
4. **Interest boosting:** Finding out from child how she or he is doing on the lesson, seeing if she or he would like some help. Sometimes should include finding out what child's interests are, then going with that rather than the assignment.
5. **Tension release:** Usually humor or playful behavior to take away the tension of the situation.
6. **Hurdle lessons:** Breaking assignment directions into smaller parts to insure understanding. Sometimes when a child doesn't understand she or he will become a behavior problem.
7. **Lesson restructuring:** Changing the lesson or particular assignment in the middle of the action. This is often done when things just aren't working out. Unfortunately, some teachers feel they must continue on the planned lesson regardless.
8. **Support from routine:** Make schedules, assignment due dates, classroom practice in general, a matter of clearly communicated routine.
9. **Direct appeal to values:** *Example:* If you continue to talk, we won't have time to plan the party.
10. **Removing seductive objects:** Athletic equipment, outside reading material, pictures, and other materials that are not part of lesson should not be around to tempt students.
11. **Antiseptic removal:** Child having some trouble, ask her or him if they would like to go get a drink of water or go get some papers you left in the office.
12. **Physical restraint:** Use only when child endangers the physical safety of herself or himself or that of others.

MS. STROKUM   I do some of these things, but I didn't know they had a
   name. That *is* a helpful list, B.J. We seem to have a lot of information.

---

* Adapted from Nicholas J. Long, "Managing Surface Behavior of Children in School," in *Conflict in the Classroom*, ed. Nicholas J. Long et al., pp. 352–362.

I guess there is really no end to it. But if we stick to our idea of making what we give the teachers short and sweet, plus providing some references for them, I think we can manage.

MS. ENERGY   Don't forget the material center we're going to set up, and that we can serve as advisors to each school.

MS. STROKUM   Right. . . . Now, I think we're ready to pull this together. I think that Bernice and I can pull together a few general principles from our interviews along with material we have read—some of it we got from Evelyn and B.J. And B.J., perhaps you and Evelyn could do the same. (Everyone nods in agreement.) So . . . perhaps we can take next week to do that and meet here the following week to grind the final product out.

MS. ENERGY   That's fine with me. I think I have an idea for some other things that could go in the material center, too.

MS. STROKUM   Good. Well, I guess that's all for today then.

(*Lights go down as the scene ends.*)


SCENE TWO

(*As the lights come up, the four principal characters are once again seated around the conference table discussing their ideas for the final set of guidelines.*)

MS. ENERGY   . . . and then I thought, if we might serve as consultants, what could we use to get teachers involved in discussing their positions and beliefs about classroom control? So, I developed this game I call the Classroom Problems Game. It's very simple really. I figured we could leave it in the material center, but also maybe use it as an opening gambit when we work with teachers. Or, for that matter, teachers could use it themselves as a self-starter for discussion. Here is the explanation of how the game works.

(*Ms. Energy provides written explanation of game
to committee members.*)


# Classroom Problems Game


**How Many Players:**   Any even number of players can play this game in one team of two, two teams of two each, and so on. In cases where more than one team is playing, each plays continuously without regard to the other teams.

**Materials Needed:**   At least twenty concise statements of classroom problems are written on sheets of paper about the size of playing cards—one statement for each sheet.

**The Classroom Problems:**  Here are some ideas for classroom problems, but you may want to include your own.

1. A student leaves the room without permission.
2. Two students are having a loud argument while class is going on.
3. A student throws a pencil at another student.
4. A student throws a pencil at you, the teacher.
5. A student from another class comes in and disrupts your class.
6. A student starts crying for no apparent reason.
7. A book is missing and you think you know which student took it.
8. A student doesn't have an assignment done which was due a week ago.
9. A student tells you, the teacher, to "go to hell."
10. Two students start chasing each other around the room.
11. A student runs out of the classroom, out of the school, and down the street.
12. Another teacher reprimands three of your students for doing something you said was all right, but the students yell very loudly that they have been shafted.
13. A male student pinches a female student on the behind.
14. Two students are playing football with a paper wad.
15. You, the teacher, overhear a student swearing at another student.
16. A student from another class walks right in front of you, the teacher, while you are teaching a lesson.
17. A student falls out of a chair and the whole class laughs loud and long.
18. You, the teacher, overhear a student swearing at you under his or her breath.
19. One student complains that another student has stolen his or or her billfold.
20. Three students are pitching pennies in the back of the room.

**How the Game Is Played:**  One playing partner draws one classroom problem from the shuffled pile, making certain not to let the other partner see what it says. After thinking it out, the partner who has drawn the problem tries to get the other partner to guess what the problem is by using hints that must be confined to statements beginning with "I would solve this problem by. . . ."

At no time can the hint-giver use any information included on the problem sheet. You are trying to get your partner to guess what the problem is from your indications of how you would solve it. The guessing partner gets one guess for each hint given. Make your hints good ones; you are limited to only five hints per problem. Once one partner has either guessed or given up on the five hints, then the other partner becomes the guesser.

**Objective of the Game:**  The primary objective of this game is to encourage discussion of various ways to solve classroom management problems. After the guessing partner has either figured out the answer or has given up, the two partners should decide what could have been better hints and what other solutions would be possible.

**To Win:**    The first partner to get the other partner to guess five classroom problems correctly wins the game or when two or more teams are playing, the first team to get five correct wins.

MR. TIRANT    You never cease to amaze me, Bernice. You must have worked on that game a long time.

MS. ENERGY    Oh, not really. It was fun to do anyway.

MS. STROKUM    Well, I guess we're ready to pull together what we have developed for the teachers. Let's see what we have here. Evelyn, you and B.J. can look at our list and Bernice and I can have a glance at what you came up with.
            (*Committee members spend a few minutes examining the work that has been completed.*)

MR. TIRANT    I see we have duplicated each other in spots, but it looks like we have a pretty good set of ideas here. Somebody is just going to have to sit down and put it in final form so that the ideas we have correspond.

MS. ENERGY    I'd be glad to do that. I'll send each of you a copy and give you a chance to react before we give it to the assistant superintendent and the teachers' council.

MS. UNEVEN    What shall we call this thing, anyway?

MR. TIRANT    How about something like "Rules of the Road for Classroom Discipline"?

MS. STROKUM    Oh, I think that sounds a little too absolute and final. These are really just some selected recommendations.

MS. ENERGY    Why not that then? "Selected Recommendations for Classroom Control and Management."

MR. TIRANT    I'll go along with that.
            (*Everyone else nods in agreement.*)

MS. UNEVEN    You know, this wasn't as bad as I thought it would be. I really didn't think we could do it.
            (*Everyone laughs as they walk off together.*)

**Postscript.**    So the committee did produce some ideas for the new or experienced teacher. Along with the information included in the play itself, here is their final product.


## Selected Recommendations for Classroom Control and Management

PREFACE

This set of ideas and references is not intended to be all-inclusive, but should provide a teacher with enough ideas so that he or she might survive in the typical classroom setting. The committee also recommends that individual teachers or individual schools should engage in training, reading, and any other means they can, to work on the problems of control and management within their own specific setting. The committee members would be available to help any individuals or groups get started on this quest for self-preservation. Also, any material mentioned will be available at the information center at the administration building.

## Selected Principles

1. *Don't overreact* or react without thinking to student misbehavior. While there are no easy remedies to solving these problems, irrational teacher responses can sometimes cause more trouble than you started out with. Many teachers feel that, being human, they must react emotionally, but in too many cases they are sorry later that they reacted without thinking it through.

2. *Expect the unexpected* and try to anticipate problems that might occur. Teachers who are successful at this know that it is important to esti-mate or at least guess in advance what problems· might occur with any given lesson or teaching situation. First-year teachers may have to learn this the hard way, but learn it they must. Small group work, large group discussions, games, and field trips all have their special contexts and things can go very wrong if you are not prepared for what could happen. And if the unexpected does occur, see the first selected principle.

3. *Don't lose your perspective* or forget who you are and where you are. Experienced teachers often say that they mistakenly get upset because a student is doing something which is distracting, only to learn too late that no one else was distracted. The teacher has to use the class as a barometer for such things or become more of a distraction him-self by making an issue of it. A teacher may also lose perspective by trying to solve a complicated discipline problem on the spot, forgetting that the remainder of the class is now totally off task. Simple problems can be solved quickly with a look or a shake of the head, but more complex difficulties deserve more time and rational thought. Also, conferring with another teacher can be a significant aid in maintaining a realistic perspective.

4. *Make your expectations clear* to the students so that any misbehavior on their part is not due to misunderstanding. If there are certain things you can't or won't allow, pick situations when these things come up to explain your limits to the students. (It's not a good idea to start off the year listing such limits, since the students either won't hear it all or can't see its meaning until a real situation arises. Also, there is no point in starting off in a negative manner which might actually induce misbehavior.) It is also important to outline expecta-tions for given days and/or particular lessons. Students need to be reminded when it is all right to talk, or when silence is necessary. In addition to this, many teachers actually list the chronological events

of the day or class period so that the students can know what the routine is going to be. (This is also a good technique for keeping organized—see #5.)

5. *Keep things organized* enough so that students know what they are supposed to be doing. This means providing reminders of what the daily or period schedule includes and organizing the subject matter so that the students do not become confused. Not knowing what to do, students get off task and sometimes into trouble. In addition to these organizational factors, the teacher must be prepared for each lesson or activity. Teachers who are unsure of the subject matter and/or unprepared to teach it on a given day often become disorganized very quickly since they themselves do not know for sure where they are headed. This might confuse the students for a time, and is likely to set up other kinds of control problems, especially if the students suspect that the teacher is in some way unsure of himself.

6. *Maintain physical proximity* with the students by moving around the room and keeping eye contact with as many students as possible. Even during seat work or small-group work, students need to know that you are part of the action. You can help keep them on task and at the same time discover potential problems before they get out of hand. Failure to project a whole-room presence and awareness leaves the teacher outside the group, putting him or her in a position of not being in touch with the minute-to-minute interactions that occur in a classroom setting. A teacher who doesn't circulate runs the risk of unintentionally ignoring behavior simply because he or she does not know that it is going on. (This is part of keeping communication open as well. See the next suggestion.)

7. *Make students aware* that you are in touch with what is going on in the classroom. This is sometimes referred to as "letting them know that you know" since your goal is to keep in-group contact with the students as they live with you in this single-room dwelling called a classroom. Students tend to think that if a teacher does not react in some way to what they are doing the teacher must not know that it is happening. This does not mean that you have to laugh or cry or scream or leap over your desk, but it does mean that in some subtle or obvious way you have to let the students know that you are aware of their behavior. "Yes, Bill, I know you're breaking pencils. What do you do for an encore?" Or perhaps a knowing look will take care of it. Teachers say that many of their student teachers begin to build problems for themselves as they let these things slip by. Some problems have been allowed to grow so serious that students begin to believe the teacher must really be "out of it" since they can do so many things without any acknowledgement at all.

8. *Deal with problems in the context* in which they occur not only by considering what might have caused the disruption in each special case, but also by paying attention to the time of day, the time of year,

and certainly where the students have been before coming to your class. Classes before or after lunch or gym can develop some strange circumstances that must be considered, as every experienced teacher knows. Also, if you are a relatively easygoing teacher and the students have just come from a very strict one, the students could overreact to their new-found freedom. This usually means that, taking this into consideration, you must change your style to fit the particular situation. Employing standard procedures for disciplining or reprimanding students without considering such special circumstances can do more harm than good. At best, the students may feel that you are not dealing with them in terms of their unique situation and therefore consider you unfair, and at worst, they could consider your tactics so unjust that they would retaliate by causing further problems.

9. *Solve problems yourself* whenever it is at all possible. While certain building principals insist upon being immersed in the discipline routine, they can seldom know the students as you know them and certainly will not be able to fully grasp either the history or the context of the problem. This is also true for other teachers. One important exception to this would occur when members of a teaching team work very closely with one another and with each other's students. Such teams have been able to work out reciprocal agreements concerning either certain kinds of misbehavior or certain students. I know of a number of cases where a team member has approached another team member and said, "Look, maybe it's me. Why don't you have a talk with her?"

10. *Work for variety* in your teaching style and in the kinds of lessons, activities, and assignments that you provide for the students. It's one thing to be organized (#5) and to make expectations clear (#4), but it is quite another to be so systematic and routine that some of the students simply lose interest out of sheer boredom. It is almost a certainty that such boredom will lead to control problems for at least a portion of the class. Variety for its own sake is something we all appreciate from time to time, and while routine provides a kind of soothing feeling of stability, it can be overdone.

**Note.** We, the committee, are certain that many of you may have other ideas to add to our list, and we welcome them. It is certain that each of you understands your school and its principal better than any of us could and can therefore see some other ideas you would like to implement. In any event, we feel that your goals should include taking a relaxed, calm approach to classroom control situations and emphasizing your trust in individual students. As many teachers told us when we talked with them about this issue, "The students usually respond to whoever the teacher is, and they'll be great if you expect that of them; but if you expect them to cause trouble they probably will."

# 4

# Credibility with Students

## Students Discuss Teacher Credibility*

INTERVIEWER   The reason I want to talk with you today is that I am doing research on what students think about classes and school in general. I am particularly interested in getting your views about teachers.

STUDENT #1   Are you going to tell our teachers what we say?

I   No. Anything you tell me will be confidential. No one will hear our taped discussion but me, and when I write it up no names will be mentioned.

s #2   Well, we have a lot of things we'd like to say, but we don't want to get into trouble.

I   I know what you mean and I promise that no one will know, but if you don't feel like telling me anything, that's your right.

s #3   What do you want to know about our teachers?

I   If you're ready, let's begin this way. Each of you think of a teacher you have had in school whom you liked, a teacher you felt could be trusted. In other words, a teacher about whom you are likely to say: "If it's good enough for him or her, it's good enough for me."

s #4   Mr. Johnson, seventh-grade math. He was really good. He knew the subject really well, but he didn't bore you. Even if you weren't doing so well, he'd help . . . he was really patient.

s #1   Ya, I had Johnson too. He really did know the math, but sometimes he would get upset, especially if you didn't do the assignment.

* The information contained in this discussion was taken from audio taped interviews with 211 high school students from three schools in Connecticut (Lapan, 1972).

s #5   I had a teacher in fourth grade, she was good. I believed her when she told us stuff. She was smart, but she was fair too.

I   Let's see if I get what you've told me so far. You're saying that when you believe what a teacher says it's because that teacher knows the subject matter but is fair too. Is that right?

s #1   Ya, that's about right, but I think there's more too. Like I had this seventh-grade teacher, she was an English teacher and she used all of them big words. . . . Nobody understood what she was talking about half the time.

s #6   Hey, I remember her. We used to call her professor all the time. She really thought that was cool, but she didn't know it was a put-down.

I   What did this teacher do or say to make you feel this way?

s #6   Well, it wasn't just the big words . . . I mean . . . she acted like we were supposed to know everything. She'd go over directions or explain something once, real fast, then that was it. We were supposed to understand it or else.

s #1   That's not all! It was almost like we weren't in the room. Sometimes I think we could have walked out while she was talking and she wouldn't have known the difference.

I   Does this mean you didn't trust her, that she wasn't credible in your eyes?

s #1   Well, it's hard to trust somebody who doesn't act like you even exist. Besides, she just couldn't seem to talk on our level so we could understand and she never asked us if we understood either. I don't think she cared.

s #3   I've had teachers like that too. I didn't trust 'em. If they didn't act like I counted for something then they didn't count either.

I   Let's see if you can think of other teachers you've had who acted in a way that made you trust what they said.

s #2   Mrs. Block, my history teacher now.

I   What is it that she says or does that makes you believe her?

s #2   She knows her subject really well and I think that's important. I mean if the teacher doesn't know what she's talking about how can you believe in what she says?

I   Anything else she says or does?

s #2   I guess what really makes her trustworthy is that if you tell her something she doesn't blab it all over school. She's not a narc.

I   A narc?

s #2   Ya, a narc. She doesn't narc on you—tell on you or tell things about you.

s #1   How do you know she doesn't?

s #2   You know, man. You know. I had a teacher last year who told me he thought something was bothering me and it was goofing up my school work. So I told him about my old man leaving us to live with some woman in Springfield. The next thing I knew two other teachers tell me how sorry they are to hear about my father clearing out. That's a narc.

ɪ   So its important that teachers not talk to other people about what you tell them.

s #2   Well, most things anyway. There are some teachers you just can't trust. But Mrs. Block, you can trust her. She doesn't tell your personal stuff to everybody. One time she said she wanted to talk to somebody about something I told her, but she asked me first if it was all right. That's what makes her cool.

ɪ   What are some other things teachers do that make you trust them?

s #4   One of the things I don't like is where teachers judge you before you even hand in work on anything.

ɪ   Could you tell me a little more?

s #4   Well, I'm thinking about my sixth-grade teacher. I'll never forget it, when I came into the room the first day she said, "Oh, I had your sister two years ago. I hope you can do as well as she did." That really got me.

ɪ   You mean that you were being compared to your sister?

s #4   Not only that, but she had already decided how good my work was supposed to be. By the end of the second week of school she was already telling me that my sister could do things that I couldn't.

ɪ   That is a bummer. What'd you do?

s #4   I quit trying. What was the use? I wasn't my sister, I was me. I sure didn't trust that teacher.

s #5   I've got a teacher now who always compares our work with grades we got last year. I think that's unfair!

ɪ   How come?

s #5   Well, just because you didn't do too hot in science because you didn't like playing with frogs doesn't mean you can't do the work in physics. Besides, he didn't have me last year anyway. How did he find out my grades? I don't trust anybody who snoops around in your records.

ɪ   Kind of like the CIA. or something, uh?

s #5   Ya! Big Brother's watching you.

ɪ   Well, we've done pretty well so far. Maybe we've talked as much about teachers we *don't* trust, but that's all right. Any more ideas about why you tend to trust what certain teachers say and do?

s #1   One thing I think is really important is that a teacher tells you exactly what she expects. I've had some teachers who are good at that and it really helps. It's good to know where they're coming from.

s #3   Miss Coughlin is like that. The first few days of school she explained how she graded and what the work was going to be . . . and she told us things she didn't want us to do.

ɪ   Could you give some examples?

s #3   What she didn't want? Well, she didn't make a big deal about it, but she made it clear that work had to be in on time. If it wasn't and you didn't have a good excuse, your grade would go down.

s #1   That's what I mean. I've had so many teachers who didn't lay that out at all. Then you hand in something late and they nail you for it. Some other teachers don't give a damn whether stuff is on time or not. But those who will nail you for it a lot of times don't tell you you're going to get nailed until it's too late.

I   So you find it hard to trust what that kind of teacher says or does in other areas too?

s #1   Right on! It's really hard to believe 'em when they pull surprises on you like that.

I   Well, let's take a break and come back to talk some more in about ten minutes. O.K.?

## What Is Credibility?

What these high-school students are discussing is of great importance to them. They feel very strongly about their perceptions of teachers and whether or not they trust them. What they are saying is, in effect, that what you as a teacher say and do makes a big difference in your ability to reach them in the classroom. And much of their conversation revolves around the believability or credibility of the teacher.

The term credibility is used to mean the believability of a person according to others who view that person—in this case student perception of teachers. Credibility has been given many other labels, such as status, trustworthiness, charisma, prestige, and image, but whichever term is used ". . . research consistently has indicated that the more 'it' the communicator [teacher] is perceived to have, the more likely the receiver [student] is to accept the transmitted information" (Berlo et al., 1970, p. 563).

In the classroom situation your credibility as a teacher is an important factor since a large portion of your time is spent message-sending. Students may vary in their judgments as to how credible they perceive you to be, but overall your credibility should be fairly good in their eyes or problems could arise. And after all, because of your extensive message-sending role, your effectiveness as a teacher could be significantly influenced by the degree of credibility you are perceived to have.

The amount of credibility a teacher is believed to have could be judged in one of two general ways: (1) according to static or stable characteristics of that teacher such as color of hair, tone of voice, or physical size; or (2) according to the perceptions of the teacher's classroom behavior, such as knowledge of the subject matter, fairness toward students, or communication effectiveness in explaining lessons. Most people who have conducted research in this field agree that the credibility of an individual depends on the perceptions of others and not on static attributes. Credibility is a fluid, changing entity which depends for the most part on the point of view of the recipient of a communication (Rosnow and Robinson, 1967). As Karlins and Abelson (1970, p. 109) have explained it, ". . . credibility is in the eye of the beholder."

What is your credibility rating? How do you know if your students perceive you as believable? One helpful way is to scrutinize what students have reported as characteristic behavior of "credible" and "not-so-credible" teachers. Let's get back then to the interview with our high school students to see what they have to say.

INTERVIEWER    O.K. Let's look at this issue of teacher believability from another angle. We have been talking about teachers you felt you could trust. This time, each of you think of a teacher about whom you would be likely to say: "If he or she says something is so, or says it's good, I would tend to doubt the statement."

STUDENT #1    You mean like old lady Turner? Man, nobody believes anything she says.

s #2    Right! Anybody'd be stupid to believe her.

I    Why? What does she do to make you feel this way?

s #1    Oh, a lot of things. For one thing she doesn't listen to anything you say to her and when you tell her she's on the wrong page she tells you to be quiet or acts like she didn't even hear you.

s #2    Ya, but she does worse things too. You never know where you are in the class. . . . She doesn't tell you what grades you're getting until it's too late. And I don't think she knows the subject either. Anyway, I don't believe anything she says whether it's about biology or not.

s #3    I've heard about her. Bob Washington told me that if you try to tell her something that might make the class go better, she gets nervous and changes the subject all the time.

s #1    She's a winner, all right. I don't think the other teachers think much of her either. They're always making jokes about her.

s #4    Give her a break, you guys. She's not so bad. I had her last year and I learned a lot.

s #2    Ya, but did you believe what she said very much?

s #4    Well, not always. She did get a little mixed up . . . but I think Stephens is worse. He's always giving speeches about how we should act and how important it is to study, but he will never listen if you have ideas that might make the class run better.

s #5    Ya, he really blows his stack if you tell him that discussing would be better sometimes rather than him lecturing all the time. He thinks he's got all the answers, that's for sure.

I    There have been some interesting ideas so far. If I understand what you're saying about these teachers they seem to not know the subject matter, be very closed to suggestions, and aren't considered very important by the other teachers.

s #6    They talk about students to other teachers too. That really bugs me. I don't trust anybody who does that.

s #2    I can think of a teacher I didn't like in eighth grade. Well, I liked her all right, but I really didn't trust what she said much.

i    Why not?

s #2    Mainly she was just boring. I mean kids would actually go to sleep in her class all the time.

i    Do you remember what she did to make things so boring?

s #2    Gee, I don't know. She was just boring that's all. . . . She talked in a monotone that kind of made you sleepy. She was just unexciting, like she really didn't want to be there. I think she was bored herself.

s #6    I've had a few teachers like that. They really don't act like they care.

i    Not very dynamic, uh?

s #6    Dead City, tired blood or something.

s #3    I had a teacher my freshman year who I really didn't trust. He taught political science and was always giving his opinions on everything.

i    You find it hard to trust a teacher who gives their own views or ideas?

s #3    It's more than that. He never considered our views on anything and always made you feel like he had the one and only answer for everything. We never got to consider both sides of an idea, it was always just his side.

s #5    Ya, I really hate teachers like that. They act like they know it all and you know they can't be right all the time. My history teacher was like that. We even proved her wrong once by showing her a book that explained our argument. She just said the book was wrong and wouldn't talk about it any more.

i    You really find a teacher like that hard to believe?

s #5    Even when you can prove they're wrong and they still won't admit it. How could you trust anything they'd say?

s #4    I don't like teachers who won't let you ask questions when you get lost or something.

i    You mean when the teacher is giving an assignment . . .

s #4    No! Anytime. Sometimes you just need to ask questions to help you understand the material better . . . like you can't seem to see how to do something even though the teacher has explained it. You just need to ask your own questions before you catch on to it.

s #1    I wouldn't trust a teacher who is disorganized. You know, they lose things like assignments you hand in or forget that they ever gave the assignment. You feel like you did all the work for nothing.

i    That is bad. What does the teacher do, tell you to forget it, throw it away?

s #1   Ya, like that, or they say keep it, we'll be working on it later. But you never work on it later. I'd never trust a teacher like that.

I   How organized a teacher is must be important. Can you think of other examples of what a disorganized teacher does that makes you not trust what they say?

s #6   One thing is when they aren't ready to teach something. That's being disorganized isn't it?

I   I would guess so. Do you mean that they haven't organized what it is they're going to teach.

s #6   Ya, like you can tell. They kind of ramble on and you can't figure out where they're going. They get mixed up and repeat things . . . just get lost.

s #2   That sounds like Mrs. Shay. I don't think she ever prepares anything . . . when she teaches she'll tell you to do something one way and then tell you to do it a different way five minutes later. That can really goof you up in home ec.

s #1   Mr. Berman is a little like that, but he does something else that really gets me. He's always blaming the whole class when just one student is goofing off. He'll make us all do extra homework or keep us all after school.

I   Are you saying that this makes him less believable because he does this.

s #1   In a way. He makes you feel like you're in trouble even if you didn't do anything. That's not fair. I don't know if that means I don't believe what he says, but its harder to accept what he says when he makes dumb moves like that.

s #4   Well, Berman does something else that bugs me more. He'll blame the whole class when things aren't going right.

I   I'm not sure I understand.

s #4   Just last week he was all prepared to show us this film on geography or archaeology or something and the projector broke. We got a little noisy I guess, but it was no big deal. He screamed at us for ten minutes and everybody knew it was because the projector broke, not what we were doing. You can't trust a teacher like that.

I   Well, we're getting fairly close to the end. Are there any other ideas you want to share before we stop?

s #5   This was fun. I wish our teachers would let us talk about things like this.

s #3   They'd learn a lot. Maybe they would do a better job.

s #6   Are you sure you're not going to tell them what we said?

I   A promise is a promise. You don't want me to, do you?

s #1   God, No! It might help them, but I don't think I want to take the chance.

s #2   Can you imagine old Stephens getting ahold of this stuff. We'd be in detention for the rest of the year.

s #4   I guess the main thing is that we got to talk about it. I thought of things that I really hadn't thought about before. You know, I guess the main thing that is important, if you trust what a teacher says, is that they have confidence.

s #5   Ya, but some teachers have confidence and still act like fools. I wouldn't believe what a teacher says just because they act like they know what they're doing.

s #6   There are a lot of things really. They have to respect us and trust us if we're going to believe what they have to say. They have to know the subject, but they have to be willing to accept criticism too.

s #4   I think that the teachers who are willing to accept criticism are the best. They wouldn't need to hear this stuff we're saying because they let us tell 'em about it in class.

s #2   Ya, that's the important thing. The teachers I believe in most are the ones that ask us to tell them how to make the class better and they don't get uptight about it.

s #4   They ask you your opinions and they really want them too. Some teachers will ask but you know that you can't tell the truth or they'd barf.

s #1   That's what Mr. Lovelace did this year.

s #4   Barf?

s #1   No, gees. I mean he told us at the beginning that if we had any ideas about how to make the class better we should let him know.

I   What happened?

s #1   Some turkey believed him and we all paid the price. He said he was the teacher and we'd better not forget it. He was trained to teach and we didn't know anything about it. That guy who told him how he could do something better has been taking crap from Lovelace ever since, too.

I   That sounds familiar. I had a professor tell our class the same thing at the beginning of the year. Then he proceeded to lecture for sixteen weeks. We didn't even get a chance to go to the bathroom much less suggest changes in the class.

s #5   That reminds me. I do have to go to the can. Are we finished?

I   I think so, yes. Thanks a lot for your ideas. I'll be able to use them for my study. And I promise not to blow the whistle on any of you.


### The Results of a Study on Teacher Credibility

The student interview information was a helpful start toward gaining insight about how students perceive teacher credibility. Their ideas should serve you well as a kind of check on how you come across in the classroom. The investigation into student perception of teacher credibility did not stop with the interview data, however. A much more extensive study (Lapan, 1972, 1976) was conducted that included examining other credibility studies as well as using statistical techniques to refine the findings.

As a result of this comprehensive inquiry into what makes teachers credible it was discovered that five areas of teacher behavior were the strongest, most important credibility determinants as far as students were concerned. No other credibility areas were found to be as significant as these five.

## THE FIVE AREAS OF TEACHER CREDIBILITY

The single strongest factor leading students to believe that teachers are credible was that of *teacher openness*. Teachers who score well on this credibility factor do so because students perceived them as willing to accept comments or criticisms about the way the class was run, and because they were seen as encouraging students to express their ideas and dislikes about the subject area or methods used in the class. Thus, if a teacher wanted to improve the openness credibility factor he or she should ask for feedback from the students about how the class is going and consider what students have to say with an open mind.

In order to judge teachers on their openness, students rated them on the following nine items on a one to five scale: 1 = almost never true; 2 = seldom true; 3 = true about half the time; 4 = true most of the time; and 5 = almost always true.

The teacher for this class:
- Encourages your comments on how the class could be improved.
- Wants to know what your opinions are.
- Encourages you to tell how the class is going.
- Listens to criticisms about the class.
- Considers what students have to say with an open mind.
- Listens to what you have to say.
- Does not like you to explain what is going wrong with the way the class is taught.
- Cannot take criticism from others.
- Doesn't give reasons for why the class is run the way it is.

Some of the items that the students used to rate their teachers are stated negatively. For this reason, the teacher interested in high credibility would want to receive low scores on those particular statements about their teaching.

The second strongest credibility area was that of *teacher qualification*. This refers to student perceptions of your knowledge and expertise in the subject areas that you teach. Teachers receiving high scores on this credibility dimension were seen as experienced in their fields and as exhibiting skill or knowledge in the material being taught. Knowing your stuff is a very important aspect of credibility according to students.

In judging teachers on this credibility factor, students rated them on the following seven items once again on the same one to five scale.

The teacher for this class:

• Is skilled in the subject of the class.
• Knows his or her stuff.
• Is not an expert in the subject area being taught.
• Is well trained in the subject area of the class.
• Knows little about the information taught in the class.
• Is knowledgeable in the subject area he or she teaches.
• Is not experienced with the subject of the class.

These items are all very similar, referring as they do to the qualification dimension of a teacher's behavior. However, students were found to rate a teacher's skill versus his or her knowledge in the subject matter, for example, slightly differently.

Yet another important aspect of teacher credibility as seen through the students' eyes was *teacher communication effectiveness*. Students found it very difficult to trust what a teacher had to say if that teacher did not communicate clearly or make material easy to understand. Thus, teachers were scored on how clear and well organized they were in presenting materials in the class. Also, teachers could do well on this factor if they were seen as making sure the students understood presentations or explanations before continuing.

In order to rate their teachers on communication effectiveness students used the one to five scale in considering their teachers on the following five items.

The teacher for this class:

• Makes presentations that are not generally understood.
• Makes material difficult to understand because it is not well organized.
• Makes material easy to understand.
• Presents material in a way that makes it hard to understand.
• Makes sure that everyone understands the material before going on.

Communication effectiveness as a teacher credibility factor was relatively important in the student view of things. If they can't understand you or feel you are not working toward communicating clearly with them, it is very hard for students to believe in what you're saying.

The teacher's ability to *define expectations* clearly for students was also considered to be a relatively important contributor to a teacher's credibility. Defining expectations means in this case that the teacher makes it clear what is expected of the students and communicates clearly how well the students are doing in the class. This would mean that the teacher expresses what he or she expects by telling students how they will be evaluated as well as how well they are doing in the class. If a teacher waited until the end of a grading period before informing students about how they were doing, students judged that such a teacher did not clearly define the expectations for the class.

The students used three items to rate their teachers on a one to five scale.

The teacher for this class:

- Lets you know how well you are doing in the class.
- Tells you how well you are doing in class.
- Doesn't let you know how you are doing until grades come out.

This credibility area is one that students find especially important if they are not doing well in school. While there can be many reasons for poor student performance, defined expectations is one area where students trace the fault back to the teachers.

A final credibility dimension, *teacher objectivity,* was found to be important to students, who expected teachers to treat them fairly and with an even hand. If teachers did not do so, students judged them to have a low credibility rating in the objectivity area. Such objectivity or fairness on the part of the teacher meant that he or she judged students according to work accomplished rather than on past performance or personal feelings toward that student. Students expected objective evaluation on the part of teachers, not popularity ratings.

Five items were used to measure student perceptions of teacher objectivity.

The teacher for this class:

- Gives good grades only to students he or she likes.
- Grades class members according to grades they have received in the past.
- Grades class members according to how popular they are.
- Is fair in giving grades.
- Gives you good grades if you do good work.

A teacher would want to work for high scores on the positively stated items and low scores on the negative ones.

## What's Your Credibility Rating?

The major goal for the classroom teacher in responding to these credibility ideas should be to make attempts at assessing his or her credibility in the classroom. As a teacher you are trying to communicate ideas, skills, and other important information to your students, and in doing so you are working to insure that the students are buying what it is you have to offer. However, if your students don't find you believable (credible) and therefore resist or in some way ignore what you are teaching, survival in the classroom could become difficult indeed.

Using feedback to improve upon your teaching was described in great detail elsewhere in this book, and collecting feedback regarding student perceptions of your credibility is one concrete approach to use. Therefore, all of the items that represent the five dimensions of teacher credibility have been organized into a questionnaire that can be completed by students at the sixth grade level or higher.* This twenty-nine–item form is called the Teacher Credibility Questionnaire and can be employed using the general ideas presented in the chapter on planning and getting feedback on teaching, and using the specific directions provided as follows.

DIRECTIONS FOR GIVING THE TEACHER
CREDIBILITY QUESTIONNAIRE

These directions are intended as a guide for giving the Teacher Credibility Questionnaire. Once you have mastered the basic principles and necessary direction steps there is no need for you to quote from it verbatim.

**Introduction.**    It is recommended that someone other than you administer the *T*eacher *C*redibility *Q*uestionnaire (TCQ) to your class. In this way your students are assured of a higher degree of anonymity, which is of the utmost importance in using such a student feedback tool.

    If you cannot find anyone to administer the TCQ, then select a student to do it for you. *In any case, under no circumstances should you, the teacher, be in the room while the students are completing the instrument.*

1. Make sure the teacher has left the room. If necessary, let him or her select a student to retrieve him or her after everything is completed.
2. Say to the students, "I'm going to hand out a questionnaire for you to fill out. It gives you a chance to react to how you feel about your teacher for this class. (Teacher's name) wants this information so that he (or she) can improve the way he (or she) teaches. So—be honest in your reactions. This is not a test, so it is your personal opinion that counts. Don't put your name on the questionnaire or on the answer sheet. This way, no one will know who answered the questions in what way.
3. Hand out the TCQ questionnaires, telling the students once again not to put their names on them. Also tell them not to write on the forms at all.
4. Read the directions printed on the questionnaire.
5. Hand out the answer sheets.** Say to the students: "You don't mark on the questionnaire because we want to use them over. Instead, you answer each question by circling the number you have chosen on the answer sheet. Please make sure that you circle only one number for each question. If you circle more than one, your answer cannot be counted."
6. Hold up the sheet and show them how you might answer the first question on the questionnaire.

---

* The teacher interested in getting feedback on credibility with kindergarten to fifth-grade youngsters is encouraged to modify the questionnaire, using a simpler format, fewer questions, and words that are more at the level of these students.
** A sample answer sheet follows these directions.

7. Students may begin. Tell them it should take them only about ten to fifteen minutes to finish.
8. Have one student collect all of the answer sheets and another collect all the questionnaires when everyone has finished.
9. After stacking the answer sheets in a pile with a paper clip holding them together, label the stack with the teacher's name, and the identity of the class that completed the TCQ.
10. Ask one of the students to inform the teacher that she or he may return to the room.

   **Note:** You may answer procedural questions for the students, but do not interpret statements or suggest answers for them. Encourage them to answer each question.

## The Teacher Credibility Questionnaire

This *Teacher Credibility Questionnaire* (TCQ)* was developed for use by the classroom teacher in order that he or she might gather information regarding his or her credibility as a teacher. It is *not* intended to be used as an evaluation tool by supervisors or administrators, nor should it be. Collecting feedback for self-improvement should be the sole purpose in utilizing the TCQ.

* Formerly called the Source Credibility Measure, Lapan, Copyright, 1973.

### SAMPLE ANSWER SHEET

*Please do not put your name on this sheet. Be sure to circle only one number for each statement.*

|  | Almost Never True | Seldom True | True About ½ the Time | True Most of the Time | Almost Always True |  | Almost Never True | Seldom True | True About ½ the Time | True Most of the Time | Almost Always True |
|---|---|---|---|---|---|---|---|---|---|---|---|
| 1. | 1 | 2 | 3 | 4 | 5 | 16. | 1 | 2 | 3 | 4 | 5 |
| 2. | 1 | 2 | 3 | 4 | 5 | 17. | 1 | 2 | 3 | 4 | 5 |
| 3. | 1 | 2 | 3 | 4 | 5 | 18. | 1 | 2 | 3 | 4 | 5 |
| 4. | 1 | 2 | 3 | 4 | 5 | 19. | 1 | 2 | 3 | 4 | 5 |
| 5. | 1 | 2 | 3 | 4 | 5 | 20. | 1 | 2 | 3 | 4 | 5 |
| 6. | 1 | 2 | 3 | 4 | 5 | 21. | 1 | 2 | 3 | 4 | 5 |
| 7. | 1 | 2 | 3 | 4 | 5 | 22. | 1 | 2 | 3 | 4 | 5 |
| 8. | 1 | 2 | 3 | 4 | 5 | 23. | 1 | 2 | 3 | 4 | 5 |
| 9. | 1 | 2 | 3 | 4 | 5 | 24. | 1 | 2 | 3 | 4 | 5 |
| 10. | 1 | 2 | 3 | 4 | 5 | 25. | 1 | 2 | 3 | 4 | 5 |
| 11. | 1 | 2 | 3 | 4 | 5 | 26. | 1 | 2 | 3 | 4 | 5 |
| 12. | 1 | 2 | 3 | 4 | 5 | 27. | 1 | 2 | 3 | 4 | 5 |
| 13. | 1 | 2 | 3 | 4 | 5 | 28. | 1 | 2 | 3 | 4 | 5 |
| 14. | 1 | 2 | 3 | 4 | 5 | 29. | 1 | 2 | 3 | 4 | 5 |
| 15. | 1 | 2 | 3 | 4 | 5 |  |  |  |  |  |  |

**Do Not Put Your Name on This or on Your Answer Sheet.**

**Directions:** *The statements on these sheets ask you to describe your teacher for this class. Each of these statements is followed by the numbers 1, 2, 3, 4 and 5. This is what these numbers mean:*

1. *Almost Never True.* This statement about what my teacher says or does is almost never true.
2. *Seldom True.* This statement about what my teacher says or does is only true occasionally.
3. *True About Half the Time.* This statement about what my teacher says or does is true about half of the time.
4. *True Most of the Time.* This statement about what my teacher says or does is true most of the time.
5. *Almost Always True.* This statement about what my teacher says or does is true almost all of the time.

**Read Each Statement Below**
*On the sheet provided circle the number that best describes your teacher for each of these statements. Be sure to answer every statement. Also, be sure not to circle more than one answer for each statement.*

| *Begin each statement with: The teacher for this class . . .* | *Almost Never True* | *Seldom True* | *True About ½ the Time* | *True Most of the Time* | *Almost Always True* |
|---|---|---|---|---|---|
| 1. . . . listens to criticisms about the class. | 1 | 2 | 3 | 4 | 5 |
| 2. . . . lets you know how well you are doing in the class. | 1 | 2 | 3 | 4 | 5 |
| 3. . . . is skilled in the subject of the class. | 1 | 2 | 3 | 4 | 5 |
| 4. . . . makes presentations that are not generally understood. | 1 | 2 | 3 | 4 | 5 |
| 5. . . . makes sure that everyone understands the material before going on. | 1 | 2 | 3 | 4 | 5 |
| 6. . . . gives good grades only to students he or she likes. | 1 | 2 | 3 | 4 | 5 |
| 7. . . . knows his or her stuff. | 1 | 2 | 3 | 4 | 5 |
| 8. . . . encourages your comments on how the class could be improved. | 1 | 2 | 3 | 4 | 5 |
| 9. . . . doesn't give reasons for why the class is run the way it is. | 1 | 2 | 3 | 4 | 5 |
| 10. . . . doesn't let you know how you are doing until grades come out. | 1 | 2 | 3 | 4 | 5 |
| 11. . . . is well trained in the subject area of the class. | 1 | 2 | 3 | 4 | 5 |
| 12. . . . makes material difficult to understand because it is not well organized. | 1 | 2 | 3 | 4 | 5 |
| 13. . . . gives you good grades if you do good work. | 1 | 2 | 3 | 4 | 5 |
| 14. . . . wants to know what your opinions are. | 1 | 2 | 3 | 4 | 5 |
| 15. . . . knows little about the information taught in class. | 1 | 2 | 3 | 4 | 5 |
| 16. . . . makes material easy to understand. | 1 | 2 | 3 | 4 | 5 |

| 17. . . . grades class members according to grades they have received in the past. | 1 | 2 | 3 | 4 | 5 |
| 18. . . . is not experienced with the subject of the class. | 1 | 2 | 3 | 4 | 5 |
| 19. . . . encourages you to tell how the class is going. | 1 | 2 | 3 | 4 | 5 |
| 20. . . . grades class members according to how popular they are. | 1 | 2 | 3 | 4 | 5 |
| 21. . . . cannot take criticism from others. | 1 | 2 | 3 | 4 | 5 |
| 22. . . . is knowledgeable in the subject area he or she teaches. | 1 | 2 | 3 | 4 | 5 |
| 23. . . . listens to what you have to say. | 1 | 2 | 3 | 4 | 5 |
| 24. . . . presents material in a way that makes it hard to understand. | 1 | 2 | 3 | 4 | 5 |
| 25. . . . is fair in giving grades. | 1 | 2 | 3 | 4 | 5 |
| 26. . . . does not like you to explain what is going wrong with the way the class is taught. | 1 | 2 | 3 | 4 | 5 |
| 27. . . . tells you how well you are doing in class. | 1 | 2 | 3 | 4 | 5 |
| 28. . . . considers what students say with an open mind. | 1 | 2 | 3 | 4 | 5 |
| 29. . . . is not an expert in the subject that is being taught. | 1 | 2 | 3 | 4 | 5 |

## WHAT YOUR RESULTS MEAN

After you have obtained completed questionnaires from your students you may either calculate an average score on each item (adding up all of your ones through fives then dividing by the number of students) or you may choose to put together the average scores for all items that represent each credibility dimension to see how you rate on areas like openness or qualification. If you select the second approach you will be able to see what specific areas you need to work on in order to improve your credibility in the eyes of the students. In so doing, you might consider fours or fives good for positively stated items and ones or twos good for negatively stated ones.

Another way to judge how well you did on each item is to compare your score with the scores of sixty-eight teachers whose students (1,477 of them) filled out Teacher Credibility Questionnaires on them.

A third way to decide how well you did according to each item on the Teacher Credibility Questionnaire is to sit down before the students complete it and mark how you want to score on each of the items. In this way you can compare your student averages with how you wanted to do and decide where improvements are needed.

In any event, be sure to discuss the questionnaire findings with your students to get ideas from them on how you can improve or change the way you do things in the class. This also lets the students know that you value what they say. And remember, student perceptions of credibility

*Average Scores For Sixty-eight Teachers*

| Item # | Score | | Item # | Score | | Item # | Score |
|---|---|---|---|---|---|---|---|
| 1. | 3.38 | | 11. | 4.43 | | 21. | 2.31 |
| 2. | 3.40 | | 12. | 1.99 | | 22. | 4.46 |
| 3. | 4.45 | | 13. | 4.35 | | 23. | 3.93 |
| 4. | 2.34 | | 14. | 3.46 | | 24. | 2.25 |
| 5. | 3.65 | | 15. | 1.54 | | 25. | 3.95 |
| 6. | 1.76 | | 16. | 3.46 | | 26. | 2.49 |
| 7. | 4.36 | | 17. | 1.89 | | 27. | 3.30 |
| 8. | 2.98 | | 18. | 1.56 | | 28. | 3.65 |
| 9. | 2.68 | | 19. | 2.57 | | 29. | 1.88 |
| 10. | 2.54 | | 20. | 1.52 | | | |

change from month to month as well as from class to class. If you get some fairly good scores from one class at one time, don't get smug or overconfident, but do find out how you did it and work on keeping your credibility at that level.

# 5

# Planning and Getting Feedback on Teaching

## What Is Feedback All About?

In the course of teaching we sometimes forget that what we are doing could be very important to know about in a more complete way. Sure, it was a good day or a good class, but why was it good? Guesses can be made, very accurate guesses sometimes. But we don't always know for sure. That is the rub, that gnawing feeling we get sometimes that successes in teaching seem so haphazard, some kind of magic synthesis of the time of day, the kind of subject matter, the attitude of the kids, how the teacher feels.

Collecting some kind of information through tape recordings or student feedback can remove some of that mystery. While such data won't answer all the questions, it gets the teacher closer to a fuller understanding of what is happening in the classroom.

### TWO KINDS OF FEEDBACK

Actually, most of us as teachers spend a great deal of time and energy interpreting what is happening in our classroom every day. You see the expression of a student's face and know immediately that he or she didn't understand the assignment. You hear a comment from a student that re-

---

* A giant piece of credit should go to Dr. William Rogge who first turned me on to the concept of feedback in his self-assessment training program at the University of Illinois. Many other teachers have Bill Rogge to thank for training them to use their own classroom for self-improvement.

minds you that you have forgotten to explain an important segment of a lesson. You hear yourself saying something, perhaps too late, that will probably "goof up" the way you had originally intended to present an activity. The better we are at picking up on these signals, the better we are able to keep our teaching on track, fitting our actual teaching with what we intended it to be.

This kind of informal interpretation procedure can be described as *involuntary-unrequested* feedback, information we receive about what is happening in the classroom as a part of the normal teaching process. It is *involuntary* in the sense that when students are sending messages or you are recognizing clues, it is part of the natural course of events— something people do without even meaning to. And it is *unrequested* because as a teacher you will get this feedback whether you want it or not. You can deal with it, ignore it, or remember it for later use, but without any formal request from you, it's there for you to act upon.

Teachers who have greater sensitivity or responsiveness to this involuntary-unrequested or I-U feedback seem to do a better job of teaching. It is sometimes called a "presence,"—being with the group of kids in a way that creates a more complete link through both verbal and nonverbal communication. Most experienced teachers know they have a certain facility for utilizing this I-U information even if they cannot explain just how it works or what they are doing to make it work.

But why leave such an important aspect of the teaching process to chance? I have heard too many administrators say, "Oh, he knows the subject matter well enough," or, "Sure, she gets the job done, I guess," but they never fail to add, "On the other hand, he just doesn't seem to be in touch with the kids," or, "She seems too reserved somehow, just not part of the classroom."

It is possible that these administrators are wrong in such judgments, for many are wrong on many occasions. It is also possible that they do sense a given teacher's inability to utilize I-U feedback well enough to keep his or her teaching flowing in a meaningful way. But why gamble? Not all of us have this magical "presence," and if we don't we had better do something to adjust for its lack. Even if we do have some ability at interpreting I-U feedback, it is still possible to improve upon that process.

One solution is to formalize the feedback process, intentionally setting out to obtain information about your teaching so that you can study it, use it to readjust your teaching strategies, and collect more information based on what you have learned. This approach can be called *voluntary-requested* information-getting and can be implemented in a number of ways. Such an approach to obtaining feedback about your teaching is *voluntary* because you choose to do it and are much more ready for its arrival; and because it is requested it is something that you can plan for, and think out ways in which the information can be obtained and used.

A teacher may make the commitment that I-U feedback is important data to be used for day-to-day classroom decisions, but that *voluntary-requested* (V-R) information can increase the kinds and quality of information from which the teacher can draw. The teacher obtains V-R data because he or she wants it and can define to some extent what kind of information it will be. He or she may want to know if lessons are too hard, assignments too long, discussions too boring. Whatever focus is selected, the teacher then decides how best to find the answers. Perhaps listening to a tape recording of a particular lesson will be the best approach, or maybe asking the students how they feel about an issue of importance is the way to go. Some teachers have opted for having a trusted colleague observe a class according to the teacher's instructions as to what to look for. (I would certainly make sure that it is a *trusted* colleague.)

Whatever V-R procedure is implemented, it will give the teacher a stronger sense of control over what is happening and what will happen in the classroom. Put simply, it increases the amount of "real live" classroom information upon which the teacher can base teaching strategy decisions.

## Implementing a Feedback Program in Your Classroom

Beginning the task of collecting classroom feedback to improve teaching should call for careful reflection by teachers regarding what it is they want to know. Some teachers know almost immediately what questions they want answered or what kinds of information they desire. However, many find it hard to get the process started because they have never participated in a feedback program before.

There are two important guidelines that will help the teacher new to the feedback collection process. First, the teacher should select kinds of feedback that are both practical and reasonable to collect. This means that the area selected to examine should be useful—such as requesting students to comment on the best and least liked things about the class or asking a colleague to observe how clearly you give directions and assignments. The information gathered from such feedback approaches can provide you with practical and useful data from which to make decisions. Other examples of practical and useful feedback information are discussed later in this chapter.

The second guideline is perhaps the more important of the two: be sure to try *something,* whether or not you are certain that it will produce any information that you would want. This "getting the feet wet" approach is strongly recommended since it will provide you with first-hand experience in what the feedback process is all about. Using feedback is not difficult or complex, but it can seem so until you have experience with it. Further, chances are very good that the information will be useful. Most feedback is helpful to some degree, and much of the newly acquired information could bring you insights not available before.

During the course of planning, the teacher interested in collecting trustworthy information should keep in mind that certain times of the year should be considered off limits for the feedback process. There is, of course, the consideration that your teaching style should be established and the classroom routine clearly defined before feedback data should be collected. You will feel that the information is more accurate if it is collected once the classroom situation is "in the groove" for the year. And surely the students would provide much more accurate responses once they know what the teaching pattern is all about. This is *not* a case of "don't smile until Christmas," but it certainly is a case of "don't collect feedback before Halloween."

Teachers should also be wary when requesting student feedback during times when the students are likely to be either anxious or pre-occupied. Generally, this would mean that it is normally unwise to attempt collecting student reactions around testing time, vacation time, or close to the end of the school year. Students are much more likely to provide stable perceptions during times when the work routine is somewhat regular and they can concentrate more upon the information requested of them.

## SETTING THE CLASSROOM ATMOSPHERE

Before you get underway with a feedback program, it is very important that you reflect upon the basic purpose for doing so—self-improvement. With this in mind, teachers who plan to collect feedback must work to create an atmosphere that will aid in making the data more trustworthy. This generally means that students and others involved in the process should be made aware of what is being done and why, so that the actual feedback collection process is clearly understood by everyone.

Problems can occur during feedback collection that might easily interrupt the routine of the class and therefore make the results less than representative. Use of video and audio recorders, classroom observers, student questionnaires, or other special collection procedures can so pre-occupy both students and teachers that normal classroom routine could be changed drastically. Such interruptions can be avoided if you discuss with the students what is going to happen and even practice some of the procedures to be employed.

Further, it is important that you discuss with your students the reasons for conducting feedback programs. Since the teacher involved is presumably engaging in this process for the purpose of self-improvement, this should be the focus of any such discussion with the students. It is here that you should make clear that by finding out feedback information you will be able to improve the way the class is run, and this will make the classroom experience more meaningful for the students.

Establishing the proper classroom atmosphere for collecting feed-back is simply and easily done, but is one of those important early stages in the process that, if not attended to, could easily affect the strength of the entire feedback program. Discussion with the students is vital and should be carried out in such a way as to help establish a mood of openness and understanding between you and the students.

The following should be considered as only one among many possible approaches to discussing the feedback issue with the students, but it can at least serve as a reference guide for your use.

## GUIDE FOR PRE-FEEDBACK STUDENT DISCUSSION

**Step #1.**   The teacher explains to the students what it is he or she plans to do and to use to collect feedback (e.g., a questionnaire, a tape recorder, an observer).

**Step #2.**   The teacher then explains in his or her own words these reasons for collecting the feedback.

a. The teacher is always trying to improve as a teacher and therefore needs to find out what is happening so things can be made better.
b. Things that are working well can be continued, while things that are not working so well can be changed.
c. The teacher needs to know what is working and what isn't before changes can be made.
d. The teacher needs the students' help in getting this information (e.g., by filling out questionnaires, by getting used to the recorder, by getting used to the observer).
e. Students can also help in discussing the feedback results and suggesting how something can be improved.

**Step #3.**   The teacher then encourages the students to ask questions or make comments. If the students need further encouragement, the teacher might try the following questions:

a. Who would like to see if they can explain what it is we're going to do?
b. Would anyone else like to comment on what we are going to do?
c. What do you think about doing this? Do you think it will work?
d. Does anyone have any other ideas of how we could go about getting information to make the class better?
e. Would you like to have more talks like this?

**Step #4.**   The teacher then thanks the students for talking this over and further thanks them for any feedback they may have provided during the discussion.

Such discussions may provide you with new insights about how to improve the class even before you have begun to collect information in a more formal way. The main issue here, of course, is that you have let the students know you care about what they think and may act on some of their ideas. You may not agree with all of their ideas, but it is important that you follow through with what they say to build a continuing trust between you and the kids.

## Implementing a Feedback Program

### PREPARING TO DEAL WITH FEEDBACK RESULTS

Another important issue that you should consider prior to collecting the feedback relates to the problem of interpreting the results that are to be received. In some situations, of course, it is necessary to wait until after the feedback results are collected to make decisions about interpretation. In the case of student open-ended questionnaires, for example, there is little you can do but wait to see what the students have said. Interpretation of the results in these instances amounts to figuring out the major positives and negatives about the class.

However, in many other situations, concerned teachers should prepare for the feedback results by committing themselves to what it is they want and expect to get. In this way you will not be as tempted to change your mind about what your intentions were. There is always that self-protection reaction, especially to unexpected feedback, that makes you want to say things like, "I really expected these results considering the type of class it is. I may have wanted to talk less than fifty percent of the time, but that's impossible with these kids." Impossible? Perhaps.

Committing yourself to expectations before the fact helps you see differences between what you want and what actually occurs and thus provides you with helpful data for self-improvement. If you have already noted, for example, that fifty percent teacher talk and fifty percent student talk is what is ideally wanted from the tape recording of a class, then it is difficult to rationalize a percentage that is far different from that ideal. By establishing ideal expectations prior to feedback collection, you have also devised a standard against which to measure the results.

**Setting Ideals.**   One of the important goals of professional teachers is that of being aware of their classroom behavior—knowing, in other words, exactly what is happening when it is occurring in the class. This is admittedly difficult because of the constant time and energy demands placed on the teacher, but one extremely helpful approach toward reaching that goal is that of working toward clearly defined ideals—ideals to which you, the teacher, make a definite commitment. Thus, in the case of interpreting feedback results, committed professional teachers have the opportunity in most cases to select well-defined ideals to which they can aspire.

In selecting these ideals prior to collecting feedback data, you may utilize one of a number of approaches, depending upon the type of feedback that is to be requested. Using the guiding principle that the ideals chosen represent those things wanted in the classroom if everything were perfect, you can then score or rate yourself according to what you would ideally want things to be like. For example, you may have chosen to use a trusted colleague to observe a class discussion regarding drug abuse in the United States. First you must decide what it is the observer should be looking for. You might decide on the following:

1. I want the students to discuss factual information, but also provide their opinions.
2. I want the students to have ample opportunity to talk during the discussion.

Given these teaching goals, you then instruct the observer to collect the following feedback information:

1. During a segment of the discussion write down the questions I ask the students and count the number that request facts and the number that request opinions.
2. During a segment of the discussion keep track of how much I talk versus how much the students talk by making a tally every ten seconds indicating who is talking at that particular time.

As a result of collecting this information, the observer will have been able to calculate percentage figures for fact questions versus opinion questions and teacher talk versus student talk. Knowing beforehand that this will be done, you can establish ideal scores in these areas. They might be something like this:

*My Ideals for This Class*
Fact Questions = 30%
Opinion Questions = 70%
Teacher Talk = 25%
Student Talk = 75%

Once the observer has recorded the information and calculated the percentage figures, you have but to compare the ideal percentages with the actual percentages provided by the observer. As can be seen, you not only have a way of judging success by comparing the ideal percentages with the actual or real figures, but are also committed to charting a course for self-improvement where discrepancies between ideal and real are found.

One additional procedure for establishing a means of interpreting feedback is to guard against establishing ideal scores that really represent predictions. For example, in establishing an ideal score for teacher talk, a teacher says, "I think I will probably talk seventy percent of the time." That teacher has just made a prediction about what will really occur, not an ideal statement. The teacher should instead be thinking, "I would ideally like to talk thirty percent of the time."

The easiest way to guard against this tendency to predict rather then idealize is to develop a second set of self-ratings prior to feedback collection. In creating both ideal and predicted real scores, you are forced to differentiate between the two and avoid the problem.

Thus, you might have a pre-feedback estimate that looks like this:

| *Ideal* | *Predicted Real* |
|---|---|
| Teacher talk = 30% | Teacher talk = 65% |
| Student talk = 70% | Student talk = 35% |

Establishing ideal and predicted real estimates prior to data collection can be of definite help by providing teachers with specific, comparative information on how well they have done according to predefined goals. It takes a little more time than just waiting for the results, but the distinct clarity it gives the interpretation of those results is worth the effort.

The chart on page 85 should provide teachers with useful examples of the ways to establish ideals and predicted reals for different kinds of feedback data.

## Formal and Informal Feedback Collection

The teacher interested in implementing a feedback program in the classroom can employ many different methods for collecting useful information for self-improvement. Teachers should utilize both of the major forms of feedback collection—formal and informal.

Formal modes of collecting feedback data are characterized by clearly defined rules for procedure and usually include some systematic format such as questionnaires or observational schemes. Informal procedures are characterized by fewer rules and a more open, give-and-take atmosphere, as in class discussions and talks with individual students. Both types of information collection processes are important in their own ways, and the teacher should attempt to use each type.

**Formal Procedures.** Formal feedback-collection procedures might be utilized systematically throughout the school year. Such procedures might include administering a questionnaire to the students, obtaining observational data from a trusted colleague, or analyzing tape-recorded lessons. Care should be taken to insure that feedback information collected in this way is objectively obtained so that the results can be trusted. Formal, systematic rules should be established so that personal judgments do not interfere with the data collection process.

In the case of questionnaires, the students must be guaranteed anonymity. Therefore, someone other than the teacher for that class should administer the questionnaire, and clear instructions should be given in administering it to the students. Also, scoring or judging the results of a questionnaire is very important and whenever possible should represent the same kind of systematic, objective procedures. If the questionnaire rates the teacher on a five-point scale or in some other way provides

| Method of Getting Feedback | Form Results Come In | Way to Establish Ideal and Predicted Real |
|---|---|---|
| Audio Tape-recording Classroom Teaching | A mirror description of what happened. Can choose some things to be counted and turned into percentages—like how many questions, what kinds of questions and how many of each, amount of teacher talk and student talk. | Numbers can be converted into percentages. Also subjective statements of expectations can be made. |
| Observing Classroom Teaching (Same as Videotaping) | Same as tape-recording, plus what can be seen but not heard. Attempt to consider things that can be counted. | Same as above. |
| Student Questionnaires | Might be ratings for each question like one equals lousy and five equals great with in-between scores, or could be two choices like agree-disagree. Also could be fill-in-the-blanks or open-ended. | If one to five scale, pick numbers for each question that are ideal and predicted real. If agree-disagree, choose one or the other. If fill-in-the-blanks you might idealize and predict what will be said. If open-ended, not much can be done except to react afterwards. |
| Other Methods, e.g., Class Discussions | Always comes as subjective, raw information. Can be recorded on predeveloped answer sheets.* | Can only react afterwards, unless answer sheets are developed. Ideal and predicted scores can be estimated if sheets have things like yes-no and how many said what. |

\* Such sheets can be prepared showing labels for each topic to be discussed. It is possible to record information such as "only a few agreed" or "many thought this," and you may want to indicate which topics students did not like to discuss.

results that can be calculated numerically, objectivity of the results can easily be maintained. On the other hand, if the questionnaire to be used is more open-ended, then such objective scoring may be impossible and fruitless to try. In this case such a questionnaire might be considered a more "informal" approach to obtaining feedback, still valuable in the overall feedback program.

By protecting student anonymity, making questionnaire administration rule-guided, and objectifying the scoring process with the use of numbers, the teacher can help make the feedback obtained more trustworthy and therefore more usable.

When considering formal observational procedures to be used as data for feedback, important formal steps should be followed as well. So that teachers being observed might trust the observation feedback they receive, the observer should have prescribed elements or specific portions of the class to observe. You would probably request that the observer look at particular facets of your teaching so that he or she is not distracted by other segments of a particular lesson. If you want to find out through observation by trusted colleagues about certain aspects of your verbal interaction with the students, you should instruct the observer regarding what areas to scrutinize. It would be of little help if the observer, not having been instructed regarding what to look for, decided to write down student names if they talked out of turn or recorded the number of times students got up to sharpen pencils.

Further, observers should be given specific instructions on methods of recording observed data and on which time segments to sample. For example, it is helpful to request observers to pick out representative time samples during the class period, such as the first ten minutes, middle ten minutes, and last ten minutes of the class. In this way you know when the recorded observations were made and that as a whole the observations are representative of the entire class time. As to method of recording, it is helpful where possible for the observer to use tallies or counting procedures to note his or her observations. In this way, amounts, percentages, and averages can be calculated, and this once again provides you with much more formal and objective feedback information. Knowing this kind of hard data (e.g., percentage of teacher talk versus percentage of student talk or amount of time spent giving directions versus amount of time teaching the lesson) gives you specific, definite notions of what went on and what needs to be done in order to improve. Discovering that he or she talks one hundred percent of the time helps a teacher recognize that he or she must talk a lot less, perhaps; or taking most of the period to give an assignment that should have taken five minutes means that the teacher has to work on assignment giving. This quantitative system provides understandable numerical reference points from which to work rather than somewhat ambiguous feedback such as "talk a little less" or "spend less time on giving assignments."

It should be pointed out that, like open-ended questionnaires, some observational information cannot be recorded in numerical or objective ways, *nor should it be*. Certain things going on in a classroom simply cannot be reduced to numbers or sampled time segments; they retain their meanings only when described in full. As has been mentioned, such subjective or informal data-collection procedures are both acceptable and needed to complement a comprehensive feedback program. Observers should be made aware of this and instructed to record informal data in addition to formal information, while not allowing the subjective recording to interfere with the more formal collection procedure.

Analysis of tape recordings is another area of formal procedure in the feedback process. This can be done in almost exactly the same way that observational data is recorded. In this case you have the opportunity to observe your own classes, as it were, by listening to and analyzing tape-recorded segments of your classroom behavior. As with observational procedures, you should utilize systematic methods for responding to tape recordings, using numerical and counting procedures where possible. Also, you can take advantage of the opportunity to collect more informal and subjective information, just as was the case with observational data collection.

**Informal Procedures.**    Unlike the more formal procedures for collecting feedback information, informal procedures are much less planned for and certainly not encumbered by many rules or numerical recording practices. While portions of more formal procedures such as of questionnaires, observations, and tape recordings contain informal feedback information, informal data collection procedures are much more spontaneous and personal in nature and provide teachers with opportunities to deal with students on a more interactive basis.

The three most often used procedures for instituting informal feedback processes are group discussions, individual interviews, and unsolicited encounters. In group discussions, teachers have the opportunity to involve students in open verbal interplay regarding how the class is progressing; in individual interviews, teachers can create a more personal, one-on-one setting with a single student, again to deal with how the class is going; and in unsolicited encounters, the teacher finds a usually unexpected situation where a student has provided an opening or made a statement which suggests to the teacher an opportunity to gather feedback for self-improvement.

Group discussions for the purpose of obtaining useful feedback can be held on a routine basis so that students expect that once a week or twice a month they will have a chance to talk of their concerns about the class. Unplanned discussions can also occur, depending upon your willingness to deviate from regular lesson plans or other class routines. Such unexpected discussions usually come about because of students' individually voiced concerns or because you have diagnosed an immediate need for a feedback session.

Feedback discussions with the class should find you serving as a listener, facilitator, and clarifier in order to provide an atmosphere that will encourage honesty and openness from the students. Teachers who attempt to probe, judge, or in other ways intimidate students will find that such discussions are less useful and that the students will become more wary of providing helpful information.

Individual interviews can also occur in both routine and unplanned manners, and a combination of both approaches increases the richness of the feedback obtained. Teachers normally need some practice in carrying on interviews with their students, especially when the content of the interviews requires a change in role for both participants. Interviews require the teacher to question unobtrusively, requesting that the student comment on how things are going. Such behavior is sometimes radically different from the teacher role of asking direct questions about subject matter and expecting satisfactory answers. Whatever the student says in the feedback interview should be considered satisfactory as long as the teacher judges it to be an honest perception. There are no right answers.

The student role also changes, usually as a result of the teacher role variation. If students believe that teachers are not teaching but are truly concerned about the feedback process, they will become more open as they sense the easing of tensions. Without fear of reprisal students can begin to "tell it like it is."

Creating an atmosphere for unsolicited encounters is one of the most difficult tasks for the classroom teacher. Such encounters require that the teacher make it known through a series of exhibited behaviors over a long period of time that honest feedback from students is acceptable at any time. This means that the teacher has not shown in any systematic way that he or she wants to hear about only the positive aspects of classroom conditions. Teachers who say they want to hear all sides but appear in the least way hostile to negative feedback will find that all useful student feedback will soon "go underground."

By their very nature, unsolicited encounters are never a matter of routine. They occur when a student brings up a point of concern or when you judge that a student is concerned about something. In this setting, you must utilize the same listening and acceptance tactics employed in the other informal feedback procedures, encouraging the student to openly express feelings and perceptions. Some say the final measure of a truly open classroom can be judged by the number of occurrences of unsolicited encounters, which take place because the students feel safe and secure in making them happen.

Formal and informal feedback procedures can be utilized in various ways. The formal procedures use many different sources of information, all based on the classroom setting. Informal procedures, on the other hand, focus solely on students as a source for feedback, with the exception of those informal kinds of data found through observations and tape recordings.

The major strength of formal feedback procedures resides with their objectivity. If the information is collected systematically and scored in numerical terms, the results contain the kind of specificity that provides you with clearly defined guidance toward self-improvement. Formal feedback also demands a certain amount of long-range planning on your part.

Conversely, informal procedures do not encourage long-range teacher planning, nor do they deal in the realm of objective information. Instead, informal feedback is mostly subjective, providing the teachers with current descriptions or interpretations of class activities without indicating how much, how often, or what to do about them. However, informal procedures have their strengths too. First, every kind of feedback information cannot be counted, averaged, and catalogued, just as many occurrences in everyday life defy quantification. Such unquantified information is no less important, however, and informal procedures must be employed to obtain it.

Second, informal procedures by their very nature are more personal and warm in approach, and thus do much more to encourage openness and extend avenues for future feedback processes. A questionnaire or a tape recording can do very little to develop an open feedback atmosphere in the classroom, but a properly handled small or large group discussion provides direct evidence to the students that you are interested in what they have to say.

**Specific Examples of Collectible Information.**    Many teachers understand the feedback process and see its merits in helping them to survive in the classroom setting. However, they still ask: "What should I look for? What is important information to get?" My response is normally that each individual teacher is the best judge of what kinds of data to look for if each of them would perhaps believe in his or her own judgment a little more.

On the other hand, it helps to have some ideas to help you get started. Here are sixteen ideas for you to consider.

*Examples of Information*

1. Classroom questions found in tests, assignments, or daily discussions.
2. Positive, neutral, and negative reinforcement you use in teaching.
3. Overall amount of teacher talk, student talk, and silence found in your daily lessons.
4. Patterns of verbal behavior exhibited by your students during class discussions.
5. Proportion of time you spend giving information to your students versus the time spent seeking information from them.
6. Length of time any one student has the opportunity to talk during class discussions.

7. Amount of student-to-student verbal interaction versus the amount of teacher-to-student and student-to-teacher interaction.
8. Proportion of time you spend accepting students and/or their ideas versus the time spent rejecting them.
9. Amount of time students spend asking for clarification of directions that you provide.
10. Habits you have unknowingly acquired that may help or hinder your teaching.
11. Ways in which you relate to your students physically regarding spatial distance and touching.
12. Patterns you have developed in correcting student work.
13. Comparative emphasis you place on intellectual versus social interactions in the class.
14. Relative emphasis you place on individual tutoring versus small-group instruction versus large-group teaching.
15. Your use of humor in the classroom and its effect on the students.
16. Patterns you have developed in the use of teaching aids, such as audio-visual aids and other devices.

## Students As a Source for Feedback: Guidelines and Examples

The concept of utilizing students as a source for feedback information depends to a large extent upon your belief as a teacher that students have important contributions to make to the workings of the classroom. If you are sincerely interested in developing a feedback program that includes student feedback information, it may be helpful for you to examine the guidelines and examples that follow.

## A Guide to the Questionnaire Approach

The use of questionnaires in obtaining student feedback can prove helpful in providing teachers with information that can lead to active self-improvement. The questionnaire approach is an efficient one, since they can be administered to students simultaneously and if used a few times a year will not consume valuable teaching time to any significant degree.

Three types of questionnaires are normally used in the classroom setting, all having their specific purposes. The open-ended questionnaire is one type employed often by teachers. It has a simple format and requires very little preparation on the part of the teacher using it. Table 1 shows two examples of the open-ended questionnaire.

As can be seen from the two examples in Table 1, all that is really needed is a single sheet of paper with simple and rather general questions to be answered by the students.

## TABLE 1    TWO EXAMPLES OF OPEN-ENDED QUESTIONNAIRES

Example #1
1. What are the things you like most about this class?
2. What things would you like to see changed?
3. Any other comments? (Use the back if you need room).

Example #2
1. Name three things you think are good about this class.
   a.
   b.
   c.
2. Name three things you don't like about this class.
   a.
   b.
   c.
3. Are there any other things you would like to say?
   (You may write on the back).

The second type of questionnaire can be labeled the semi-open-ended or comprehensive open-ended questionnaire. This form takes a bit longer to prepare, but does provide more specific information. Table 2 provides an example of this questionnaire type.

This type of questionnaire is characterized by a larger number of questions and by more specific questions, and while it is open-ended yes and no answers are also requested.

The third questionnaire type can be called the closed-end or specific-answer questionnaire. While this kind of questionnaire requests student judgments, perceptions, and opinions, there is usually no opportunity for writing responses or going in directions other than those specifically requested by the questions. This form takes a much longer time for the

## TABLE 2    EXAMPLE OF SEMI-OPEN-ENDED QUESTIONNAIRE

1. What is the one most important thing you like about this class?
2. What one thing would you definitely want to change?
3. Is there something the teacher does that you really like?
   YES_____          NO_____
   If yes, what is it?
4. Is there something the teacher does that you don't like?
   YES_____          NO_____
   If yes, what is it?
5. Would you say that, in general, you enjoy this class most of the time?
   YES_____          NO_____
   Why or why not?
6. If you were in charge of this class, what would be the first thing you would do?
7. Any other comments you would like to make about this class?
   (You may write on the back.)

teacher to prepare, since the questions are much more specific and more difficult to create. While it is possible for teachers to develop the closed-end type, it is usually recommended that they seek out copies of such questionnaires which have already been developed.*

Table 3 shows how such a questionnaire might look. It should be kept in mind that these types of questionnaires usually contain many statements or questions, and Table 3 shows only five examples from the Teacher Credibility Questionnaire, which actually contains twenty-nine statements.

As can be seen from examining Table 3, the closed-end question-naire provides very concrete questions to which the students are requested to respond. In many cases, this type of questionnaire provides some kind of response format such as the one to five scale shown here, which allows the teacher to calculate numerical class averages for each of the state-ments. Examples of other closed-end response styles include "agree-disagree," "yes-no," "positive-negative," "too much-about right-not enough," and "more-same-less." Some also include a "no opinion" or "undecided" category.

The previous questionnaire descriptions and examples do not, of course, provide a complete and comprehensive look at all possible format variations that such instruments could take. These will serve though to give you a solid grasp on what questionnaires can be like.

Each of these three types of questionnaires has advantages and disadvantages when put to practical use. An examination of Table 4 will provide you with a summary of these strengths and weaknesses.

* See Chapter 4 for one example of a twenty-nine–statement questionnaire that is suitable for classroom use (grades six through college).

---

**TABLE 3***

| Begin each statement with: "The teacher for this class . . ." | Almost Never True | Seldom True | True About ½ the Time | True Most of the Time | Almost Always True |
|---|---|---|---|---|---|
| 1. . . . makes presentations that are not generally understood. | 1 | 2 | 3 | 4 | 5 |
| 2. . . . encourages your comments on how the class could be improved. | 1 | 2 | 3 | 4 | 5 |
| 3. . . . is well trained in the subject area of the class. | 1 | 2 | 3 | 4 | 5 |
| 4. . . . gives you good grades if you do good work. | 1 | 2 | 3 | 4 | 5 |
| 5. . . . lets you know how well you are doing in the class. | 1 | 2 | 3 | 4 | 5 |

* Taken from the Teacher Credibility Questionnaire formerly called the Source Credibility Measure, copyright Lapan (1973).

## TABLE 4    ADVANTAGES AND DISADVANTAGES TO QUESTIONNAIRE TYPES

| Open-Ended | Semi-Open-Ended | Closed-Ended |
|---|---|---|
| *Strengths* | *Strengths* | *Strengths* |
| —Easy to prepare and duplicate | —Fairly easy to prepare and duplicate | —Provides very concrete answers to questions |
| —Provides open forum for any opinions students might have | —Provides for some opinion | —Easy to quantify results into class averages for each question |
| —Can be repeated often | —Is specific enough to get at some answers teachers may want | —Usually deals with a greater number of important areas |
| | | —Gives students way to rate teacher comparatively using numbers |
| *Weaknesses* | *Weaknesses* | *Weaknesses* |
| —Questions sometimes too general for students to know how to respond | —Sometimes too general for students to know how to respond | —Usually provides no opportunity for opinions not specifically asked for |
| —Sometimes difficult to understand the meaning of the results | —Difficult to understand meaning of some results | —Can be boring if given too often |
| —Doesn't always provide answers to specific questions teacher may have | —Only deals with a few specific areas | —Subject to student error in marking answers |

## Giving Questionnaires to the Students

Certain principles should guide the teacher in administering questionnaires to a class of students. These guides are intended to serve as recommendations that can improve both the procedures of administration and the trustworthiness of results.

### Questionnaire Administration Guidelines

1. Be sure that all questionnaire copies are clear and easy to read.
2. If the students are to write on the questionnaire itself, be sure to have enough extra copies available in case of student errors.
3. If the questionnaire was long and time-consuming to type, have students respond on easily reproducible answer sheets.

4. Talk with the students beforehand explaining what you intend to do, communicating clearly your interest in obtaining feedback for improvement.
5. To insure student anonymity require no student names on any questionnaires or answer sheets to be used. It's not so important who said what, but how the class reacts as a group.
6. Request that someone else such as a trusted colleague or older student give the questionnaire for you. Leaving the room provides the students with a necessary extra guarantee of anonymity.
7. Provide the person who is to administer the questionnaire with a clear explanation or written instructions on how to give it properly. These instructions should be as follows:
   a. Stay removed from the students so you cannot see what they are writing.
   b. If someone does not want to fill out the questionnaire, let him or her read a book or work on something quietly.
   c. Provide no opinions on how to answer questions. Just say either, "Answer it the best way you can," or "Your opinion is what counts."
   d. Make clear to the students that this is not a test. Each student's personal opinion is what counts.
   e. If students have procedural questions or questions about word meanings, try to answer them. Be sure not to suggest how to answer.
   f. If something unusual happens or if students seem to be having unusual problems with one or more of the questions, make a note of what the difficulty was. In this way the teacher can take the problem into account when looking at the results.
   g. When students have finished, have a student collect the questionnaires and place them in one pile. Send one student to retrieve the teacher for the class.
8. Be sure to thank the students for spending the time and ask them if they have any questions or comments.

## A Guide to the Discussion Approach

Employing classroom discussion procedures for the purpose of obtaining feedback from students is sometimes a difficult task. Students have little or no opportunity to protect their anonymity while expressing opinions and perceptions. The teacher's presence and involvement in the discussion can put students on the defensive and make them wary of saying anything that might get them into trouble. For this reason, you must work doubly hard to develop a secure and open atmosphere in which students can feel safe in providing honest feedback about how the class is run. This, however, is sometimes easier said than done.

Developing the proper classroom atmosphere for feedback discussions is a sensitive and time-consuming procedure, and teachers interested in implementing the concept should not expect overnight success. As one teacher reported, ". . . the kids do have some ideas, but the last time we tried to talk about problems in the class, we set the school record for silence and squirming."

This comment is a very accurate one and represents what often happens when teachers, sometimes without warning, suddenly request verbal feedback through discussion. Students usually are not used to such experiences and need practice before they can develop ways of expressing themselves on subjects related to how the class should operate. This practice is normally best experienced in small (four to six students) discussion groups where all students have a chance to talk and where you can be much more warm and personal with the students. You may decide to try these practice sessions with the entire class also, but more success could be expected with smaller group experiences.

The content of the actual discussions will, of course, vary with the directions in which both students and teachers take them. In any case, three stages can be seen operating in group discussions used to obtain useful feedback. These stages or phases normally come about over a period of time and seldom operate simultaneously.

The first phase can be called the "warm-up" stage wherein the teacher is attempting to get the students involved by suggesting areas they might want to discuss. One example of moving the students through the warm-up stage includes a small group discussion where the students have the opportunity to talk about some school-related issue that might be on their minds. Such issues might include cheating, drug use, how to run the school, and fights on the playground.

There are two basic advantages to involving students in school-related issue discussions. First, the students begin the important process of working in a group discussion dealing with an area other than "school work." This provides them with practice in discussing issues of a controversial nature. Second, the students come to learn what to expect regarding your role in such warm-up talks. They can judge if you are a listener, facilitator, and mediator in the discussion process; or if you tend to take over by attempting to mold the opinions of the group. The teacher as facilitator and mediator will soon experience success in using the warm-up procedure, since the students will learn that their opinions count for something and are not rejected by the teacher.

The warm-up phase usually leads almost automatically to the "pre-feedback" stage, which is the second phase of the discussion process. Once the students begin to feel secure in discussing controversial school-related issues, interaction regarding classroom issues is the next step in a rather natural progression. You may provide certain classroom-related topics for discussion, such as seating arrangements, availability of resource material, and whether or not the classroom is a good place to work. While such topics may need suggesting, some small groups will progress on their own toward discussing classroom issues that concern them.

An important guideline to remember here is *not* to move too swiftly from the warm-up to the pre-feedback stage. Some groups may take only two or three weeks of biweekly discussions to progress beyond warm-up, but others may take much longer and should not be pushed too quickly.

The pre-feedback phase is characterized by students discussing issues about the classroom, but not really getting down to dealing with how conditions can be improved. This is an important stage nonetheless, because students are developing ways of talking about circumstances within the classroom setting that very well may not have been points of open discussion in the past. It is important also because the students are carrying on these discussions in your presence as the teacher, and are therefore building toward the time when openly expressed feedback about the class can be explored.

The third and most important stage of discussion development can be classified as the "feedback" phase, which is the goal of the entire program. This level has been reached when the students and teacher have developed the kind of give-and-take atmosphere necessary to support a feedback effort. During the pre-feedback stage students might well experiment with the feedback stage by suggesting some small, rather inconsequential issue about how the teacher may change or improve. During this time, you should take advantage of any such experimentation by responding positively and exhibiting appreciation for the students' contributions. You may also experiment in attempting to turn the students' attentions toward more direct feedback-oriented discussions. Combining both experimental efforts will soon point out the time when feedback discussions can begin in a comprehensive way.

Because it is so important, the feedback stage of discussion places you in the position of carefully watching yourself as you work through the process. One workable way to maintain this vigil is by tape-recording discussion sessions every so often to insure that your verbal behavior is not in some way curtailing the quality and quantity of student feedback available. You can then analyze these recordings, either through listening and subjectively deciding on how things are working or by utilizing a simple checklist approach to insure that your behavior is not impeding student expression. The checklist approach provides you with a most trustworthy and objective means for assessing your effectiveness in feedback discussions. The checklist with instructions for use found in Table 5 can provide teachers with a way of analyzing discussion tapes.

Some teachers agree that the discussion approach to collecting feedback is a useful idea but question exactly how to go about it. In addition to following the three-stage process of warm-up, pre-feedback, and feedback along with occasional analysis of taped discussions, you might want to consider one or more of the following suggestions to help you initiate and conduct feedback discussions with your students.

1. Have each student write on a small slip of paper the one thing he or she would change about the class. Put the slips of paper together in a box, have a student draw one out, and begin the discussion on that topic. If little interest is shown, draw another topic from the box.
2. The teacher can list on the board four to eight statements related to things that might be examined through student discussion. Examples might include: (a) homework, too much or not enough; (b) free study time, too much or not enough; (c) pleasure reading materials in the classroom, need more or different kinds; (d) class discussions, too many or too few; (e) teacher explains assignments, too much or not enough; (f) classwork, too easy or too hard; and (g) class rules, what liked or what not liked. Separate students into three to five groups, then let each group select a topic they want to discuss. The teacher monitors the various discussions and at the end of a reasonable time, each group explains to the other students the results of their discussion.
3. Using the same type of list developed in #2, the teacher has students volunteer to be on the "for" and "against" teams for a debate. About

---

**TABLE 5  CHECKLIST PROCEDURE FOR ANALYZING TAPE OF FEEDBACK DISCUSSION***

**Step #1:**  Listen to the first five minutes of the tape to get oriented to the mood and direction of the discussion.

**Step #2:**  Listen to three or four more five-minute segments of the tape sampled from the entire taped discussion (or listen to all of it if you want to take the time) and focus very closely on your verbal statements. Using the checklist below, make a tally mark for each time a statement you make fits one or more of the items in the checklist.

1.  A———— I sought information from the student(s).
    B———— I gave information to the student(s).

2.  A———— I accepted what the student(s) said.
    B———— I rejected what the student(s) said.

3.  A———— I restated exactly what the student(s) said.
    B———— I changed the meaning of what the student(s) said.

4.  A———— I asked the student(s) what they thought.
    B———— I told the student(s) what I thought.

**Step #3:**  Grade yourself for the discussion by comparing the number of tallies you received for each of the four pairs on the checklist. You should work to get more "As" than "Bs." "A" statements are positive approaches to conducting feedback discussions. "B" statements tend to impede students from expressing their true feelings. The teacher should ideally work for all "As" and no "Bs."

---

* I wish to thank Patrick Walsh for providing me with the kernel for this idea some years ago.

three on a team should be sufficient. The other students observe and then vote on who won the debate. This can be done as many times as there are topics available to debate.

4. The teacher works with one small group at a time discussing feedback for improving the class. The teacher helps each group prepare results of their discussion to report to the other members of the class. In these reports, topics should be explained, arguments for and against should be presented, and any resolution to the problems should be included.

5. Hold a mock class election for "teacher for a day" in which each student candidate runs on a platform of how they would improve the class for the other students. Each candidate gives a campaign speech and the students vote to elect a winner. Besides indicating to the students what was useful from the exercise, the teacher can also allow the winning student to team-teach a lesson for an upcoming class.

6. Hold a total class discussion built around the concept of "brainstorming." Have all the students in the class brainstorm (think of all the things they can, with all answers acceptable) things they would change about the school and the class. The teacher should list all of the ideas on the board. Next, have the students separate into small groups and select from the list a topic for discussion.

7. Using the same brainstorming idea described in #6, have the entire class discuss which problems on the list could be changed and eliminate those that cannot be. Next, have the students pick the two or three they would most like to see changed, discuss the ways in which changes should occur, and develop a cooperative plan to see that the changes are made.

8. Each week appoint a different group of three or four students to serve as a review panel. Their job would be to ask the other students in the class how the class is going, if they would like something changed, or if something special happened in class they didn't like. Then, without using any student names, the review panel reports their findings to the class. These reports can be used to initiate feedback discussions.

9. Have interested students put on a skit showing how *not* to run a class. Tell them to think of all the things a teacher could do that they would think wrong or unfair and act them out for the remainder of the class. The teacher should use this to initiate discussion and get opinions in response to the ideas presented in the skit. Teachers sometimes recognize a bit of themselves in such student playacting.

10. Have a receptacle of some kind placed in a prominent location in the room. Place a sign over it saying, "Don't put your name on it, but if there was something you liked or didn't like about class today, write it down and put it here." This provides good daily feedback for the teacher and introduces new topics for discussion. An important advantage to this approach is that student anonymity is maintained.

**A Guide to the Interview Approach:**   Interviewing individual students for the purpose of obtaining useful feedback is a delicate business requiring special commitment on the teacher's part. Since most teachers are not trained in the techniques of conducting interviews, it is sometimes difficult for them to adjust to this novel style of working with students.

In the process of collecting feedback for self-improvement, the interview approach has certain advantages over the questionnaire and discussion procedures. The interview is the most personal type of data collection procedure, depending as it does on the development of clear communication between two individuals. When a student is involved in an interview experience there is little doubt that the student has your full attention and that you have the student's. The two of you can be in a world all your own without the concerns and distractions of others.

Because of this one-to-one setting, the interview approach also has the advantage of being more in-depth. You have the opportunity to seek out the interests and concerns of one student, checking on what the student is saying to insure agreement of meaning. This increases the likelihood of getting more information that is more accurate as well. The interview's major shortcoming, however, is its time-consuming nature. Interviewing all students in a given class could take many hours away from other important responsibilities.

Though it is time-consuming, the interview approach should be utilized, even if sparingly, to gain from at least a few students in-depth insights impossible to obtain in other ways.

A realistic interview plan for the interested teacher would be to seek out those students who seem more willing to talk and who show evidence of wanting to contribute to improving how the class is operated. Once these few students have been identified, you must then decide how to conduct the interview to serve the needs of self-improvement. The list that follows should provide you with the guidelines needed in preparing for the interview:

*Interview Guidelines*

1. First decide what it is you want to find out from the students. This can be done by going over information gleaned from questionnaires and group discussions. Other wanted information may be decided upon either because the particular student would know it or because you feel a need to know it.
2. Make a list of the areas of information wanted, choosing those issues that seem most important. Too much variation in content can confuse the student and make the interview results too superficial.
3. Examine the list of chosen issues and develop a list of questions that will help the student focus on the kind of information wanted. These questions should be used by you during the interview so that the student recognizes a definite organization in the interview.

4. Practice the interview questions alone or with a friend and attempt to create possible answers to the questions. This is an excellent way to test whether or not the questions are worthwhile. Some questions sound good until tried, but then get no response or a different response from what was expected.

5. Explain to each student involved what is being done and why. Make clear your interest in getting information that will help you improve.

6. With student consent, tape-record each of the interviews so that you will have the information for later reference. Also, use the checklist procedure in Table 5, page 97, to analyze each interview recorded. The same rules apply for analyzing interview tapes as do for group discussion recordings.

7. Be sure to give the students the opportunity to hear themselves on tape if they desire. This will help reduce the anxiety that tape-recording sometimes causes.

8. Thank each student for participating in the class improvement program and share the information with the class without identifying individual student contributions.

## Making Your Own Feedback Tools

Some teachers find it workable to use questionnaires and discussion or interview formats that have already been developed by others. This, of course, is the least time-consuming approach and affords teachers more opportunity to carry out other responsibilities. However, these tools may not be readily available or in many cases do not contain the specific areas that concern you at the moment. In this case, the next best approach is to locate as many developed forms as are available, such as the Teacher Credibility Questionnaire in Chapter 4, and choose those items that fit your particular needs.

If neither of these procedures seems feasible, the only choice left is to develop the tool from scratch, constructing it to include the kinds of information wanted. The set of guidelines below are intended to provide you with helpful clues in developing tools for collecting student feedback.

### Development Guidelines

1. Before initiating your own work on developing a questionnaire, discussion guide, or interview format, be sure to examine any available tools already developed. Using instruments already completed could save valuable time.

2. Whether using the work of others or developing your own, carefully formulate the ideas you want to cover. This will help you decide which method of collection to use.

3. Formulate your ideas around subject headings or categories. This will keep the information you request in an organized form and protect against duplication.
4. Select only a few categories or major headings to start with. You can always expand later once you have examined your purposes more closely. If you don't keep your categories limited, it could result in something so lengthy as to be unmanageable.
5. Decide on the format to be used in requesting the information. This is especially relevant in developing a questionnaire. The format should be consistent and easy to understand.
6. Once you have developed the tool you plan to use, test it out with colleagues or friends before using it with students. Use their suggestions for making revisions.
7. Be sure to request student feedback about the tool itself. Since students are the object of its use, they can provide helpful hints on how to improve it.

Whether you are using questionnaires, discussions, or interviews to obtain student feedback for self-improvement, involving the students in a class-improvement procedure of this type will make them feel more a part of the decision-making process. The two-way exchange of ideas is essential to making this kind of communication process work, and students with the necessary orientation to the process will contribute useful input that can make everyone feel involved in something worthwhile.

*6*

# How to Raise Test Scores (when necessary)

## How I Raised My Students' Test Scores

After a few years as a young beginning teacher, I finally got my discipline problems under control—not an easy task. I began to look for new horizons and new challenges, beyond the humdrum of everyday routine. I noticed that one teacher's test scores seemed to be consistently higher than those of the other English classes, including my own. (The first few years I hadn't given a damn about esoteric things like test scores. I was just trying to keep myself bodily in the room and to keep the breakage down.)

The other teacher was a very nice, middle-aged woman, who had been teaching for a good many years and who was also a part-time counselor. One day, with the rather quiet effrontery with which I have learned many important lessons in life (and have suffered an equal number of embarrassments), I asked her directly why her classes seemed to do so well.

"Betty," I said, "Why do your classes always seem to do so well on the English part of the standardized achievement test?" (I omit the name of the test in deference to the legal power of the testing industry.) I hoped I had asked the question with sufficient humility, rather than undisguised impertinence, because asking another teacher about what's happening in her class is not an accepted practice among teachers.

"Well," she said, "It's partly because I get the better students and naturally they do better on tests too. But there is another reason. The test is very big on commas. A great number of the items in the English part deal with comma punctuation. A few weeks before the test is given every year, I spend all my time teaching punctuation, particularly commas. My students always do well."

Being a counselor, Betty had had a chance to examine the tests since she administered them to the students. She also had a chance to interpret the results. As an English teacher, she put this information to good advantage.

Armed with this knowledge, I went back to my class and thought it over. Most punctuation rules, particularly about commas, revolve around being able to tell the difference between a dependent and an independent clause and between a phrase and a clause. In those days commas were used somewhat more generously than today. I planned and brooded. The next year, three weeks before the tests were to be administered, I put all my classes at that grade level into a crash unit on punctuation, with special emphasis on commas.

I taught the holy hell out of phrases and clauses. I had dependent and independent clauses strung out through all the backrooms of their minds. For those three weeks I prepped them like a coach, exhorting and steadying simultaneously. I was excited myself. Of course, it was a pace none of us could have maintained over the year. We (pardon me, they) took the test later and I settled back into empty casual free library periods, browsing among the books while the kids tried to find dirty pictures in the news magazines, feeling we all deserved a good rest.

So I waited for the test results to come back, and I waited and I waited. I waited so long that I forgot about them and didn't care any more. Of course, it always takes months to get back the results. But finally they came. And I looked upon the results and, lo and behold, the percentiles were uniformly high across my classes, and I was well pleased.

Of course, the results were not spectacular. Not all my students scored in the ninety-ninth percentile on the tests. There is no way my students who regularly scored in the thirtieth or fortieth percentile (our classes were ability-grouped) would score in the ninety-ninth. The kids who usually dawdled with their pencils because they didn't care still were not motivated. But they got one or two extra items right before they quit.

The kids who couldn't read still couldn't read, but they recognized something that looked vaguely familiar to them from all the drills, exercises, and perorations they had been through, and they guessed one or two right that they wouldn't ordinarily have guessed. The bright kids who ordinarily would have gotten most of them right were particularly well-honed and they slaughtered the items en masse.

And that's all it took. That's all it ever takes. A few more items correct by each kid will boost tremendously the percentiles, the grade equivalents, or however the scores are reported. Everyone didn't "top" the test, but the scores were much better than the kids would normally be expected to get. So I was a great teacher. Or was I?

For the remaining years that I taught I did pretty much the same thing with much the same results. There was no particular reward for me. Unlike today there was no strong pressure in certain quarters to raise test scores. The principal benignly noted and nodded his head over my achievement (after I had pointed it out to him without telling him how I did it). I was never impressed enough with the accomplishment to try to analyze tests at other grade levels I was teaching and to wage a similar campaign. I simply didn't bother. It was not important enough. I did it more as a challenge than anything else. As I say, there was no pressure then, and no reward.

There is a postscript though. Later the head of the business education department had become increasingly unhappy with the punctuation, spelling, and so on, of the girls she got in her senior vocational business courses. Where I taught, a few girls would go on to college, but many of the brightest would stay on in the area and become secretaries in the many surrounding industries. The English department set up a special section of these students for their junior year so they could be adequately prepared in punctuation and spelling. Although their bosses couldn't spell, they could.

I was asked to teach the special section every year, no doubt because of my brilliant and innate ability to teach punctuation and such business writing skills. I never knew but I suspect the decision was made either on the basis of the test scores, or more likely on the basis of the fact that I spent several intense weeks teaching such skills, with students going home saying so.


WHAT TEST SCORES DON'T MEAN
(NOBODY KNOWS WHAT THEY DO MEAN)

Implicit in this incident is all that a teacher really need understand about tests, I believe. I would like to make some of these facts explicit in the rest of the chapter and to suggest how the teacher can raise test scores— legitimately or illegitimately. It's often hard to tell the difference. At the same time I would like to emphasize that test scores are of very little use to the teacher and can be, in fact, rather dangerous. Nonetheless, because of external pressure, it has become difficult to ignore them entirely, particularly in recent years. The information I wish to convey in this chapter on how to manipulate test scores for your own protection cannot be found in your test and measurement courses.

From the incident I have related from my own teaching experience, note that the test results really depend on a very narrow set of questions and an even narrower piece of human behavior. Something as common and as specific as comma usage can be blown out of all proportion if it is interpreted as reflecting general ability in English and is rendered in such absolute and impressive form as percentiles or grade equivalents. It gives one the impression of absolute certainty. Unfortunately, that is the way most people interpret test scores.

In fact, standardized achievement tests are highly arbitrary devices. They are good for measuring only a tiny segment of experience (if that). How well a test measures what it is supposed to measure is what we call the test's "validity." If a test is supposed to be for measuring comma usage, has a lot of comma items on it, and is so labeled, it may have high validity. On the other hand, if it is interpreted as reflecting general ability in English (if there is such a thing), it would be absolutely invalid. To push the situation to an extreme, if you interpreted the comma test as a measure of mathematical ability, the invalidity is obvious.

All this is fairly clear. But the validity of tests for what teachers are ordinarily teaching is not at all clear. Most standardized achievement tests are not based on something as specific and as easily identifiable as comma usage. Quite naturally, test makers want to sell their tests to as large an audience as possible. They may try to key some of the test items to what is taught in some of the most widely used textbooks. However, the further the item is abstracted and removed from what the teacher is actually teaching in the classroom, the less valid the standardized test is for measuring what the students have learned in that particular class. The teacher's own tests are much more likely to reflect what the teacher has taught, but no test maker wants to gear his test to a particular teacher. There's no profit in it.

Now it is true that a student is not going to answer many questions on algebra if he has not had an algebra class. But what about on a test category labeled "verbal reasoning"? (This is one of my favorite categories because I always did so well on it.) Is the teacher responsible for improving the student's score on such a test? If so, what's the subject matter? Or does the student improve his verbal reasoning at the dinner table conversation? Or is it in his or her genes? You see, the trouble with standardized tests is that, even if you believe they measure something important, you aren't sure how they relate to what's learned in school. A great deal of damage can be done if the teacher believes that the tests accurately summarize a student's ability or if other people believe that test scores reflect the teacher's teaching ability.

What do teachers themselves usually think of tests? Too much I fear, although they seem not to make much use of the results. When I was a teacher and used to get back test results, my usual practice (excluding the incident above) was to look at each student's score on verbal abilities to see whether it confirmed or disconfirmed my own assessment of the student's capacity. If the test and I were in serious disagreement, I made a mental note of that and tossed the results in a drawer to await I knew not what.

I suspect that using tests thus for confirmation (or disconfirmation) of judgments about kids is the usual practice. Generally, studies done about teachers' attitudes towards standardized tests indicate that teachers believe they need them but do not use the results in any meaningful way. Even when the teachers have expert test help available, they rely on the tests very little in constructing a curriculum. In fact, the tests offer little help in instruction. (Hotvedt, 1971) So I believe the main function tests serve is to confirm psychologically and justify the terrible sorting judgments teachers make about kids. At the same time teachers feel, almost unanimously, that test results should not be used to evaluate their own effectiveness.

HOW TESTS SAVED ME—A PARADOX

After considerable deliberation on the subject, I have come to the conclusion that standardized tests do more harm than good. (No doubt for that judgment, I will be called a traitor to the evaluation profession—but there are worse things.) My judgment is not without some ambivalence. It is ironic and only a slight distortion to say that the tests that enabled me to escape working in a factory, and that were used to evaluate my students some years later when I was a teacher, were administered by the same organization in which I now sit as a senior staff member denouncing tests.

Growing up in a mill town laden with heavy industry, and having somewhat less than affluent family backing, I was by high school age headed for the factories. One day I discovered that machinists made more money than electricians, or perhaps it was the other way around. I decided to change my course program and take the string of vocational machinist courses rather than vocational electricity. Our high school had elaborate vocational training programs. Why, other than as a symbolic gesture, I don't know since the local trade unions were "blood" unions—you had to have a relative in one before you could get in. We didn't have a course on how to be related to the union business manager.

I don't believe I knew *one* guy who graduated from the three-year training required and got the job for which he was vocationally trained. The unions really controlled "job entry" (as I later learned to say) through apprenticeships. The only alternative if one had no relatives in the right union was to work as a laborer, to pump gas, or to become an insurance salesman or other door-to-door type and fleece the naive union men out of their dollars.

In any case, I was pursuing the dream of becoming a skilled craftsman, and in order to change my course schedule I had to see the dean. Ordinarily I would not see the dean unless I was in trouble, because he would be busy quelling revolts. But this happened to be in the summer and, like most administrators, he had nothing to do. He took some time with me. He had a lot.

"Well, House," he said, looking through my folder. The dean never failed to impress us by calling us by our last names. The other teachers were still calling us Bobby or Timmy or something childish. His blurting out last names like that made us feel manly. We almost felt as if we were in the army. This was the age of the black leather jacket.

"Well, House," he said, "you've got some pretty good test scores here."

I searched through my mind trying to remember taking the tests. Yes, when we first entered high school, the first few days. Early September, the temperature in the nineties, the humidity one hundred and ten. The windows open, the teacher reading us the questions over the roar of the trucks outside. Late at the end of the day, everyone hot and fatigued and trying to look on each other's papers. The teacher tired and not caring. I had pretty well written off that experience. It seemed of no consequence at the time and of less later on.

"House, these scores are pretty good. Have you ever thought about going to college?" the dean asked.

"Not really," I said. "My mother has mentioned it before. I thought I would go into the vocational program."

"Who in the hell put you in the shop curriculum?" he asked. If the last name was good, "hell" from an administrator was really big time.

"The counselor, sir," I said. Two could play the army game. "When I came in the summer before my freshman year for a counseling session, he put the shop courses on my schedule. He said I could change them later if I wanted to."

The dean shook his head. He looked through my papers and didn't say anything for a long time. I waited expectantly.

"Well, I think you should go to college," he said, leaning back in his chair, relaxing. In a soft, confidential voice, the reassuring voice of experience now, he told me a little about college, what it was like. This personal touch was persuasive.

"Well," I said, "maybe I will go to college." At precisely that time we changed my course schedule for the coming year to the college prep curriculum and away from the shop courses. Of course, there is much more to it than that, but from that time on I began to think about and plan to go to college. My mother had been pressing the issue, but in the dean I found the first official confirmation that I might have the ability to do it. And in this my test scores played an important part. A year later may well have been too late. Yet the scores would have meant nothing without the personal influence of the dean. When I go back to my home town and drive along the rows of mills and factories I shudder at the luck of the chance encounter that enabled me to get out, for many of my colleagues with higher test scores are working behind those gates.

So it is not without ambivalence that I declare standardized tests essentially harmful. At their best, they can help an academically talented student to escape from a setting such as I have described, although other factors related to social mobility, such as social class and family resources, are far more influential in effecting that escape. If standardized tests can sometimes be put to good purposes, more frequently they misguide, disrupt, and misinterpret good teaching.

The main issue is one of validity. The tests do not measure what teachers teach. There are also problems of test bias. Ethnic group children and lower-class children score lower on standardized tests than middle-class white children. Why this happens is a highly controversial question. Many claim that the tests are constructed by middle-class whites and field tested only on white, middle-class children. Historically this has indeed been true. Consequently, they claim, the test items are biased toward white middle-class children.

Whatever the truth of this charge, it is clear that a middle-class child whose parents have instilled him or her with the idea of being a doctor and the idea of the importance of taking tests is going to be more motivated and do better on a test than a student of the same ability who intends to be a machinist and for whom tests are unimportant. Considerable differences are built into scores through the aspirations of the parents for their children. The counterargument is that the motivated child who does well on the tests will also do well in classes. The same abilities, such as the ability to follow directions, will enable him or her to do better in school. And, indeed, it is true that those who do well on the tests tend to do well in school, though there are a great many exceptions to this tendency.

## WHAT TO DO (LEGITIMATE OR OTHERWISE) IF TEST PRESSURE IS EXCESSIVE

Validity is the first problem then, and standardized tests are not likely to reflect validly what the individual teacher does. Even tests of basics like reading vary tremendously in what they measure. So the teacher does well to avoid using standardized tests to evaluate the effects of instruction. What if such avoidance is impossible? Then the teacher should exercise great care in selecting the test that measures what the teacher is teaching. Forget the labels on the tests. You can only tell by looking at individual items themselves.

What if test avoidance or selection is not possible? Then we must revert to the general rule: *The closer the test items are to what the teacher is teaching, the better the teacher's students will do on the test.* The ultimate recourse is to teach the actual test items. Without a doubt this is the most effective way to help your students score well on tests.

A few years ago business interests were pushing "performance contracting," a technique in which the school district contracted out part of its educational program to a corporation. The business firms would be paid to raise test scores based upon a previously agreed-upon contract. A certain increase in test scores would result in a certain financial payoff. The results from the first few contracts looked great—until it was discovered that a few weeks before the payoff tests were administered, the students were taught many of the actual items on the test. Once this advantage was removed, businesses did no better in raising test scores than did the schools.

Of course, teaching the test items requires that you know them in advance. This is not always possible, and it is also a trifle illegitimate in the eyes of some people. Somewhat more acceptable socially is to teach testlike items. This again requires that you know both the content and the form of the test. To approach the problem of proper coaching for taking the test, think of the test as divided into its specific content on the one hand, and the form of the items on the test on the other.

Generally, research indicates that it only helps a little bit to teach for the content—mainly, I think, because tests measure something other than what is taught in school anyway. An exception is the test I mentioned before with such a heavy loading on commas. Knowing that the content is so specific and concrete as it was in that case, you could teach the devil out of the test without ever using actual test items. The great majority of standardized tests are so diffuse that they don't lend themselves to that approach, however.

The form of the test items is another story. You can increase scores dramatically by having students practice answering the kinds of questions they will encounter on the test itself. For example, if the items are multiple-choice, scores can be dramatically improved by having students practice and work on multiple-choice items—preferably on similar content to those on the test. Motivating students for the test, emphasizing the careful reading of instructions, coaching them to examine all the alternatives, and giving them other test-taking advice are also of great benefit.

To understand some manipulations of the test-taking environment, it is necessary to look at how test scores are constructed and reported. When people read a term like "fifth-grade equivalent" or "sixth-grade equivalent" they tend to believe that somehow the tests analyze all the things a student at the sixth-grade level would know and verify that the student has the skills of an average student in the sixth grade. This is far, far from the true situation.

In fact, grade equivalents are based upon the total number of items right on a given test, and few people realize how few items separate one grade equivalent from another. For example, on the reading comprehension part of the Comprehensive Test of Basic Skills, level three, only three items separate the fifth-grade equivalent from the sixth-grade equivalent. Most people would see these two scores as being very significantly different from one another.

Properly interpreted, a fifth-grade equivalent score compared to a sixth-grade score means not that one student is verified in the skills of the fifth grade rather than the sixth, but rather that he got three fewer items correct on the test! This is quite a different piece of information, isn't it? Knowing this you can appreciate how fragile test scores are and how easy they are to manipulate in certain ways.

Now almost all the tests are conducted under rigorous time constraints. How many items can the student do in this amount of time? A
little distraction from external noise that causes a class to lose a minute
or so and forces every child to get one item less will cause the class scores
to read at the level of 5.0 instead of 5.3. If a child gets confused on
instructions for a *few minutes,* he may score at the 5.0 rather than 6.0—
quite a difference! When one considers that the child's future or a teacher's
reputation may rest on test performance, our reliance on these devices is
astounding. But we still use them.

Some experts have criticized the use of "grade equivalence" scores,
since the term gives quite a false impression of what is being measured
and reported. The testing industry has been very reluctant to change its
reporting for the obvious reason that if people really knew what they were
buying, they wouldn't be happy with them at all. Generally, the public and
the press, and even educators, tend to interpret the tests as being literally
true. A 6.0 grade equivalent means that the child has the skills of the
average sixth-grader, they think.

There is not much good that can be said about this institutionalized
debacle, but fortunately there are a few things that can be done about it.
One possibility might be political pressure by organized teachers. Also,
the individual teacher is not entirely defenseless. Consider, for example,
if the person administering the test allows the students to spend an extra
five minutes taking it—perhaps enough time for every student to get two
more items correct. The class score will now average a 5.6 grade equivalent rather than a 5.0—a marvelous example of modern educational
technique!

Since the tests depend on so few items, they are extremely sensitive
to manipulation of test-taking circumstances, as a few more items right
or wrong makes a big difference in the final test results. The quietness of
the room, its temperature, other environmental factors—these can make
a substantial difference.

The time of year tests are given also makes a difference. As teachers
have long suspected, students do forget a lot over the summer and also
might not be used to school and taking tests at the beginning of the
school year. In addition, getting school organized causes major distractions early in the year. Standardized tests given early in the year yield
lower results than those given later. If a teacher wanted to show good
results during the academic year, he or she could give tests in the early
weeks of school. (The September results for the kids may actually be
lower than results from the previous spring.) If he or she then gave the
tests later in the spring, he or she will find considerable improvement
simply from the change in the time of the year. However, the teacher
can't wait too late in the year because of the distractions at the end of
the school term.

There is another trick to test scores. Because of the unreliability and
invalidity of the tests, there is considerable fluctuation in the scores for an

individual. This is known as the standard error of the test and it cannot be eliminated. It is well understood by test experts but not by other people. Most people believe that if a student takes the same test four times his score will be pretty much the same each time, but this is not so. Because of the standard error effect, four administrations of the test may result in differences of a whole grade equivalent.

The practical import of this little-understood phenomenon is this: if a student is given a test several times, some of his scores will be much better than others. If one is aiming for a particular level of performance, the chances of a student's reaching it are greatly enhanced by his or her repeatedly taking the test.

People from private agencies were often paid for each student who reached a certain level on the test. By giving the test on several occasions they could, in fact, be paid on the basis of the error of measurement— whether the students were being given instruction or not. A student who wishes to reach a certain level on a test has greatly improved chances if he takes the test several times—provided he gets to select his best performance. Interesting, eh? You may need it some time.

THE SHIFTING POPULATION GAME—
HOW TO WIN EVERY TIME

One of the most flagrant misinterpretations and misuses of test scores results from the intrinsic social-class bias of the tests. A common situation goes something like this. A school principal comes to our office seeking some evaluation advice. The following conversation is typical.

PRINCIPAL    I have started a new program in my school—a program for humanistic education. The school board is pressuring me to evaluate it to see if I want to expand it or keep it. What tests do I use to evaluate it?

EVALUATOR    Well, standardized achievement tests aren't really good indicators of what is taught in school. Not to mention that they won't begin to measure whatever your humanistic education is. You have to use something else.

PRINCIPAL    But the board wants to see if the humanistic class is better on the tests. I don't think they will accept anything else.

EVALUATOR    Better than what?

PRINCIPAL    Better than the other class that's not in the humanistic program. We have two classes, one in and one out.

EVALUATOR    Okay, if you insist on putting yourself at a disadvantage, here's the way to do it. Mix the kids' names together next year; randomly put kids in each of the classes. Teach one the humanistic stuff. Give both classes the test at the end of the year. Since the test won't measure what you are doing, your kids won't look any worse off either.

PRINCIPAL    Oh, my God! We can't put kids into classes that way! It was the local doctors' wives who pressured us into starting the program to begin with. We asked for volunteers for the new program. I'd have a civil war on my hands if I did what you suggested.

EVALUATOR    Well, who's in the new program? What kind of kids?

PRINCIPAL    Mostly doctors' kids and other kids from Ritzy Heights. Those doctors' wives drummed up a lot of business out there.

EVALUATOR    What's Ritzy Heights like?

PRINCIPAL    The homes there start at about $100,000. Doctors, lawyers, businessmen live there. They pretty much run the school district. If this program doesn't work, those wives will skin me alive. Those women don't have much else to do with their time, you know.

EVALUATOR    Who's in the other class?

PRINCIPAL    Mostly kids from Hardluck Haven. That's the other part of my attendance area. It's a public housing project. If you make over $5,000 a year and have ever held a job, you can't live there.

EVALUATOR    Well, if you give the XYZ Test or any standardized test to your two classes, the humanistic group is going to score much better. Not because they have learned anything necessarily, but because test scores are strongly linked to social class. The people who have all the money and advantages also have higher test scores too. It keeps the social class structure neater that way.

PRINCIPAL    Are you sure you know what you're talking about?

EVALUATOR    I guarantee the results. The people who want the new programs tend to be from the better side of the tracks generally. By accepting volunteers, you've heavily loaded the classes in terms of social-class bias.

PRINCIPAL    You're right.

EVALUATOR    If your new class doesn't score better on the achievement test than the other one, it will be an educational miracle. You will have found in the humanities program an inhibitor of all the social advantages that the well-off enjoy. You could make a fortune— although I'm not sure whom you could sell it to. The antidote seems to be more widely sought.

PRINCIPAL    I don't care about that. I just want to get those goddamn doctors' wives off my neck!

EVALUATOR    The school board would misinterpret such scores terribly. They would believe the test scores were different because of what was taught. Actually, it's just a difference between the two populations you've got there. It's a common mistake but I don't know if you could ever explain it to them.

PRINCIPAL    Right.

EVALUATOR    Where are you going?

PRINCIPAL    (getting up to leave) I just remembered that my parking meter has expired. I have to go.

EVALUATOR   Go? We haven't gotten around to talking about how to evaluate your program properly.

PRINCIPAL   I remember now I told my wife I would be home early for dinner. It's a long drive.

EVALUATOR   I feel bad about wasting your time without giving you something you could use.

PRINCIPAL   Well, don't feel bad. I think I've learned something. So long.

Shifts in population are often the reason behind shifting test scores in different geographical areas. Test scores in a large city may decline, not because teaching is not as good, but because more and more poor people are moving into the city. The city's population is changing.

Likewise, scores on national tests like the Scholastic Aptitude Tests, used extensively for college entrance, may decline over time. The reason may be that more and more students can afford to go to college so that the test-taking population is drawn more and more from lower socio-economic groups.

Evidence of a decline in the scores of nationally administered tests invariably elicits great outcries in the press about declining educational quality. Actually, there may be any number of reasons for the decline. No one really knows why test scores decline (or increase). For example, students probably watch more television now, and there are some indications that they don't take tests as seriously as they used to. There are at least a dozen plausible reasons, and there is no way to tell from the test scores themselves.

## COACHING THE KIDS

Besides the methods suggested for manipulating test scores, there are methods of preparing students for tests that some people claim produce dramatic results (Whimby, 1976). Poorer students, especially, tend to jump at the first obvious answer on achievement tests and to be rather careless in thinking scholastic problems through. Having students practice taking tests of a similar type seems to be the best way to prepare them for test taking.

The teacher can have the student think through aloud a problem he has not done correctly. Getting direct feedback on his or her errors enables a student to do better in problem solving. This is, in effect, how middle-class parents help their children on their homework, and it is this type of attention to the child's problem-solving errors that lower-class children rarely get. Of course, this technique approaches a tutorial session, and the classroom teacher is very limited in the number of students with whom he or she can work in this fashion and the time he or she can spend with each one. The teacher must patiently probe the student's reasoning. Getting students to take time to think through the problem is critical. Better students seem to carry out an internal dialogue with themselves which poorer students do not.

Of course, ultimately the teacher must balance the time spent on preparing for tests against what it is that would be more valuable for the students to learn.

# 7

# Communicating
# with Parents

## A Few Teachers Talk

ALICE   I guess it's a case of misunderstanding or something. It just seems that everytime I have to contact her, I put it off because I know there's going to be trouble.

TONY   Well, I had the same trouble last year. I really don't know what to tell you. John's a good kid, but he sure has his moods . . . wouldn't do a thing for two weeks and then everything was just fine again. And he seemed to always make a comeback just in time for the parent conferences, too. I hated to say anything negative by that time because he really had caught up.

ALICE   Parent conferences. Ugh! The thing with conferences is that they are regularly scheduled, but the problems that come up with the kids aren't. I have even overheard parents say that they thought parent conferences were a waste of time, since they really didn't find out anything they didn't know already.

TONY   It's sure a helluva thing to prepare for. I'll say that. Sometimes I really don't have much to tell them they don't already know.

KAY   What are you guys agonizing over this time? So serious you look!

ALICE   Hi, Kay. Oh, it's just parents again. It's getting to be quite a hassle dealing with Mrs. Sylvester. Her son just won't get with it sometimes, but his mother is more of a problem than he is. She's always questioning what I'm doing that might cause John to have trouble and says that he's never this way at home. There are times

**115**

when I'd like to tell her off, but I'm afraid that would just cause more trouble.

KAY   I know Mrs. Sylvester fairly well, Alice. I'm surprised to hear this about her. Are you sure it's as bad as you say?

ALICE   Oh, I'm sure alright. Why, I think that woman is neurotic and she may give me a neurosis before it's all over.

TONY   Alice is right, Kay. You weren't here last year, so you wouldn't know, but she can be hell on wheels.

KAY   Well, that's not the Helen Sylvester that I know. I've always felt she was very reasonable and willing to consider other points of view. Since I'm new here, you would have no way of knowing, of course, but she's my sister-in-law. I guess I should know her fairly well myself.

ALICE   I had no idea . . .

TONY   Hey, I may have come on a little strong . . .

Not a typical situation perhaps, but one that can help focus on a few issues essential to the teacher's survival, especially in dealing with parents. One of the things parents and teachers can do is get a bit careless in their judgments of each other. Parents learn certain categorical information about teachers and use this limited information to make decisions that will aid their children in school. "She's a tough grader," "She doesn't know how to teach reading," "He doesn't assign enough homework"— these are all examples of information parents may have to go on.

Teachers make similar judgments based on limited information. The scenario just portrayed provides a case in point: "hell on wheels," "neurotic," "a problem." This partial information may be accurate as far as it goes, but how far *does* it go toward explaining the whole situation, defining the problem, or solving the problem with the child's own best interest in mind? And teachers really don't need this added burden, anyway. They certainly have enough to worry about without having to battle with parents.

How differently Kay viewed the behavior of Mrs. Sylvester, a view from an entirely different context. She knew her personally and could think about her in circumstances in which Alice and Tony were very unlikely to find themselves. It's not that Kay is right or wrong about what kind of person Mrs. Sylvester really is. Nor can we say anything about the accuracy of Tony's and Alice's perceptions. Kay has different information, that's all. I, of course, do not recommend becoming the in-law of troublesome parents in order to solve school problems.

Seeing parents in a different light can be helpful to a teacher's survival, though. Getting to know what their situations are can provide the teacher with ways of dealing with parents in a much more realistic and complete way. Even knowing how parents in general view the school situation and its teachers can balance the teacher's view and thus give that teacher a better information base from which to operate.

## THE PARENT PERSPECTIVE*

It's very difficult to know how any particular parent or parent group views you or the school, but some parent perceptions seem to hold constant. When we become teachers, it is quite possible that taking on this new role we simultaneously shed other roles or views of the past. Seeing the school setting as a teacher makes one all but forget what he or she thought about it as a student, and it becomes confusing to experience it as both a teacher and a parent.

The school is our "turf," our place of daily circumstance. We learn the politics, the informal dos and don'ts, and the special language that goes along with surviving in our work setting. But parents really can't know all of this, and they feel quite differently when they must deal with the school one way or another. A note comes home attached to cute little Agnes saying something about "lacks motivation." "What does this mean?" the parent may ask. Or more often than not, parents will either comply willingly with whatever the school suggests or perhaps give little Agnes a "good talking to" about doing what the teacher says at school.

The teacher may be deeply concerned that Alfred is really not working up to his potential, call Alfred's mother to communicate this concern, and perhaps suggest that she drop by for a talk sometime soon. Will the parent come? Probably. Especially if it seems to be important to Alfred. But if there is any way out of it, many parents will avoid coming to the school. It can be a scary place if you are not used to it, and most parents are not used to it at all.

Conversely, there are parents who seem to be joiners or helpers by nature and would certainly come running if you called them about anything at all. In addition, they are always present at school functions and more than willing to volunteer time for bake sales, car washes, you name it. Although these helpers can be wearing at times, it is usually essential to the school's operation that they be available. But a warning: be very careful not to use the helpers as your standard for judging all parents. Not even the helpers all view the school in the same way. Those parents who are seldom seen have their own perceptions of the worth and proper role of education. Perhaps the most important idea to keep in mind is that parent absenteeism is not a good measure of their interest in their child's education. Seldom-seen parents could have many reasons for their absences—for example, both parents working, other outside interests, family demands, or particular professional demands.

What else can you expect parents to see as they look at the school from their special vantage point? The following list summarizes the most commonly mentioned general perceptions and experiences I have discovered in talking to parents.

---

* My thanks to the parents with whom I have talked and in particular to Denver Fox, who provided many insights into the parents' view of things.

- Always want what is best for their child even though it may not always seem so
- Would like to know what the year's program and objectives are going to be
- Need to know how home environment can help the child in school
- Feel ultimately responsible for their child's life and future even though the teacher may contribute to it
- Want to have a say in what happens to their child at school
- Want to be informed of any school policy changes or classroom rule changes and of reasons for such alterations
- Some teachers act as if afraid of parents but should not since parents only want to help
- Would like teacher to involve children in activities that the parents could attend and observe
- Would like to hear about positive work by child, not just shortcomings
- If something is wrong, parents want to hear about it immediately
- Would like teacher to realize that school is not their child's whole world and other activities place demands on the children, too
- Want teachers really to get to know the family unit, not just the child
- Would like to be treated as equals and would like for the teacher to be more informal and friendly
- Appreciate parent conferences only when there is a need for them

Perhaps this list can provide some insight into how parents think. While some of the ideas may seem rather mundane or obvious, these are very real and important issues to parents. Knowing this could save your backside someday, remembering that parents can wield a mighty sword if riled to the point of attack. And for your own psychological as well as job survival, it would be best if *you* solved any such problems or made certain they did not occur to begin with. To quote a principal I had the extreme misfortune to work under:

> Look! I don't much care what you do in there [the classroom] as long as you teach 'em something and keep 'em quiet. But you push something to a point where I got some momma in my office, don't look for no sympathy from me. My job depends on keepin' those mommas and papas happy—and your job depends on keepin' me happy. (Source conveniently forgotten)

A real sweetheart, he was and there are still some around like him. But even more rational- and/or modern-thinking school principals do not like to be embroiled in problems between parents and teachers. Thus, even if you are right, the principal isn't going to forget the inconvenience or problem you have caused him or her.

Of course, no teacher is going to cause such problems for him or herself if they can be avoided. Some further ideas from parents might better guarantee that such difficulties won't occur. Specifically, the last general parent idea on the list previously provided ("Appreciate parent conferences only when there is a need for them") creates some additional ideas for the concerned teacher to consider. Indeed, several parents have said that they purposely avoid parent-teacher conferences unless there is a communicated need for a conference. One parent said that teacher conferences are ". . . mostly meaningless, and if you have a problem the teacher usually can't solve it anyway." And another parent pointed out that she was not sure that ". . . conferences are really necessary for all parents, but I personally want to talk with the teacher as many times as possible."

What's the hang-up with these conferences anyway? I always thought that I was doing the parents a favor by taking this extra time to prepare for and hold meetings to discuss the progress of their children. Not so, say some; definitely, say others. I guess the teacher can always make it a volunteer program, and not be overly concerned when some parents don't show. Many schools operate this way already and seem to feel that such an approach is a successful one. But what lies underneath this "conference versus no conference" syndrome?

Among other things, parents report that in some cases they fear that what they might say could be used to damage their child's school growth. My colleague* tells the story of going into a school to talk with his son's teacher, mainly because he was concerned that the teacher was holding his son back in reading unnecessarily. "He can read more advanced books than this one," he told the teacher. "Would it be all right if you moved him ahead some?" The teacher reluctantly complied, but knowingly or unknowingly used my colleague's suggestion to motivate his son in other ways. "Your father says you do much better than this at home. You had better get on the ball." "I'll bet you're better than this in math. According to your dad, you always seem to drag your feet."

Probably a very unusual situation—at least I hope it was. But parents fear such things nonetheless, and as teachers we can assuage some of these anxieties by the way we operate in the conference. One way to get a handle on better parent conference techniques is to look into how we behave in conferences. For example, we could examine our listening habits as teachers, for there are certain things that each of us does that probably irritate others. The following is a self-test you could take to judge your listening habits. It is only intended as a helpful set of reminders that could keep you out of trouble in dealing with parents. This list was gathered from subordinates who found the listening habits of their supervisors to be particularly irritating. It could easily apply to the teacher-parent conference as well.

* Personal communication with Denver Fox

## Irritating Listening Habits*

Test yourself by thinking of the teacher-parent conference setting, then rate yourself on each of the forty-four items below the way in which you think parents would rate you.

$$1 = \text{never true}$$
$$2 = \text{seldom true}$$
$$3 = \text{true about half of the time}$$
$$4 = \text{true most of the time}$$
$$5 = \text{always true}$$

Add up the numbers you gave yourself for each item. Chances are good that the higher total score you give yourself, the more irritating you are to parents.

44 is a perfect score (nobody should get that)
132 is an average score (that's about where I'd score)
220 is the lowest possible score (nobody got this, did they?)

_____ 1. Doesn't give me a chance to talk. I go in with a problem and never do get a chance to tell about it.

_____ 2. Interrupts me when I talk.

_____ 3. Never looks at me when I talk. I don't know whether he or she is listening or not.

_____ 4. Makes me feel that I'm wasting his or her time. Doodles and draws pictures all the time.

_____ 5. Continually fidgets with a pencil, a paper, or something, looking at it and examining it as if studying it rather than listening to me.

_____ 6. Paces back and forth as if impatient with the way I am telling my story.

_____ 7. Has such a poker face and manner that I never know whether he or she is listening or understands me.

_____ 8. Treats me like a child, ignoring me at times.

_____ 9. Never smiles—I'm afraid to talk to him or her.

_____10. Asks questions as if he or she doubted everything I say.

_____11. Always gets me off the subject with his or her questions and comments.

_____12. Whenever I make a suggestion, he or she throws cold water on it. I've quit making suggestions.

_____13. Always tries to get ahead of me—pre-stating my point or pre-finishing my sentence.

_____14. Rephrases what I say in a way that puts words into my mouth that I didn't mean.

* After Nichols (undated mimeo)

_____15. Talks me around into a corner, and makes me feel like a fool.

_____16. Frequently answers a question with another question—and usually it's one I can't answer. It embarrasses me.

_____17. Occasionally asks a question about what I have just said and shows he or she just wasn't listening. For example, just after I finish telling about a problem, he or she might then ask, "Let's see, what was the problem you wanted to talk to me about?"

_____18. Always takes notes when I am talking. I get so worried about what he or she is writing, and so worried about how I am saying things, that I forget what I am saying.

_____19. Argues with everything I say—even before I have a chance to state my case.

_____20. Everything I say reminds him or her of a personal experience or a happening that he or she heard of recently. I get frustrated when he or she continually interrupts to say, "That reminds me . . ."

_____21. Sits there picking hangnails, or clipping or cleaning fingernails, or cleaning his or her glasses, etc. I know he or she can't do that and listen, too.

_____22. Rummages through papers on the desk or through desk drawers, instead of listening.

_____23. Twitches and turns constantly, just waiting for me to stop so he or she can take over.

_____24. When I have a good idea, he or she says, "Oh, yes, I've been thinking about that for some time."

_____25. Whenever I talk, he or she swings around and looks out the window.

_____26. Smiles all the time, even when I am talking about a serious problem of mine.

_____27. Stares at me as if trying to outstare me.

_____28. Looks at me as if appraising me. I begin to wonder if I have a smudge on my face, or a tear in my coat, etc.

_____29. Looks me in the eye too much . . . for unnaturally long times.

_____30. Overdoes trying to show me he or she is following what I'm saying . . . too many nods of the head, or mm-hms and uh-huhs.

_____31. Inserts humorous remarks when I'm trying to be serious.

_____32. After apparently listening, he or she says something like, "It looks to me as though your problem is . . ." _and what he or she suggests usually isn't my problem at all._

_____33. Blows smoke in my face. It almost makes me dizzy at times.

_____34. Asks personal questions when other people are in the same room with us.

_____35. Frequently looks at a watch or clock while I am talking.

_____36. Closes his or her eyes, rests head on hand, as if resting.

_____37. Doesn't put down what he or she is doing when I come in, and turn his or her attention to me completely.

_____38. Doesn't seem to take personal interest in me—is completely withdrawn and distant.

_____39. Always makes some remark that indicates that he or she is doing me a favor in seeing me.

_____40. Is always rushed for time, and makes comments about his or her busy day. Won't sit still.

_____41. Passes the buck on problems, saying things like, "We'll have to think about it."

_____42. Acts as if he or she knows it all, frequently relating incidents in which he or she was the hero.

_____43. Says something and then denies it at the next meeting.

_____44. Asks questions that demand agreement—for example, he or she makes a statement and then says, "Don't you think so?" or "Don't you agree?"

## TEACHERS AS COUNSELORS

Certainly after some in-school experience, most teachers recognize the need for getting and maintaining parental support for the school and its teachers. In most cases this task can be carried off without a great deal of preoccupation over the problems that only occasionally occur—problems that might be caused by misunderstanding between teacher and parent or perhaps by a lack of real concern on the part of either. Of course, some parents are going to be a headache no matter what you do and it is best not to let them get you down as long as you have tried your best to work with them.

But working with parents in a way that will help you survive in the classroom still means that you have to understand *your* role in the communication process. One such role that has proven successful for teachers and others is the "client centered" (Rogers, 1951) or counselor role of the teacher. Teachers often utilize this approach with children, especially when dealing with them on an individual basis. It requires the teacher to listen carefully to what each child is saying and in some cases restate each child's statement to:

1. be absolutely certain that you are both on the same wave length, saying things like "so what you're saying is . . ."
2. prove to the child through your actions or words that you are indeed listening.

This kind of listening can be utilized when you are communicating with parents as well. A counselor approach can be employed whether you are talking with a parent for a short time on the telephone or in a conference, or can be used equally well with parent groups where interchanges are bound to occur. The essential ingredient to this counseling approach is that of listening and getting a few steps beyond those things that irritate (How did you do on the self-test?).

The teacher as counselor or listener may have already developed some fairly sophisticated tactics while working with the students in the class. However, being aware of these strategies to the extent that they can be reapplied with parents may be a bit much to ask of the busy teacher. In addition, the teacher should have some way of assessing whether or not he or she has developed workable listening strategies with the students in the first place. This can be done by running a little self-check to be sure that you are not blocking communication instead of enhancing it. Gordon (1970, 1974) has provided a handy set of "Roadblocks to Communication" which can help you get in touch with your present communication approach. Put in the context of working with parents, the roadblocks provide a guide of what *not* to do.

## Communication Roadblocks[*]

**Directing:**  Suggests that parents do not know what to do without your telling them.

> *Ex.* "You'll have to see that Leroy studies every night from now on."

**Warning:**  Similar to directing but also suggests consequences that might border on threat.

> *Ex.* "If you don't see that Leroy studies every night, he's not going to make it in this class."

**Moralizing:**  Providing information on what is "right" or "wrong," which can produce either guilt or defensiveness in parents.

> *Ex.* "You know, Leroy's education should be much more important to you than basketball or music."

**Advising:**  By solving the problem for them, the teacher does not appear to have confidence in parents' ability to solve it.

> *Ex.* "I think the best solution is to cut out basketball and get Leroy a tutor."

**Blaming:**  Using judgments to move the blame onto the parents.

> *Ex.* "You probably have not helped Leroy by letting him engage in all of these distractions."

[*] After Gordon (1974, pp. 80–87).

**Interpreting:**    Analyzing parent behavior by using one's own diagnosis and frame of reference.

> *Ex.* "You probably wouldn't let Leroy get away with so much playing if you weren't so fond of sports, Mr. Stein."

**Questioning:**    Probing to find out information that may not be clearly relevant in the parents' eyes.

> *Ex.* "Do you expect Leroy to become a great jazz musician?"

**Distracting:**    Putting parents off by changing the subject or directing with humor.

> *Ex.* "You know, Leroy reminds me of a boy I had three years ago and he always . . ."

I have recorded discussions with some of my students to see if I employed any of these blocking tactics with them. I do. My three worst areas are advising, questioning, and distracting—all of which I am willing to defend until my last fatal gasp. But if my *advising* makes the student feel that he or she cannot be trusted to solve his or her own problem, or if my *questioning* makes the student feel as if I am invading his or her privacy, and if my *distracting* makes the student feel that I would rather joke around than listen to his or her problem, no matter how long I defend these approaches, I am still blocking the communication. They block the communication by suggesting that you are not willing to listen. I'm certain this applies in dealing with parents as well.

I have a colleague who uses humor on occasion to distract me when we are conversing and I really don't appreciate it at all. I get the feeling that he is tired of listening or for some other reason does not want to deal with the subject at hand. I usually walk away wondering what our meeting was about, in some cases forgetting what I went in for.

Unfortunately, something about advising and questioning seems to fit the teacher's role so well that it is difficult for teachers to break the habit. Many times we don't even know that we are doing these things. Working in a classroom all day with kids makes questioning and advising second-nature procedures, legitimately used to see if students understand and to provide information to help them move ahead. However, these procedures can turn parents off, especially if used very often.

One alternative in working with parents, even on a short-term basis, is the use of listening techniques. Listening is a tricky business and requires hard, concentrated effort to keep it going. Nichols suggests that the reason that listening is not a natural behavior and one that just anyone could perform stems from the fact that people are really not willing to work at it. Problems in listening come from:

- a mistaken belief that you can relax and listen at the same time
- a desire to break into the act with your own thoughts or words

- an emotional reaction to certain words or ideas that blot out the rest of the message (Nichols, 1967, p. 1)


PASSIVE AND ACTIVE LISTENING

When discussing children with their parents, the teacher may want to employ some combination of these two kinds of listening strategies described by Gordon (1970, 1974). "Passive" listening consists of essential nonverbal messages by which you communicate that you are attentive, concerned, interested, and in other ways listening without intervening verbally. Beier and Gill (1974) have identified nine separate classes of nonverbal communication, six of which have application for the teacher-parent situations. They are body language, facial expression, posture, eye contact, proximity, and paralinguistic messages (sounds other than words). The way in which such passive (nonverbal) listening is used can communicate acceptance or rejection to the parent. As Gordon (1970, p. 37) has said, " 'passive listening' . . . is a potent nonverbal message and can be used effectively to make a person feel genuinely accepted."

"Active listening" on the other hand, consists of verbal signals teachers can send to demonstrate to the parent that they are listening. Such signals might be a restatement of what the parent has said, essentially feeding back the information to insure that you have decoded their message correctly. But to avoid parroting or sounding phony, varied listening statements should be used. You simply cannot keep saying, "So what you're saying is . . ." and then repeat exactly what you have been told. Instead you must tell them your understanding of what they've said, or, if it is quite clear to begin with, some of the following statements might be employed:

- I think I see your point
- I see what you're driving at now
- I think I get what you're saying
- Yes, I understand the direction you're headed
- I hadn't thought about that before
- Tell me more about this idea you have
- Would you mind explaining that a little further?

As Edwards (1971) has pointed out, these kinds of statements show acceptance, but at the same time: (1) demonstrate that you have been listening, (2) grant that the ideas have some importance, and (3) can encourage further talk from the parent. In addition, such statements do *not* back parents into a corner but provide them with the opportunity to stop pursuing an issue if they have no more to say.

The application of passive or active listening depends solely on the situation in which you find yourself with the parent. Certainly if a parent has a question or wants to inquire about the child's progress, this kind of response would seem warped indeed. One could easily imagine how ludicrous it would sound if a parent asked, "How is Mary doing in spelling now, Ms. Jones?", and the teacher, faithful to the active listening approach, says, "You're wondering if Mary is doing better in spelling, Mrs. Hotch-kins?" However, one does apply the listening strategies when problems occur involving the child's work in school, and most importantly when the parents are concerned or perhaps even upset by what has been happening at school. When parents seem to think the teacher is at fault is where passive and active listening can be utilized to save your hide. Your position is simply to keep your cool and let them spill it all, and in many cases the tempers and the issue have been defused, not only providing a calmer setting but also giving you the upper hand. By keeping your mouth closed or reflecting on the ideas and feelings of the parents, you know where they are coming from and have had time to think about what you will say.

## TWO EXAMPLES OF PARENT CONFERENCES

Examining two different approaches to discussing issues with parents might clarify how the listening strategies can help you survive. The first example illustrates a teacher using some roadblocks to communication; the second, a practical application of passive and active listening.

# Example #1: The Roadblock Approach

TEACHER   Oh, come in Mr. Dempsey. Have a seat right there, if you will. Now let me begin by explaining to you why I have called you in today.

PARENT   I think I know why I'm here, Ms. Greene. This isn't the first time, you know. I'm beginning to wonder if it's all Danny's fault.

T   Are you suggesting that the fault is mine, Mr. Dempsey? Have you asked Danny about this, has he said something? (Questioning)

P   Now, hold on. Let's not bring Danny into this just yet. What I'm saying is that he seems to be a fairly normal kid for his age, but somehow he's in a lot more trouble here than his friends are.

T   I'm sure that there are times when his friends put him up to it. But he is the one who gets caught, and he should know better. (Blaming, Moralizing)

P   But why him all the time? I cut up in school just like any healthy boy his age. This whole thing has got me just a little bit mad! I think . . .

T   Look, Mr. Dempsey, don't get upset with me because Danny is a troublemaker. If he keeps it up, he's going to be in real trouble. (Interpreting, Warning)

P Don't you think you're picking on him just a bit? Hell, around the neighborhood there are kids from this class who break windows for kicks. You won't ever catch Danny doing something like that! Believe me!

T Danny is a little bit like my brother, Mr. Dempsey. He was always an angel around our father, but when he was out of sight, he changed to a devil in a hurry. (Distracting, Interpreting)

P Well, Danny ain't your brother and I'm a little tired of this run-around. We'll see what the principal has to say about this.

## Example #2: Passive and Active Listening Approach

T Oh, come in Mr. Dempsey. Have a seat right there, if you will. Would you like me to explain why I called you in for this conference?

P I really don't think that will be necessary, Ms. Greene. We've traveled this road before and I'm beginning to wonder if it's all Danny's fault.

T You think that other things might contribute to Danny's troubles other than what we've talked about before?

P Well, yes, I do. It seems to me that he's pretty much like some of the other boys in your class, but he's always the one who's in trouble.

T (Nods in encouragement)

P Well, why him all of the time? This is getting to be a pain in the neck.

T You really wonder if Danny is getting a fair shake then?

P That's part of it, yes. And he really doesn't get into this much trouble at home when he's not around some of the other boys in your class.

T You think that perhaps the other boys may have something to do with his troubles?

P Well, it's either that or maybe he just gets caught and they don't. I don't know exactly what to make of it. He tells us that you have been fair with him, but he doesn't seem to see why he's in trouble either.

T You really feel confused about this whole thing and would like to figure out what's going wrong?

P You said it! I'm getting tired of running over here every two weeks trying to bail him out. I know he's energetic and apt to get into some trouble. But he's in trouble all the time, it seems!

T You would really like to get this thing solved and help Danny get along better in school. I guess we do have a real problem here.

P We sure do. Do you have any ideas, Ms. Greene?

T Well, I think we can work something out together on this. I'm sure we'll both have some ideas.

Now, these two examples were purposely set up to show the contrast between the two approaches. In many cases, a combination of the two approaches probably occurs and this could lead to problems as well. The major advantage to using the second approach (passive and active listening) is that it can lead to a shared problem-solving situation where parent and teacher negotiate alternative solutions to the difficulty. Such negotiated settlements ultimately provide both parent and teacher with a sense of satisfaction derived from the personal contribution each was able to make.

### YOU HAVE TO WANT TO

Gordon (1970, 1974) has best described some of the shortcomings and traps to watch out for when utilizing the listening approach. However, his main advice is that certain attitudes must prevail if you are going to employ the listening strategies with parents. These are perhaps best summarized by Lichter (1976, pp. 70–71).

1. You must want to hear, and have the time to hear, what the parent has to say. If you don't, say so.
2. You must want to be helpful with the parent's problem at that time. Otherwise, wait until you do.
3. You must be able to accept the parent's feelings, whatever they may be or however different they are from yours. To accept his feelings does not mean that you must accept them as your own, but simply that you allow him the right to feel as he does. It is a way of saying, "I can be me, and you can be you."
4. You must believe in the parent's ability to find solutions to his own problems. This requires the teacher to give up decision making power over the parent's life.

# A Few Teachers Talk Again

ALICE   I'm really very sorry about what I said yesterday, Kay . . . about Mrs. Sylvester, I mean. I really put my foot in my mouth.
KAY   Forget it, Alice. We all make mistakes. As a matter of fact you may be interested to know that a similar thing happened to me.
TONY   You mean you blew it in front of somebody's sister-in-law?
KAY   No, of course not. But the experience had essentially the same effect. Only in my case another parent overheard me in the lounge saying some rather questionable things. Believe me, I heard about it. Unfortunately the parent told the mother who in turn called the

principal. Needless to say, I was not only embarrassed but in hot water for a time. It taught me a lesson I won't soon forget.

ALICE    I think I got the message too. You know, there really ought to be better ways to solve these problems with kids and parents besides resorting to lounge gossip and bitching all of the time.

TONY    Well, because of our little incident yesterday I did some reading and talked to a few teachers I know about dealing with parents. I think I found some pretty good ideas.

KAY    Oh? Like what for instance?

TONY    Well, one teacher* I talked to said he feels that it is important to organize a regular parent communication program to insure parent support. He says it helps with the kids too—like with discipline and their studies.

ALICE    What's he do?

TONY    At the end of August just before school starts each year he calls all of the parents of the children he will have for that year. He tells 'em who he is and some of the things he plans to do during the year. Also, he let's them know that sometime between September and the end of November he will drop by their house after school just to bring them up to date on how things are going.

KAY    All the parents? That sounds like a whole lot of work. I've got thirty-five kids this year. I don't know if it would be worth it.

TONY    You may be right, but he says it's worth it. He said he hardly ever has a problem with parents and if there is a problem, they are able to work it out together. You know . . . no hassle, no involving the principal. See, I guess when he called them he gave them his home phone number and also his schedule at school. That way they felt like he was accessible, that they could talk with him if they really felt it was necessary.

ALICE    It would be a lot of work, though. What else did he tell you?

TONY    Not a whole lot more. . . . Oh ya, he said that it really made a big difference in the classroom discipline area. He remembers that before he started this program he used to have a lot more problems. I guess now it's that the kids know he knows their parents. He's talked with them, and by December he has visited all their homes. It would make a difference, I'm sure about that.

KAY    Does he hold regular parent conferences besides doing all of this?

TONY    Well, he still holds conferences when they're needed, but not on a regular basis. A couple times a year he invites all of the parents in to see what the kids have done in class. He says almost every parent shows. Can you imagine that . . . volunteering to come in? I usually get about 30 percent if I'm lucky.

ALICE    Ya. Me too. I still don't know though. It sounds like a great deal of time just for parents alone.

---

* My thanks to Mr. Richard Landman for this valuable idea.

KAY   Well, it's not just for parents really. It pays off with the kids, I guess. But I agree. That's a lot of time and work. Especially that visiting every home, that could take forever.

TONY   It does sound like a lot. He says he takes about three days a week for the first ten to twelve weeks of school before he has it all done. It only takes him about a half hour for each visit, I guess.

ALICE   I don't know. I do like his results though.

KAY   Maybe you could do part of it. I think I might try that next year. Call all the parents and let them know what's up for the year and that I'm available. You wouldn't *have* to visit the homes except in special cases. Maybe with three or four kids who are really having trouble.

ALICE   Probably a good idea, Kay. I'll give it some thought.

TONY   What I don't get, though, is what you do after the parents do come when you invite them. I mean thirty parents all at once, what do you do? I had parents in last spring and set up conference times for those who wanted to talk. And I invited the rest into the room for coffee and stuff. I had all of the materials and bulletin boards prepared, but they didn't seem too interested.

KAY   They want to see the kids do something or see what they have produced. They could care less about materials and bulletin boards, Tony.

ALICE   Kay's right, Tony. I made the same mistake you did.

KAY   I set up programs that really turned parents on, I think. I had the kids doing plays in the room and invited the parents. I had projects all around with the kids' names on them so parents could see what their child had done. But my biggest success was with video tape.

TONY   Video tape? What'd you do?

KAY   My students wrote and acted out a television program and even included news, weather, and sports in it. It was really very well done. So, after a few run-throughs I video taped it and we invited the parents in soon after that to see it. All the kids were involved in one way or another. It really went over. The kids who had smaller parts in the program answered questions and explained how they set up the program. The parents really ate that up.

TONY   I'd like to try that. I'm impressed, Kay.

KAY   You're a pushover, Tony. Everybody knows that. Right, Alice?

ALICE   This guy visited the homes of all his students? Are you sure, Tony?

*part three*

# The School

# 8

## Dealing with Bosses

Now we all know that we teach for the good of the kids. But no one, however indifferent to external surroundings, is unconcerned about his boss and how his boss perceives him. He may fight with the boss, he may ignore him, he may torture him day by day, or he may polish his shoes. But make no mistake—everyone is concerned about his boss.

There are three major types of bosses with whom the teacher is intimately concerned: the superintendent, the people who run in and out of central offices and who accrue titles of anything from assistant superintendent to consultant to viceroy; and the ubiquitous, lovable (or bastardly) principal.

One way of dealing with one's boss—the best way short of blackmail over something particularly juicy—is to understand where he is coming from. Understanding is not easy. You usually see the boss in a peculiar and highly constrained setting. This is particularly true of school administrators, who must be the most constrained group around. They are not likely to reveal their personal concerns, ambitions, and fears, especially to their subordinates.

In fact, it sometimes seems that the only emotion school administrators allow themselves to express publicly are the stereotyped jokes about busty secretaries, teachers, and students, which they tell each other at administrator meetings. The off-color joke—never too raw—is a basic mode of expression by which they indicate to each other, and perhaps to themselves, that they are still alive, a reminder that they have not succumbed completely to the stuffiness and make-believe respectability of their jobs.

Underneath it all, hard as it is to believe, they are people—a fact which even some of them may find surprising. They are shaped by social pressures and by their own ambitions into something that they may not always like themselves. To a smaller extent, perhaps, that is true of all of us. To deal with them most effectively, one must understand the kind of people they are, where they came from, and where they think they are going.

## What Type Person Is the Superintendent? WASP-ish

First of all, the superintendent is a man—almost always. A woman was recently hired as superintendent in Washington, D.C., but she did not last long. It has been almost entirely a male position, which one acquired by working his way up the administrative ladder of the school from teacher through principal. Since men are always chosen superintendent, those male teachers who simply persist in the schools and work their way up through the ranks have the best chance, although the elementary principalship is often a dead end for those aiming for the top.

Not only is the superintendent male but he is almost certain to be white. He is likely to come originally from a small town of under 10,000 population. The overwhelming majority are Protestant in religion, with the Methodist church preferred by more than forty percent. Seventy-five percent say they attend church weekly. In fact, when employability traits for superintendents were rated by school-board members, laypeople, teachers, and students, the best possible thing a superintendent could be was a Protestant. The worst thing he could be was a communist. There are no communist school superintendents that we know of in the United States.

Of course, the fact that superintendents are Protestants is no accident, since the vast majority of school-board members are themselves Protestant. Like school-board members, the superintendent is conservative politically, with a far larger percentage of superintendents being Republicans than is true of the general population. It goes without saying that the superintendent is married. The superintendent's wife is considered an important asset to his job. No superintendents are single and very few are divorced. In fact, divorce is ten times more common among the general population than among superintendents. Apparently, they are not allowed to admit marital mistakes. Too bad. They have obviously made some.

Superintendents are recruited heavily from the lower and lower-middle social classes. Only one in ten have fathers who were also professionals. It is not too farfetched to imagine that some of the stuffiness and stiffness that characterizes school administrators results from feeling not quite comfortable in more genteel settings and not quite secure in their newly won status. Most have risen from working-class status to become teachers and eventually administrators. It is a position in which they are defensive and unsure. In such cases convention is a safe harbor.

Since this is also my own background, I am not without sympathy for their perspective. But it does make them stuffy. It is no fun to be forever concerned about one's propriety. If administrators have attained the high status they cherish, I suspect they pay a high price for it in their lifestyles. But then again, their small-town fundamentalist backgrounds prepare them for a life of severe rectitude.

In their college education superintendents attend the lower quality colleges, more a reflection of their social backgrounds perhaps than of anything else. As undergraduates, education majors in general rank at just about the mean test score of all college graduates. Among graduate programs, students in educational administration rank lowest among all seventeen fields on the Miller Analogy Test. Superintendents are recruited from these groups and must have an advanced degree in administration. So whatever else they are, administrators are not scholars.

Superintendents judge success by the type of position held. The highest status jobs are the superintendencies in the largest school districts and the wealthiest suburbs, which also happen to be the best paying jobs. Superintendents grade each other's status by this measure and many are constantly searching for what they think will be better jobs. But as in every other occupation, those who start near the top end up at the top.

### The Superintendent's Job and His Limited Power

Apparently the most important thing one can know about the superintendent is whether he is promoted to the job from within or whether he is brought in from the outside. Being brought in from the outside indicates he is mobile and intends to build his career by moving from one superintendency to a better one. In other words he is "career-bound" (Carlson, 1972). His career is more important to him than where he lives.

On the other hand, if he stays in one district, working his way up through the ranks, then he prefers living where he is rather than hopping around in pursuit of something better. In other words, he is "place-bound." The career-bound and place-bound superintendents have different backgrounds and quite different effects on the school district. If you know whether the superintendent came from outside or inside the district, you can predict on this basis what kinds of things will happen.

Consider the career-bound man coming in. We know he is an ambitious man who wants to further his career by moving into better jobs. His task in his new job is to build a good reputation so that a bigger and wealthier school district will hire him eventually. Furthermore the board has hired him presumably because they want some change. If they were entirely satisfied with the last superintendent why not simply hire his assistant, who will continue the same policies? No, they want change, so the new incoming superintendent has at least a mild mandate for change.

Consider the place-bound superintendent. Perhaps he never thought he would be higher than a principal. His behavior has been much less purposive and restless than that of the career-bound man. As he is promoted to higher and higher positions, his aspirations rise with each new job. He picks up a few courses on the side at the most convenient campus in order to qualify for his new positions. He has no burning vision of what education in the district should be like, no intention of moving on to bigger and better things as he builds a reputation.

Perhaps more significantly, as he moves up through the ranks over the years he has built friendships and made enemies. He does not come into the district a free man. The place-bound man knows the district well, but he also has many personal obligations. He is not in any position to make sweeping changes. He has incurred social debts in his rise to the top. He cannot radically transform the system that produced him.

Why does the school board hire him if he is not going to change things? Perhaps they do not want change. Particularly if they are satisfied with the last superintendent, they are inclined to hire from inside. Perhaps the inside man has established strong personal ties with school board members with whom he has been in frequent contact. In bad financial times, the district is more likely to hire from inside. The inside man is cheaper.

The new career-bound superintendent, on the other hand, comes in with the image of a knight in shining armor, with visor down. He is unknown, a mystery to the people in the district. Only his strong points have been publicized so that no one knows his weaknesses yet. People are more afraid of him since he is an unknown quantity. He can, and he does, shake up the district much more. He introduces more innovations and more changes than the place-bound man does (which is not to say that the innovations are successfully implemented).

Of course, this magic aura cannot last forever, and the magic is totally gone within five years. The great majority of innovations the superintendent will cause to be introduced come during the first few years of his reign. In a sense, the social structure of the school district is temporarily suspended when he comes in. New coalitions and alliances essential to introducing new innovations can be formed. The old cliques of power are weakened vis-a-vis the new superintendent. So it is possible to do things that could not be done before.

Naturally those highest in the system are most threatened by the change in administration. They tend to retreat into their own levels of hierarchy—e.g., principals with principals—in order to protect themselves against any untoward changes. This defensiveness is much less evident with place-bound superintendents since the old power groups still prevail.

The new career-bound superintendent does have some loyalty problems, however. On whom he can count? He usually brings in his own set of assistants whose loyalty to him is guaranteed. Thus there is usually an addition of new central office staff. In order to demonstrate that he is in control of the situation, and to feel that way himself, the new superintendent makes an extraordinary number of new rules and regulations.

What about the teachers? *There is almost nothing the new superintendent can do to influence the teachers directly.* While he may order about the other employees or even remove them from their jobs, the teachers are fairly impervious to attack or threat. His main method of influence must be by persuasion or by example. He can inspire but he cannot directly command classroom performance. In a very real sense the superintendent's power over teachers is greatly restricted, however they might quake when he enters the teacher's lounge. His effects are primarily psychological.

Finally, when a place-bound man steps down, he is rarely replaced by another place-bound man. Since the average superintendent's tenure is nine or ten years, that would make twenty years of relatively no change. Few districts have been willing to buy that much status quo. Even school boards have limits on conservatism.

## The Politics of Fooling with the Central Office Staff

In a much more fundamental way than either the superintendent of the principal, the people on the central office staff operate from *derived* authority. They rule by association with someone else. The staff members have a need to appear to be in control of things, even when they are not. They manage this by controlling communication and access to the superintendent and school board and by differential allocation of resources. The cooperation of the central office staff is critical to doing anything new or different.

Two researchers studied the operations of a central office staff in a fairly large district (McGivney and Haught, 1973). They found that the staff had two major subgroups. One of the subgroups consisted of the finance and the personnel man. Their offices were close together and they interacted frequently on a day-to-day basis. In fact, they were also good social friends. They focused attention on the superintendent and the school board and were, in fact, able to control most information flowing to either.

The other major subgroup, based around the former superintendent, also had offices close together and interacted on a day-by-day basis. Both of the major subgroups in turn consisted of *minor* subgroups of a couple or three people. Other people in this rather large central office did not belong to either of the major groups. But it was the major subgroups that determined all the important policies.

Here's how they worked. Any new idea had to start in one of the smallest groups. If the two or three people there decided to promote it, the idea was advanced to the major subgroup. There it would be discussed and argued. If agreement were reached, it would be advanced to the full central office staff meeting. Only if agreement were reached by the staff would the idea be advanced to the school board. Any idea had to run this full gauntlet of consensus before it could be presented to the school board. *There was no other way for an idea to be seriously considered as district policy.*

Even when the successful ideas were presented to the board, it would be in informal closed study session. Before the public meeting, the central staff would know exactly how each board member would vote. The staff never presented ideas they had not discussed previously, and they never showed any signs of disagreement among themselves in front of the school board. A united front was maintained at all times. The school board almost always accepted central staff proposals.

If an outside group or a teacher managed to present a new idea at a public board meeting, it was inevitably referred to the central office staff for "study." The subgroups would dispose of the idea as they saw fit. In fact, no ideas of school personnel other than the central office staff were acted upon at a board meeting.

Proposals by dissident outside citizens' groups that did not agree with the central staff were usually intercepted by the staff before they reached the school board. If the ideas were presented to the board, the central staff impugned the credibility and sincerity of the sponsors. In this fashion, the central office staff maintained complete control over the formal policy making of the school district.

Another control device was gaining control of hiring committees and manipulating hiring practices. For example, it was felt that one principal always hired teachers for his school who were too "intellectual" rather than more "well-rounded" types. When he was sent out to hire teachers, two central office staff members went along to outvote him on whom to hire.

Of course, the central staff also controls discretionary funds. In a school where the budget is always tight, a few dollars here or there can make quite a bit of difference. The money can provide books, supplies, trips, or a number of rewards for the cooperative teacher.

The gatekeeping function of the central office staff must be taken very seriously by the teacher. While there is little a staff member can do directly to affect the teacher's classroom, most things outside the class are subject to staff influence for good or for ill. Needless to say, proposals and ideas that threaten the status quo or the central office staff position will not be dealt with favorably. It is also essential that the central staff member *appear* to be in control of a project, even if he or she is not. *The semblance of power is critical.*

The best way to gain central staff cooperation is to have a staff member champion one's idea within the small groups. He or she can take credit for it there and galvanize the rest of the central staff behind it. A close relationship with the staff member is the surest access. Failing that, if the idea is too threatening, there are at least three other options.

One option is to find another sponsor within the central staff and play the staff members off against one another. This works on politicized staffs, but it is a dangerous alternative and requires some knowledge of the informal staff relationships. Another alternative is to make a more formal demand through an organized group of teachers or some organized support in the community. This way is somewhat more protracted and laborious but is more comfortable if one is allergic to kissing someone's feet.

The third alternative is to be quiet and do what one was going to do anyhow. Of course this works only if what one intended to do is rather small-scale. If one needs resources and public endorsement, then dealing with the central staff in some manner is essential.

It is not difficult to see why a new superintendent from outside is so unsettling to the central office staff. He upsets all the informal relationships and the delicate power balance. The staff members are directly under his purview. In addition, the superintendent is highly likely to bring in his own troops to reform the informal power blocs more to his liking. And you thought national politics were complicated. If you ever wondered why central office staff members don't do more, the answer is that they are busy plotting and politicking—necessary part of their jobs.

## The Principal: Where Is He Coming From?

Now, we all know that the principal is the instructional leader of the school and that he is the helpmate of the teachers, the inspiration of the kids, etc., etc. That is what the principals are taught in administration classes. The teachers' view may be a little more jaundiced than that. What does the principal really do? To find out, an anthropologist followed one around for a year (Wolcott, 1973). Perhaps his study will help dispel a few myths.

First of all, the principal is neither an inspirational leader nor a field commander. He is a mediator. He spends an overwhelming part of his time in meetings, trying to iron out differences between various groups. He has little time for instructional tasks, if indeed he has the talent or desire to be helpful.

In and of itself, I would not see this role as a necessarily bad thing. That there are so many conflicts that must be mediated means there are a number of pressures operating in the school from groups that feel they have legitimate demands. These groups are powerful enough that they must be attended to both internally and externally. In other words, a balance of forces prevails. In a more hierarchical setting, mediation might not be necessary because the orders come from the top down and are simply to be obeyed. There is nothing to mediate.

On the other hand, it may be that the schools are so vulnerable to pressures that an inordinate amount of time is spent by both principals and teachers in appeasing parents and other groups. My own feeling is that perhaps this is so and that perhaps the schools are so susceptible to pressures that the instructional tasks are imperiled. But back to the principal.

Let us take an elementary principal as the typical case since that is the guy Harry Wolcott, the anthropologist, followed around for a year. The average elementary school principal is between thirty-five and forty-nine years old. He is married, of course, and invariably comes from a teaching background. He has between ten and nineteen years experience, anywhere from two to nine years as a teacher. The typical school has fifteen to twenty-four teaching positions. The average principal feels he spends forty-eight to fifty-three hours a week at school. Most say their goal is to be and to remain a principal.

The average principal sees himself as the leader of the school. His role in formulating school district policy is one of encouraging certain viewpoints. He usually has the power to accept or reject teachers coming to his school. On his own school's budget he can make recommendations, but he does not have the power to determine what it shall be. On school curriculum matters, he sees his role as modifying and adapting. The pronoun "he" is used advisedly since about eighty percent of the principals are men.

But these kinds of "averages" are pale shadows of the job and the people in it. Most principals are men who have had a hard time gaining an education. They have sacrificed to go to college, coming as they have from farms and working-class backgrounds. They have worked hard to go to the not-so-good schools and have risen to professional status as teachers. They have spent years in the teaching ranks, living on low salaries, and waiting patiently for the opportunity to break into administrative ranks. They have despaired at the long wait and at the great number of other men waiting for the same opportunity, for one of the few administrative posts.

Finally, they have made it. And when they do, they feel they have arrived, after a long arduous climb. They feel they have paid the price. For example, when Ed, the principal we focus on here, left Kansas in order to take a job in the west, his father would not come to the car to say good-bye but, knowing his youngest son was going for good, went into his house and cried. The price these men pay is not only one of labor and years, but one of sentiment and affection.

These men are recruited from social classes that believe in upward social mobility but often are not prepared for the subjugation of personal concerns to career as are the upper classes. Of course, by the time they "arrive" in their positions, they are as committed to career as any young executive. It is not surprising that some characteristics acquired in the upward struggle express themselves in the principal's job performance: perseverence with routine tasks, frugality, dominance, perhaps an impatience with those—both children and teachers—who cannot master their own affairs and who cannot discipline their personal lives to their duties. These traits are as indelibly etched into the person of the principal as acid carves out stained glass.

The average principal is likely to have had such a background, to be industrious, to work hours at many routine tasks, to attend church regularly (likely a more fundamentalist denomination), to belong to one or more social clubs, and to carry his work problems home with him. His wife is dutiful and has consciously subordinated her life to her husband's career. Perhaps there is an implicit recognition that his routine work, self-discipline, devotion to career, and adherence to social conventions make the average principal a pretty dull person to talk to. He did not necessarily start out that way.

He very much sees the school as "his" school. He is possessive about it and takes any criticism of it personally. He likes to see the school faculty as his extended family with himself as something of the patriarch. In situations in which he clearly has power over the other party, such as an individual student, teacher, or lower-class parent, he is likely to use that power and to resort to ultimatums frequently.

Like others from his class background, including teachers, he is very conscious and solicitous of the upper-class neighborhoods within his attendance area. Without directly experiencing it, one cannot appreciate the differences in the way service employees treat people in different types of neighborhoods. If, for example, you get a parking ticket for an expired meter in an upper-class suburb like Highland Park, Illinois, the police officer is likely to apologize profusely to you in an almost servile way, no doubt believing you are a member of a social group far above him. In contrast, observe the behavior of police officers in impoverished areas, particularly black ghettos, where the police represent a higher class than that of the residents. They behave like storm troopers, entering restaurants with overbearing demeanors and treating inhabitants most rudely. The difference in behavior is incredible and is the cause of much interclass hostility and misunderstanding.

Educators are not nearly so discriminatory in their behavior, but they do tend to be very solicitous of residents of the "better" neighborhoods, who win considerations far beyond what their numbers would indicate. Of course, part of the differential treatment is because the upper-class groups have the vocal ability, personal contacts, and desire to cause trouble. To them, educators represent a distinctly lower social group, which can be attacked directly. For any reason, these groups can ring the principal's bell.

Within the school setting itself, the employee system is set up in such a way as to maximize differences among types of employees. The authority for the entire district is seen by the principal as residing in the central office, and ultimately in the person and office of the superintendent. But the real concern of the principal is with "his" school.

## How Does He Really Do? How Did He Get His Job?

How does he actually spend his time? From the time he enters the building until he goes home at night almost all his time is spent in personal encounters. About ninety percent of these encounters are face-to-face meetings while another ten percent are on the phone or intercom. About one-fourth of his time is spent in prearranged meetings, another one-fourth in deliberate but not prearranged meetings, and another fifteen percent in casual, unplanned encounters. *The principal has only fifteen percent of his time to spend in his office alone.* He can hardly be an instructional leader with that much thinking time.

About half of the contacts are with the school staff—teachers, secretaries, custodians, etc. One-quarter of the interactions are with pupils, perhaps another fifteen percent with other principals and the central-office staff, and about ten percent with parents. That is a lot of meetings.

The formal meetings—teacher meetings, administrative meetings, PTA meetings—are supposed to serve the purpose of facilitating communication among groups and of arriving at collective decisions. The anthropologist Wolcott sees it differently, however. He believes the meetings are quite unsuccessful in these terms. The communication at the meetings is unilateral rather than bilateral. Most often the decisions have already been reached before the meeting is held. In the meeting they are *revealed* rather than arrived at.

Wolcott believes the underlying function of all these formal meetings is to "validate" the roles that different people have in the system and to reinforce the status structure. By attending meetings one can publicly demonstrate that one is concerned about curriculum or whatever problem is under discussion. At the same time, one can review his or her own status within the overall social structure and be reminded of his or her position.

Who has a right to call certain kinds of meetings and who must attend, whether they want to or not, are constant reminders of people's places in the system. One's presence at a meeting is acknowledgement and acceptance of one's status. Not attending regularly is akin to advocating anarchy. Hence, even though the principal may dislike attending general administrative staff meetings because the superintendent simply lectures the troops, he would never miss one. Similarly, the principal's teachers will come to the school biweekly staff meetings and listen to him talk. Whether Wolcott is correct about the underlying purpose of the formal meetings the reader can determine from his or her own experience—but without doubt Wolcott is a sharp observer.

Now if a man has worked all his life and has denied himself constantly in order to get into an authority position, and if his status is fed by attending meetings in which he is head honcho, he is not going to be happy with you if you continually miss his staff meetings. You had better have a good reason for doing so.

I have heard it said that there are a few teachers who simply like to bait the administrators. Missing meetings is one of the better ways to do it. But such behavior damages long-term prospects. If you want something important in the long run, you would do better to comply in the unimportant matters. Unlike the hippies, true revolutionaries like the Maoists wear sharp suits and have short hair. They are intent on instrumentally changing the system, not simply on expressing themselves. Think long.

The principal is, of course, socialized into his job by many pressures. The principal's job is usually acquired through "sponsorship." What this means is that someone in the administration, usually another principal, takes an interest in the young teacher and promotes his reputation within administration circles. He sees that the teacher is put on the right committees, keeps his name to the fore, and generally increases his visibility before the central-office staff and the school board. When a position opens up, here's the obvious man for the job.

The sponsor also encourages the man to think about administration, take the proper courses, and conduct himself in a seemly manner. Naturally, the young man is highly influenced by this voice of the experienced administrator. After all, he is getting encouragement while his colleagues are not. When a principal's job opens up, it is presumably open to all applicants in a free competition, but of course it is really not. It is only open to the few who have sufficiently strong sponsorship to compete.

Those men who aspire to be administrators start from the beginning of their careers to solicit the attention of their superiors. This is done by demonstrating acceptance of the authority system, being willing to take responsibility for school-related but nonteaching assignments, and for proper decorum. It is not good to attract too much attention. The man is then regarded as too ambitious.

The average principal does not read too much. He must take appropriate administration courses for advancement into the principalship, but he tends to see his university coursework as being of little help on his job. Privately, he will comment to his colleagues about the worthlessness of coursework. Only on-the-job experience is seen as being beneficial. At the same time the principal relies on his academic credentials for advancement and he often hires teachers on the basis of their academic records. In spite of not being scholastically oriented, he often uses "research" authority to back up his opinions—"Studies show. . . ." This technique is frequently employed with audiences like parents and teachers who would be greatly disinclined to challenge the authority of the principal or of "science."

## The Principal's Vulnerability and Conservatism

Once a man has achieved the status of principal, a profound change comes over his behavior. It is no longer to his advantage to attract attention to himself. In fact, he perceives attention as harmful. His attitude becomes one of preventing unfavorable publicity for the school, publicity that might reach the superintendent and the central-office staff. As is true with the teacher in the classroom, it is presumed that not hearing anything means that all is smooth and running well. Frequent noise indicates trouble.

The established principal's strategy is to keep dissatisfaction to a minimum and to prevent the imagined phone call from the superintendent rebuking the principal for a poor job. The principal does nothing controversial and does not make publicity. He expects his teachers to behave accordingly. The principal perceives himself as an exceedingly vulnerable man. He has no tenure and is a fat target for anyone who has something to throw.

Most principals highly value autonomy to run their school, and they see this as being threatened by unfavorable publicity. They must constantly work around the rules and regulations emanating from the central office in order to keep from being forced into the position of a functionary in a bureaucratic system. It is in his fear of "making waves" that the typical principal is most vulnerable to both teachers and the community. (Along with the older teachers, the principal plays an important role in socializing new teachers into the school. That role is discussed in the chapter on teacher evaluation.)

The extreme vulnerability and visibility of the principal leads to great role confusion. He feels that he must satisfy the demands of all the various groups impinging on him. Of course, many of those demands are contradictory. Trying to respond to everyone, he has no set role. This ambivalence about what he should be doing is reflected in endless discussions about what the principal's role should be.

For example, principals are not sure whether they belong with teachers or with superintendent and management on labor issues. They like to see themselves as closely identifying with their teachers and with classroom problems, yet they know that much of their life is controlled from the central office, and that in a sense, they are functionaries of the central-office bureaucracy. The increasing power of teacher organizations is a threat to their autonomy, for negotiations progressively narrow what they may do.

The principal cannot possibly meet all the divergent demands made of him. Survival becomes a paramount problem, and simply staying in the job often becomes the overridding goal. Such a concern prevents the principal from exercising much of a leadership role. His authority, which he constantly worries about, is limited by the expectations of others. Wolcott outlines the principal's position beautifully: "His freedom was to make no serious mistakes." A serious mistake could mean dreaded demotion "back to the classroom."

Although he is exhorted to be the great agent of change in education, in fact the principal may represent the point of least change in the system. The way the innovation system now operates (or malfunctions, whichever you prefer), innovation proceeds from the top down—from the state government for example, and through or from the central-office staff (House, 1974). Generally the principal works to constrain change, to make sure that change does not occur too fast. For example, in our studies of how gifted-student programs entered Illinois schools, we found that the school was much more likely to develop a good program if a central-office administrator or a teacher were appointed director rather than a principal.

The principal generally works to maintain the school's stability. He becomes a master of the rhetoric of innovation in order that he may appease groups clamoring for innovation. At the same time he tries to go very slow with implementing any new ideas for fear that they might upset various other groups. He becomes an expert in rationalizing new programs in terms of traditional justifications. For example, in a large-scale implementation of aesthetic-educational materials in Pennsylvania, the use of the materials was justified on the grounds that they would improve basic skills, an argument much more likely to gain wide acceptance.

If one group of parents clamors for innovative instruction and another group is strongly in favor of maintaining traditional instruction, the rational thing for the principal to do is to give them both. Have some teachers teach innovatively and keep others involved in traditional instruction. Contrary to the desire of reformers outside the school, the principal would work to keep the innovation from spreading throughout the school. This would upset the traditionalists. Of course, maintaining some teachers as innovators and some as traditional instructors may lead to some conflict on the staff.

One of the best techniques for maintaining order is for the principal to tell one group one thing and to tell another something else. As with a politician, this works fine as long as he does not have to speak to both groups simultaneously. Usually he does not, for he can conduct his business through bilateral meetings.

Another facet of trying to please everyone and to avoid any trouble that might reach the central office is to deal with any problem that arises. The principal has no set of priorities except to keep small problems from becoming big ones. His is a continuous task of crisis management. His door is almost always open, and he responds to emergencies daily. He is always on call. All problems are seen as important. This global response to any and all concerns means he never has the time, energy, or inclination to develop or carry out a set of premeditated plans of his own. Containment of all problems is his theme. The principal cannot be a change agent or leader under those conditions.

In spite of the obvious disapprobation that one might heap upon such a role in a society in which change is the norm, the principal's resistance to change must be seen as at least partly beneficial and partly necessary. If we are to have comprehensive schools that serve the diverse and even contradictory interests of the entire public, and if those schools are to be open to external pressures as American schools are, then there must be ways of fending off change. Otherwise the school would bounce around like a ping-pong ball. If the school responded to all the critics, the reading program would be changed every two weeks. Most of us would agree that children need a relatively stable environment for an extended period of time in order to learn to read. Defenses must be built into an institution as vulnerable as the school. The principal is the main line of defense.

## BOOKS TO READ

In our analysis in this chapter we have drawn heavily on the following two books. While they are research books, they are the best accounts we know of the superintendency and the principalship.

Carlson, Richard O. *School Superintendents: Careers and Performance.* Columbus, Ohio: Charles E. Merrill, 1972.

> Carlson synthesizes a number of studies on superintendents into a comprehensive picture of where they are coming from and where they are going. Researchy but excellent.

Wolcott, Harry F. *The Man in the Principal's Office.* New York: Holt, Rinehart and Winston, 1973.

> An anthropologist follows a principal around for a year in order to see what he says and does. Unparalleled in its view of the principal's job.

# 9

# Surviving Teacher Evaluation and Getting Tenure
## A Play in Three Acts

## Act One: The Typical Evaluation

## Act Two: Enter the Evaluation Expert

## Act Three: Tit for Tat on Tenure

## Cast

TEACHER     Bill Ferguson
PRINCIPAL     John Hammel
ASSISTANT SUPERINTENDENT     Dr. Leonard Wylie
EVALUATOR     An Anonymous Professor

# Surviving Teacher Evaluation and Getting Tenure:
## A Play in Three Acts

### Act One: The Typical Evaluation

**Scene 1:    The Teacher and Principal in the Principal's Office**

(*The principal is seated in a large, spacious office working routinely at his desk. The teacher enters, a coffee cup in his hand.*)

TEACHER    Hi, John. Is it all right to come in? Your secretary isn't out there at her desk.

PRINCIPAL    Sure, Bill. She took a break.

T    Sorry I'm a little late. I stopped by the lounge to get some coffee. Want some?

P    No thanks. I've been drinking too much already.

T    Me, too.

P    (*Leaning back in his chair*) Bill, the reason I asked you to come in was to discuss your class tenure. You know you're eligible this year.

T    Oh, oh. The guillotine, huh.

P    Seriously, I've been looking at these forms I filled out in your class. You know I've visited your class several times in the last few years. And I've decided not to recommend tenure to the superintendent. (*Looks directly at him*)

T    (*Long silence—he is obviously stunned*) How come?

P    Well, I've visited your class—uh, six times in the past two years. You know we've had a talk—a conference—after each visit.

T    Yeah, but I didn't think I was in any trouble. (*Tears are beginning to well up in his eyes*)

P    Well, we talked after each one of the visits, and I told you you were having discipline problems. The class was very noisy and some kids weren't working.

T    Yeah, but I didn't think it was that bad. You gave me some ideas, and I tried them out but they didn't work either.

P    The main purpose of the evaluation is to improve instruction. Some people can handle a class and some can't.

T    Why didn't you tell me then that I might not get tenure?

P    I tried to indicate to you that you were having problems. You signed all the forms. I have your signature here on all the forms.

T    Yeah, yeah. But I thought everybody had some kind of problems when they started teaching. I think you should have told me before, John.

P   I'm supposed to visit the class of each nontenured teacher at least once but no more than four times a year. Each time I visit I write up my report and give you a copy. I talked to you about it.

T   Is that what I signed?

P   Right. You signed it, and I filed it. Here they all are.

T   But I still didn't think they were that bad.

P   I told you that you could write out your objections to the evaluation report and file it with the report. That's in the contract.

T   I just didn't think they were that bad. I thought it was a formality.

P   Look, Bill. It's not just the classroom visits I'm going on. I've gone past your classroom several times, and it's almost always noisy. I've got some reports here I've written out. I haven't always talked to you about it because it's the same stuff.

T   It's not *always* noisy. You know I'm trying to do some different things in class.

P   I've talked to some of the teachers, particularly some of the senior ones.

T   Yeah, I'll bet I know who.

P   There's kind of a general agreement that you might do better some place else. (*Pauses*)

T   (*No response*)

P   You know I've always thought of this school as *my* school, *my* faculty. I like to think of us working together as a team. Having a common approach. Maybe we're a little more traditional than some of the other schools in the district. But I don't think that's bad.

T   You think one guy trying something a little more progressive is going to mess up the whole school?

P   No. Of course not. But you don't quite fit into the spirit of things either. I've always tried to hire teachers that fit into the school. Even the young ones I've hired have fit into the Barnum approach. You know that, Bill. You've talked to them.

T   Yes, I have.

P   Even the young ones are conservative. That's how they think they can get the best job done for these kids. These kids need more structure. I've handpicked the teachers here, and I know that's how they feel.

T   I don't necessarily disagree with that, John. But that doesn't fit me. That's not what I'm trying to do.

P   But you can't keep control of the class with what you're trying to do. That's exactly what I mean.

T   There's a difference between being quiet and being in control.

P   Sure, there is. Look, we've been all over this before. Several times. You don't quite fit what we're trying to do here, rightly or wrongly. You may do a lot better in a school where they agree with your philosophy.

T   Is this a transfer or are we talking about tenure?

P   Well, it may be that some other principal may want you at his school. Maybe something can be worked out.

T   Maybe not.

P   Come on, Bill. It's not the end of the world.

T   It's not the beginning either. I'm twenty-six years old.

P   Well, I know how you feel. This isn't easy for me either.

T   Thanks.

P   O.K. In any case, I'm making my recommendation to the super-intendent in writing. You'll get a copy. According to the teachers' contract, I have to submit the recommendation by March fifth. I just wanted to tell you first.

T   Thanks.

P   So you'll be getting the letter in a few days. Any questions?

T   Am I the only one in the school, eh, not getting tenure?

P   Let's see. The only ones up this year are Francis Ackerman and Pat Greer. I guess I'll recommend tenure for them. See, they fit in better. By the way, I hope you won't mention this to anyone for awhile.

T   (*No response*)

P   I'm really sorry it worked out this way, Bill. I really am. I'm just trying to do my job the best way I can. (*Standing up*) Anything else?

T   Yeah. My coffee's cold.

### Act I, Scene 2:    The Principal at the Central Office a Few Days Later

(*The assistant superintendent for instruction, Dr. Leonard Wylie, is sitting behind his desk. It is a very large office with a conference table and a window looking onto some commercial buildings. The principal, John Hammel, enters the office and sits in one of the chairs in front of the desk.*)

ASSISTANT SUPERINTENDENT    Hi, John. Sorry to keep you waiting. I had a phone call from McIntyre in District Twenty-three. Same problems over there as here. Money.

PRINCIPAL    That's all right. I haven't been here too long. I got here about ten minutes early anyway.

AS    I've got a tight schedule today. Most of the principals are coming in so let's get down to business. You know that the school board has requested that the administrators in this district be evaluated. This meeting is our evaluation conference to meet that requirement.

P   Yes, I'm aware of the regulation.

AS    Good. Now, what do you see as the educational philosophy of your school?

P   Educating every child to his fullest potential.

AS    Could you elaborate a little on that, John?

P   Well, we hold that all facets of the child's personality—the emotional, the social, the cognitive, the academic, the physical—should be developed in the school. We have a responsibility for all those things.

We're a little more traditional in our approach than some, as you know.

AS  How is your individualized reading program going?

P  Pretty good. The teachers seem to be adjusting to it better than the last time I talked to you. And the parents seem enthusiastic about it.

AS  You haven't had any more trouble with it?

P  Well, of course, not everybody has accepted it. There are still a few teachers that haven't accepted it. Bill Ferguson for one.

AS  Yeah, I wanted to talk to you about Ferguson. We'll get to that in a moment. What about the clerical demands of the program? Can you keep up?

P  That's really a major problem. It's a struggle all the way. I could use another clerk. The girls are barely keeping their heads above water.

AS  You should be getting the new budget request forms within a month. As soon as they're run off. It seems like everything hits at once.

P  Well, the program does cost more money. I don't see any way around that.

AS  What about the in-service workshop?

P  It's going pretty well, too. Except I've got a few teachers who can't seem to stand to stay an extra hour a week.

AS  You've always got those. Community relations—how do you think you're doing there?

P  Well, I try to get out and meet as many parents as I can. But it's tough. I just don't have as much time as I would like.

AS  Do you think you should give that area a little higher priority?

P  I don't know. I don't really want to take more time away from my other duties. I just don't know.

AS  You had a good turn-out for open house.

P  Yes, we did. Although, you know, it's always the same parents who come. The ones who always come.

AS  What about staff relations?

P  I think that I'm doing pretty good there. I like to think that my teachers share the school philosophy and are happy there. Generally I think they are. I have one or two who haven't yet fit in too well.

AS  Ferguson.

P  Yeah, Ferguson for one.

AS  I saw your final evaluation report on him. You told me before that he didn't fit in too well.

P  No. He can't seem to adjust to the kids. His classroom is always noisy.

AS  You've tried to work with him?

P  Yes, I've tried. You know I don't like to be too obtrusive in my classroom visits. When I go by the room or go in for some reason, his room is usually a mess. Nine times out of ten.

AS  You've talked to him about it?

P  Several times. It doesn't seem to do any good.

AS   You said before that he was resistant to authority.

P   He is. He's just got a different slant on things. Maybe he would fit in better somewhere else. But not in my school.

AS   After looking at your reports, we're inclined to agree with you.

P   I wish I had followed my original instinct about him. I had the feeling when I interviewed him for the job that he was the wrong type. But I felt I wanted another male teacher in the school to balance things up a bit. I would have saved us both some grief if I had followed my own impressions.

AS   You had a conference with him? How did he take it?

P   Not too good I think. He was a little morose. I think he blames it on me.

AS   How's that?

P   He feels I haven't been fair with him. He doesn't think I spent enough time observing his classroom. You know how I don't like to be too obtrusive about going into classes. He doesn't know all the times I observed that he wasn't aware of.

AS   You did follow the proper procedures according to the contract?

P   Oh, yeah. This isn't the first time I've had to let a teacher go.

AS   Well, we've had some changes in the contract language this year, John. They were on that green sheet I sent out in the fall.

P   You guys send out so much stuff I can't remember everything I read. But I'm sure I followed proper procedure.

AS   Check it when you get back. Is that all he said?

P   He also said he was disappointed in me and also that my rating of him was too subjective.

AS   Have you heard anything more since your conference with him?

P   No. Just that he was disappointed in me.

AS   Well, sad but unavoidable. (A long pause when neither man says anything) What about Frances Ackerman?

P   She's come along all right. I had a little trouble with her for a while but she's all right now. For the first year especially she used to take off from school early, right after the kids were gone. I used to wonder to myself, "Is she really interested in teaching or in rushing off to meet her boyfriend somewhere?" I had a talk with her and she's all right now.

AS   You have her rated very high in classroom performance.

P   Yes, she's really a pretty good teacher, for only a few years experience.

AS   Good. And Greer's okay too.

P   Yes, Greer is good too. At first I thought she was too aloof. I couldn't really get to know her. But she's turned out fine. She's just a little less social than most people.

AS   Okay. Any other problems with staff?

P   No. None that I know of.

AS   What about Jeanette Parrish?

P   Well, you know Jeanette. She's always up and down. Up one week, down the next. It varies from day to day. She just has personal problems.

AS  Okay, John. The superintendent and I have filled out a rating form on you. Why don't you take a look at it and I'll be back in a few minutes.

(The assistant superintendent gets up and leaves the room. He is gone for about five minutes. Meanwhile the principal takes the rating form and looks at it. From the look on his face he is not particularly happy with what he sees. He stares at it as if trying to read some meaning into it. Finally the assistant superintendent returns with a handful of papers he places at the edge of his desk.)

AS  You've had a chance to look at our ratings on you. Notice that we rated you particularly high on community relations but a little low on staff relations.

P  Christ, Leonard, I would have turned it around the other way. I thought I had real good relations with my staff. Just because Ferguson is upset . . .

AS  No, it's not Ferguson. We agree with you on that one. If the man can't handle a class, he can't. That's all there is to it. No, it's other people on the staff we've been hearing from. And maybe we're just wrong on it.

P  Well, I really don't see it. But maybe you're right. I'll have to think about it. I've thought about my school as kind of a happy family.

AS  We rated you high on community relations, John. You had a good turn-out for the open house. You started the parent committee on vandalism. You've done a lot of good things there.

P  Well, I guess I wouldn't have rated myself higher there than on staff relations. I've thought maybe I should be putting a little more effort into working with parents. Maybe not.

AS  Your rating on demeanor is also good. People say you are a little too grim most of the time but you always represent the school district well in public. Maybe it would help if you would smile a little more.

P  I'm not a TV commercial for toothpaste, Leonard.

AS  Just a suggestion. All these comments are just suggestions, John.

P  I do agree that I'm not the best principal in the world at starting new programs. I think I deserve my rating there. At my school we have always seen things as more traditional. Traditional programs seem to work best and we don't need a lot of new things.

AS  Yes, getting new things going is not really your strength, John. That's true, I think.

P  Yeah. I could be a little less formal too sometimes.

AS  Overall this is a good evaluation, John. That's what both the superintendent and I think. You can be proud of your school and the job you're doing this year.

P  (No response. The principal doesn't look very convinced of this right now.)

AS   Do you have questions on any of the other ratings?

P   (Pause) No, not really. It's a little hard to figure out what some of these ratings mean.

AS   Well, why don't you look them over for a few days and then if you have any questions, give me a call.

P   Okay. What's going to happen to these ratings now?

AS   Well, the school board, partly at the prodding of the teacher's organization, I think, asked for these. So I guess we'll show them to the board.

P   Could I see how mine compares to the other principals'?

AS   That's not a good idea. We promised everyone we would keep them confidential. If we showed them around you know they would get out. We'd have principal ratings plastered all over the district. We're going to show them to the board in executive session. I just hope they know how to handle them.

P   It would be helpful to know how you stand in comparison to the other people doing the job.

AS   Yes, I know, John. But just think what would happen if some of those guys in the teachers' organization got hold of these. I shudder to think what would happen. They've been bitching and moaning about our administrators as it is. They want a written procedure for selecting principals.

P   Why don't they just run the whole district?

AS   That's how I feel sometimes. Sometimes I'm ready to give it to them. *(The superintendent stands up on this note of concord, signaling an end to the meeting. The principal still looks a little puzzled and is not ready to quit but he sees he has no choice. He stands up too.)*

AS   Well, John, I think you really came out well in your evaluation. And I know that's what the superintendent thinks. You don't have anything to worry about. You're really running a tight ship there. And a smooth-sailing one, and we appreciate it up here.

P   Thanks. Sometimes I think the ship is taking a little water. These ratings make me a little more appreciative of the way the teachers feel when I rate them. It's a funny feeling.

AS   Yeah, John. The seas are rough these days. Every man has to look out for himself so he doesn't fall overboard.

P   Yeah. I'd better leave before we both get seasick.

AS   If you have any questions, give me a call. I've got to meet with three more principals today.

P   That's a long day.

AS   I don't like this business.

P   I don't think I do either. See you later. (He leaves.)

## Act Two: Enter the Evaluation Expert

### Scene 1:   The Teacher and Evaluator at Big Time University

(*The evaluator sits at his desk, slack-jawed and staring into vacant space —obviously a college professor. From the looks of his clothes, he is not very affluent—or if he is, he has forgotten it. The office is very small, with just enough room for one visitor's chair. Papers and books litter everything. The teacher enters with a coffee cup in his hand and immediately sits in the chair.*)

EVALUATOR   Hi, Mr. Ferguson.

TEACHER   I hope you don't mind my helping myself to some coffee. The secretary said I could have some.

E   Did she make you pay for it?

T   No. She said I didn't have to pay. Should I?

E   No. Of course not. I just wish I was that lucky. She's been after me for a week. Very suspicious lady. What can I do for you?

T   I hope I'm not taking up too much of your time. You're not too busy, are you?

E   Yeah, I'm always busy. I've got a book manuscript due in June which I've hardly begun. I've got to give a speech next week. And the students keep bothering me. The university would be a great place to work if it weren't for the students.

T   I won't take up too much of your time. The reason I called is I'm in trouble and someone who had a class from you said you might be able to help me.

E   Someone from one of my classes? You are in trouble.

T   I'm a teacher at P.T. Barnum School and I've been bounced. Canned.

E   Fired?

T   Well, not outright. But, you know, they aren't going to give me tenure.

E   So you're looking for a job?

T   Yes, I am going to look for a job, but that's not why I came to talk to you. A guy I work with said you were an expert on evaluation. You see, what happened was that the principal visited my classroom a few times and evaluated me. He said he didn't like my classes, the way I was teaching, and wouldn't recommend me for tenure.

E   Why not?

T   Discipline, he said. Actually I don't fit in too well. The other teachers, the whole school, is very traditional. I was trying out some open classroom stuff. I thought maybe you would give me some pointers in evaluation.

E   Ah, I don't think what we have to offer will be much help. Most professional evaluators evaluate programs rather than personnel. You know, federal and state programs. Sometimes local programs.

It's been that way since the big money came into education in the mid-sixties.

T  That's not what I need.

E  No. I could tell you what we know though. If that'll be any help.

T  O.K. I took part of the day off so I may as well do something.

E  First, there's a difference between the way a teacher is evaluated by a principal in a school and the way someone with research training would attack the problem. The principal came to class and filled out a form, right?

T  Right. Our district has a Teacher Evaluation Form developed by a professor at Marineland Community College, I believe. He has it copyrighted and sells it to school districts. I don't remember his name right now.

E  Never mind. Don't tell me. The form has a bunch of items like, "Teacher presents a neat appearance," or "Teacher keeps kids working"?

T  Yeah, something like that.

E  And then the principal rates the teacher "excellent," "superior," "high," or "low" on each item.

T  On this one there are numbers for each one and the principal circles a number. So you can be "one" or "five" on each one. I think there are five numbers. I could get you a copy.

E  Don't bother. There are a lot of forms like that. You could make up one yourself. The problem is that how you come out is pretty much dependent on the judgment of the principal.

T  That's right.

E  This judgment may be good—or it may be bad. There's no real way of knowing from the form.

T  I don't have too high an opinion of his judgment at the moment.

E  Well, there's nothing wrong with that type of evaluation in a sense. It's like a boss evaluating a subordinate. It *is* a boss evaluating a subordinate. But from a scientific, quote, unquote, point of view it leaves something to be desired. It may not be very impartial, very objective.

T  You mean it's just his opinion.
      (*Teacher takes out note pad and begins taking notes*).

E  Something like that. His opinion may be very good. After all, he is close to the action and experienced in the field presumably. He may be able to tell good teaching from bad. On the other hand, he may simply not like you. There's no way of telling. You're going to take notes now?

T  Yes. I think you just said something I can use.

E  So there's no way of telling what kind of *biases* are creeping into his judgments. So the professional evaluator looks for ways of *reducing* possible biases. Not of eliminating them. That's impossible. But a way of reducing them.

T   So the real evaluator looks for scientific methods. For objective methods.

E   Something like that. Only I wouldn't push that idea too far. The principal is also a real evaluator. What you want in order to be fair is to eliminate bias. Really, to be impartial. An objective method is one everyone can do the same way. It may or may not be impartial. In fact some minority groups contend that tests are biased against them even though objective. Impartiality and objectivity are not synonomous, even though they are used that way.

T   I think you are getting a little esoteric for me.

E   O.K. look. What if your best friend took the P.T. Barnum Teacher Evaluation Form and administered it. What would happen?

T   I'd be on tenure.

E   Besides that. The principal would say your friend was biased even though he used the same procedure. Right?

T   I can hear it now.

E   At the same time there is no safeguard from the principal being biased against you. Or *for* you for that matter.

T   Yeah! In fact, this one gal who got tenure is pretty good looking and pretty chummy with the principal. One time after school, I saw the principal . . .

E   Let's not get into that. Write that up in your memoirs. The point is that there are ways of guarding against bias.

T   How?

E   Lots of ways. For one thing, you could have *several* people rate you. That would reduce the influence of any person who might have it in for you.

T   Our principal would never buy that.

E   Of course not. That would reduce his power too much. He has other things in mind other than fair evaluation. He's protecting his position.

T   You'd better believe it.

E   Another thing would be to put the evaluation forms of all the teachers together without names and let a panel who doesn't know the teachers decide.

T   That's a little dangerous when they don't know the teachers. They may not know something that's important to know that's not on the form.

E   True. The form itself specifies the type of things a teacher may be judged on.

T   Yeah. The teachers' organization agreed on the use of that particular form. They used to not have any.

E   How do they add all the items up?

T   What do you mean?

E   I mean do they take all the items on the form and average them for a total score to see who gets tenure?

T   Oh, no. Some items are much more important than others. I scored good on most of the items except the discipline ones. The principal said those were so important they overrode the others.

E   That makes sense, but it also gives the principal the power to determine what is and isn't important.

T   Every time I turn around, the principal gets more power.

E   Essentially the teacher evaluation system you have operating gives the administration a clear shot at you for most any reason up until the time you have tenure. Then you are home free and clear.

T   Why would the teachers' organization agree to such a system?

E   I don't know. That's the way it is almost everywhere. Maybe it grew up historically. That's the way it is in business, and educational administrators sometimes like to think of themselves as business executives and to copy things from business. It gives the bosses more control.

T   Too much.

E   I don't know. The teacher organizations haven't moved very aggressively into changing the area. Maybe they figure extreme vulnerability for a few years is worth it for tenure later. Maybe they just don't know what else to do.

T   *Is* there any thing else to do?

E   From a research viewpoint, there are better ways. I don't know about from a political viewpoint. A few years ago California instigated a teacher evaluation act for *all* teachers. One of the leading researchers, a man named Glass from Colorado, investigated the problem and concluded there are three distinct ways of evaluating teachers from a research viewpoint.

T   What are they?

E   Don't get too excited. The first way is with tests. Standardized tests.

T   Oh.

E   You don't like that one. Neither did Glass. He concluded that standardized achievement tests don't really measure what teachers usually teach for. Even if they did, it would be extremely difficult to say that such and such a test score was the result of the teacher's ability.

T   What do they measure?

E   That's a matter of great dispute. But there's no doubt that tests don't get at a million and one things that the teacher is striving for and spends time on.

T   I've never found them very useful.

E   No, most teachers don't. They may look at test scores when they come back saying to themselves, "Hmmm, this kid is high, just as

I thought, that one low. Oh, that one is a surprise!" That's about the extent of it.

T   If you have smart kids, the scores are high, and dumb ones they're low. There's not much you can do about it.

E   Right. There's also a very high relationship between test scores and socioeconomic class of the kid. So it's really difficult to see the relationship between test scores and what the teacher is doing in class.

T   I'm with you there.

E   So overall, test scores are not a good way of evaluating teachers—though many people still try. Some people have tried to remedy these problems of tests by constructing criterion-referenced tests.

T   What?

E   These are tests specially geared to a particular content. Say I have a history textbook, and I take Chapter Five and I develop a test on that material. Then I have a test keyed to only that material.

T   Teachers do that all the time.

E   Right. In order to evaluate their students. The technique can also be used to evaluate teachers by having teachers teach the same material and comparing them to each other.

T   I don't get it. Different kids would do better than others.

E   Here's how it works. You take a bunch of kids the teacher hasn't seen before and *randomly* assign them to classes. A while before class the teacher is given the material they are to teach to review. They teach the kids the material. Immediately afterward the kids are given a special test which has been prepared previously. Since the kids are randomly assigned to classes, the classes are presumably equal in ability. The teaching ability of the teachers can then be compared to each other directly.

T   Are you deliberately trying to upset me?

E   No. This has actually been done.

T   Where?

E   In California.

T   That figures. But what about rapport with the kids, long-term teaching effects, motivation, in-depth understanding, all the things that are important in teaching and learning?

E   It does leave something to be desired, doesn't it?

T   I'd rather take my chances with the principal. The cure is worse than the disease.

E   From a research standpoint, it has an overwhelming liability. It has zero reliability.

T   What does that mean?

E   It means that in one situation, with one set of materials and kids, a teacher will look good. In another he or she might look bad.

T   That figures.

E   So that's not the way to go either. The third way, and the preferred way according to Professor Glass, is with instruments that look at the classroom.

T   Instruments?

E   Well, that's what we call them. It makes them sound more scientific. What they are are forms that people fill out, something like your teacher evaluation form.

T   I had a vision of a bunch of shining equipment being wheeled into the room.

E   No, these are forms that people fill out on what's going on in the classrooms. But the people who fill them out are not the principal. There are two different kinds. One kind is called "classroom observation schedules." These are filled out by observers in the classroom who are specially trained in the particular instrument. Presumably they would treat every classroom the same way and would not be biased towards anyone.

T   What do these forms have on them?

E   Well, that's the catch. There are all kinds of these instruments, at least two hundred of them. They look for all different kinds of things in the classroom. The most popular one, the Flander's Interaction Analysis, sorts all classroom talk into ten categories, roughly divided between teacher talk and student talk.

T   Which is better—teacher talk or student talk?

E   Again, that's the rub. Teaching is so complex that sometimes one is better and sometimes the other. Since teachers usually talk eighty to ninety percent of the time, letting students talk more is generally considered a good idea. But one can easily imagine situations when the opposite is true. People do studies on which is best, but the results are never conclusive because what's good in one situation may not be good in another.

T   What's the advantage of this approach then?

E   Well, once you decide what you want to do, you are reasonably assured of having it measured accurately and with a minimum of bias. The producers are reliable and valid. What you called objective.

T   What if it's not what you want to do?

E   Precisely. You choose one of the other two hundred approaches. None will be perfect. There is always a strong element of human judgment involved in saying what good teaching is. Teacher-student talk leaves an enormous amount out. It would be foolish to rely on that alone or on any one thing.

T   You still have to use your own judgment in deciding what's good in the classroom. Measuring it doesn't tell you that.

E   Right. Also those procedures are expensive. Having a trained observer come in for several visits runs into some money.

T   The school district would never foot the bill for that.

E   Another approach—which I prefer—is to use instruments which the students fill out.

T   The kids?

E   Right. The students have forms that say things like, "The teacher is well prepared for this class." When you average these across all the students in the class, many of the personal biases cancel out. You don't ask question like, "I like the teacher." That elicits too emotional a response rather than describing the classroom.

T   I think I have seen some of those forms.

E   If you have had a course at this university, you have probably filled out such a form in the course. The student scores are added up, anonymously, and reported to the instructor in different categories.

T   What happens to them?

E   In order to be promoted here at Big Time University, you have to submit some student evaluations of your teaching. However, at a university like this, teaching is not nearly as important for getting tenure and being promoted as are publications. The promotions committees can judge the student ratings as they wish. However, they must be included. Other universities have similar systems.

T   But the students rating the teachers? That might be all right for college, but my students in the seventh grade are too young.

E   Generally, it has been shown that students do an accurate and fair job of rating their teachers—much better than what teachers think. And much kinder than teachers expect. But you're right. The seventh grade is about the lower limit. I don't know of any good rating scales off hand for kids that young.

T   The idea does appeal to me. With my kids rating me, I'd look great as a teacher.

E   Yeah, I like it too. The students are in the room all the time all year long so they know what's going on. Visitors can just come in for a few days altogether.

T   There's also a certain justice in having them judge us since we judge them all the time.

E   True. It's also very cheap. Most forms only take a few minutes to fill out. They usually require some specialized scoring though. Usually it's a few bucks a class.

T   Why doesn't everyone use this approach?

E   Well, you're into the same problem again. There are hundred of these forms. What's good and what's bad? There has to be some agreement on that. On an item that said, "This class is always quiet," you wouldn't look so good.

T   That's true.

E   Also these forms leave out a hell of a lot, although less than most other approaches. They're only part of the story.

T   Well, where does that leave me? I feel that I've learned a lot, but somehow I don't feel any better off.

E   That's the problem with a lot of education. I tell you what. I have an evaluation class this afternoon in an hour. Why don't you come with me, present your problem to the class, and let them work on it for a while.

T   I feel that would be an imposition.

E   Are you kidding? I don't have anything prepared at all.

### Act II, Scene 2:   The Principal Visits the Evaluator

(*A few days after the teacher's visit, the principal enters the evaluator's office which is no less cluttered than before. The evaluator doesn't look any better either.*)

PRINCIPAL   Hi, I'm John Hammel, principal over at Barnum.

EVALUATOR   Mr. Hammel. What can I do for you?

P   What in the hell have you been telling my teachers?

E   What do you mean?

P   I passed Bill Ferguson in the hall the other day at school, and he said you said my evaluation of him wasn't any good.

E   That's not exactly what I said.

P   You guys sit over here at the university, philosophize, theorize, and second-guess us on everything. Why don't you be helpful for a change?

E   We are trying to be, Mr. Hammel. We are trying to be.

P   It's not very helpful to have him running around the school, shooting his mouth off in the lounge that I don't know my job.

E   I didn't say that.

P   That could get back to the superintendent. That could get back to the parents. It could cause me trouble.

E   I'm sorry for the confusion.

P   Did you tell him I didn't know what I was doing?

E   What I told him was that from his description of what you did, you evaluated teachers much the same as any principal. No better, no worse. From the research point of view, the procedure you used is not likely to have high reliability.

P   Reliability! Like in statistics? I had a statistics course once. What do you mean?

E   I mean that if you were to do it again, or, better yet, if someone else were to do it, they would be likely to get different results.

P   Of course. They might look for different things.

E   Exactly. So another principal might judge Mr. Ferguson's performance and judge him to be a good teacher. He would get tenure.

P   I grant the possibility. But it's not quite *that* arbitrary. A lot of principals would have judged him to be a bad teacher.

E  I grant that possibility. But your evaluation procedure has no way
   of *demonstrating* that that's the case. To the teacher it looks like
   the arbitrary whim of one man—you.

P  But it's *my* school.

E  Then you don't have to explain or justify your actions to me,
   to Mr. Ferguson, or anyone else, do you?

P  Well, I want my teachers to be happy. And my parents, and the
   superintendent.

E  One of the funny things about a public evaluation, particularly of
   a person, is that it not only has to be accurate and fair, but has
   to *appear* to be that way. You have to justify it to other people.
   You are not in *technical* trouble on your evaluation, Mr. Hammel.
   You are in *political* trouble.

P  Political trouble? I can ride this out.

E  No doubt. But the real issue is whether you gave Ferguson the bounce
   because he was a bad teacher or for personal reasons which would
   not be legitimate. People will treat you differently in the future
   depending on what they believe.

P  O.K., O.K. I am the principal of the school. Don't I have some say
   on what goes on there? I am held publicly accountable to the parents
   and the superintendent for what happens—whether I want to be
   or not.

E  True. But your procedures must be perceived as being fair.

P  Look, I visit the the classroom, judge the teacher, and make my
   recommendation. That's how the teacher's contract says it should
   be done. I'm the principal. How else can I hold these teachers
   accountable for what they do?

E  I confess I don't have an easy answer for that one. Most of the
   solutions I've seen I don't like.

P  Like what?

E  Well, most states have some kind of teacher "accountability scheme"
   in development, which usually amounts to a statewide testing
   program.

P  I don't like the sound of that.

E  Neither do I. The most developed such scheme is in Michigan where
   the state education agency has written educational objectives for
   each grade level and has constructed tests to measure those
   objectives.

P  What!

E  For example, in fourth-grade math there might be thirty-five
   objectives. Each fourth-grade class in the state is given a special
   test to measure those thirty-five objectives. This information is fed
   back at the state, district, school, and classroom level. Each
   teacher could be judged by how well the objectives were accomplished.

P  But every school and every class is different. Maybe they don't need those particular objectives. There are all kinds of special circumstances.

E  I agree. I would not recommend trying to hold teachers accountable for achieving a prescribed set of objectives. It's too inflexible. What's more, some state officials want to tie some state funding to how many objectives a district achieves.

P  That's crazy!

E  That's what a lot of people have tried to tell them—the teachers, the principals. But sometimes they don't listen so good.

P  Why?

E  There's a lot of power at stake. A lot. That's why I prefer a system where the accountability arrangements are worked out at the local level. That's where the kids are.

P  At least we agree on something.

E  I do not think it should be worked out though. With the people involved. Not just one person passing judgment on another. That's a little arbitrary for my taste.

P  The principal still has his obligations.

E  So does the teacher.

P  I have to go. We have a track meet this afternoon, and I should be there in case anything goes wrong. I think I understand your position a little better. One more question.

E  Sure.

P  Would your type of reasoning apply to supervisor relationships as well?

E  What do you mean?

P  Well, the way the superintendent treats his assistants. Or his principals. Or the way the school board treats them.

E  I haven't thought about it too much, but I don't see why not. In a hierarchical arrangement, the person higher up has an obligation just as much as the people lower down. Accountability is a two-way street. Individuals should not only be accountable to the institution. The institution should also be accountable to the individuals. This fairness should be reflected in evaluation procedures. I think I would also apply it to the teachers and the kids. Though I'm not sure what it would look like there either.

P  Well, you're consistent anyhow. I'm not sure I agree with everything you say, but it's been interesting talking to you. I'm glad I came over.

E  Good luck. I hope things work out all right.

P  Look. I don't always feel that great about evaluating teachers either. I put it off as long as I can but it's part of my job.

E  I understand that.

P  I also get evaluated myself. I just went through an evaluation and I didn't come out perfect either. Overall it was pretty good though.

E  What kind of evaluation was it?

P  The superintendent and the assistant superintendent filled out a rating form on me. Something like I fill out on the teachers.

E  But not the same type items though.

P  No, not the same type stuff. They have things like staff relations, community relations, starting new programs, and so on. Then they rate the principal on each one. There were five points on each one.

E  The whole world is rated on a five-point scale. Someday no doubt as we sink into the coffin, someone will give us a form to rate the world on a five-point scale.

P  Huh?

E  So you did pretty good?

P  Yeah, I did pretty good. That's what Wylie, the assistant superintendent said. Of course, I don't know. Maybe they tell that to everybody to keep them happy. There were some things I didn't do so good on.

E  Like what?

P  Like staff relations, for instance. They rated me down in staff relations. I mean they gave me a three but I wouldn't consider that too good. By my own standards.

E  I know what you mean. Everytime I give someone a B in class I have to give them a long explanation why they didn't get an A.

P  In this case I think they are wrong. I don't know. I always thought I had pretty good working relations with the faculty.

E  Why do you think you got the rating?

P  I think they got a few bellyaches from a couple of people on the staff. That's all they probably had to go on.

E  You don't think that's fair?

P  No, not really. I don't think it's representative of the whole staff. But it's all the central office has to go on. It makes me wonder about my ratings of teachers.

E  What do you mean?

P  Frankly, no principal feels very secure in rating teachers. We don't have enough time to do a good job.

E  And the teachers don't think you're teaching experts either.

P  That's right. But it's our job and we do it. The central office has their job to do, too. I just wish they had a little more to go on.

E  Ferguson says the same thing about your evaluation of him.

P  Yes, but I'm not bellyaching about mine. It's just not quite as good as I thought it would be. Oh, well, it's just an evaluation. None of the principals take it too seriously. We just joke around about them.

E  Do you talk to each other about how you were evaluated?

P  No, not in specific terms. You never know how somebody else was rated.

E  Have you ever thought that part of the reason for the evaluation conference might be to remind you of your position in the hierarchy? To let you know who's boss?

P  Oh, no, I hadn't thought about that. I really do have to go to the

track meet. Otherwise I'll get rated down in my evaluation next
year. (Stands up)

E   Right. Well, nice talking to you. I hope things work out for everybody.

P   Me, too. Sometimes things are sticky no matter what. Thanks for
your time.
*(The principal leaves. The evaluator goes back to staring out the
window.)*


## Act Three: Tit for Tat on Tenure

### Scene 1:   The Teacher and Principal Back in the Principal's Office

*(The teacher knocks on the open door, looks in, and comes in slowly.
The principal looks up from his desk.)*

PRINCIPAL   Hello, Bill.

TEACHER   Hi. I wanted to tell you what I'm going to do on the tenure
thing.

P   Okay.

T   I'm going to file a grievance.

P   On what?

T   I don't think you followed the procedure properly.

P   Bill, I've been principal here for years. I know what I'm doing.
I've documented the case properly.

T   This year there's been a change in contract language.

P   On what?

T   You have to have a conference with me every time you add a written
report to my record. Within ten days.

P   I know that. We *had* a conference every time.

T   Not on the informal reports you made. Not on the write-ups you
made on passing my classroom. You didn't mention those to me.

P   On the informal ones too?

T   Yes. There's been a change in the new contract. In the old one you
didn't have to have a conference on the informal observations.

P   Well, there may have been a few minor reports in your file that we
didn't talk about. But nothing major.

T   I'm going to protest it anyhow.

P   I don't see how that's going to make any difference. The letter's
already gone out.

T   Well, the teachers' organization thinks I have a case.

P   Trivial stuff, Bill. You're pretty bitter about the whole thing, aren't you?

T   I think it's accurate to say I'm not too happy with it. I feel I got the
shaft.

P   Look. I did the best job I could. Any mistakes I made were honest
ones. With the best of intentions. How else could I have done it?

T   For one thing, I wish you had collected information from the kids. They are some of my strongest supporters.

P   We don't collect information like that from the kids. Do you think they're competent to judge whether you're a good teacher?

T   Maybe not. But there are things about the class that they're competent to judge. Things that might make a difference. I also would have been happier to be judged by my peers.

P   By your peers! I didn't want to tell you this, Bill, but some of the teachers here don't think you're a very good teacher.

T   Yeah, I know who they are. The old guard. Still complaining because we can't use corporal punishment anymore. Even so, I think I would have felt better if a committee of teachers considered information collected about my teaching.

P   What kind of stuff?

T   Stuff from the kids. Opinions of the parents, observations of my class on objective rating forms. Opinions of other teachers. I sat in on a university class last week, and we came up with a whole bunch of things that might indicate whether my teaching was any good.

P   I thought this sounded a little too familiar. Why don't we just turn things over to the professors and let them run it if they're so damn smart! Have you got any role for the principal in your new grand order. Or is the principal obsolete?

T   No. I'd let you sit in on the committee and consider and present evidence like everyone else.

P   Thanks.

T   Parents, too. I'd have a parent or two sit in to represent that viewpoint.

P   Do you know how many complaints I've had from parents about your class?

T   Yeah, but you've just heard from a few of the most vocal ones. You don't really know what most parents think about my class.

P   Enough of this nonsense. This isn't getting us anywhere.

T   You're just not willing to open these issues up to public discussion, John. You want to keep control of everything yourself.

P   That's bull. Do you think I run everything around here? Then you don't know what you're talking about. I'm just one voice among many. I get evaluated and criticized just like you do. But I don't bellyache about it.

T   Maybe that's your own fault.

P   All the big decisions around here, tenure and everything else, are done by joint action of the administrators. We talk things over and decide. No one man has the whole say. This isn't a dictatorship.

T   All I'm saying is I don't think I got a fair shake. If it had been handled differently, I might have felt better about it. Even if it had still turned out bad for me.

P   If it had turned out bad for you, you would still be complaining no matter how it was done. It's the result you don't like. You never complained about the procedure before.

T   It never lopped off my head before.

P   Look, Bill. This isn't getting either one of us any place. You've told me what you're going to do. Anything else?

T   No, I think that does it. You'll be hearing from us.

P   I'm sure. I still think your position is hopeless.

T   We'll see. (*The teacher walks out.*)

(*After six months litigation, Bill Ferguson was given an additional year's probation on the basis of technicalities*).

# *10*

# *Starting New Programs and Getting Promoted*

## A Typical Case: New Programs for Red-Headed Children

Once upon a time deep in the state of Euphoria (not to be confused with California), District 119 started an educational program for red-headed children. The story begins, as most such stories do, in the state capital. The state of Euphoria launches a new statewide program for the education of red-headed children. Studies have been done showing that red-headed children do not achieve up to their full potential, that they are often slighted by teachers, who tend to stereotype them as troublemakers, and that each red-headed child will make $140,000 more in his lifetime if he receives special instruction in school. Many are unhappy in school. Besides, word is out that the Russians have started a new national program for red-headed children, and if they should get ahead in this area, who knows what the consequences may be?

These arguments are skillfully advanced by Lance Sterling, who is principal of State University High School. It so happens that Sterling's school has specialized in developing special programs for red-headed children, both boys and girls, and now wishes to export those programs and materials to schools all over the state. By lobbying in the state legislature for a budget for his school, Sterling has become personally acquainted with members of the key legislative committees. He also knows the governor, who happens to have a red-headed daughter.

Sterling convinces the state superintendent of schools, whom he also knows personally, to assign a high priority to programs for red-headed kids. The superintendent is interested in higher office and he can count red-headed votes as well as anyone. Besides, his brother, whom he has hired as an assistant, has just been on an official tour to Russia, where he has discovered they are teaching communism in the schools to red-headed children.

Special studies are mounted. Special hearings are held. Sterling brings in leading scholars to testify on red-headed children. Parents of red-headed children demonstrate in the state capitol. After much work the state legislature passes a bill providing ten million dollars for local districts to develop such programs. The money will be administered by the state education agency. Local school districts can apply for money on a voluntary basis.

To inform the local districts of the new state program, the state agency holds a series of two-day conferences. One of these is attended by Bill Small, curriculum director for District 119 in the central part of the state. Small has just come from the east coast to start this new job, and he is anxious to show that he is doing something. After being told how to apply for funds and what type of programs the state will support, Small returns to District 119 where he convinces the superintendent of the desirability of programs for red-headed children.

The superintendent isn't entirely persuaded because he doesn't want it to appear that some children are getting special advantages. That could spell trouble with parents. However, the school district can always use extra money and the new program might pop for $100,000 for the district. He gives the go-ahead.

After working the idea through the central office staff and the school board, Small must select teachers to be involved in the plan. He wants teachers who are willing to change because they must implement new programs developed at Euphoria State University High School. On the other hand, he wants to remain in control of the project so he can get credit for it. He wants teachers who are tractable and not too wild.

Small selects ten teachers, several from each academic subject area, and a teacher he is personally close to as project director. The teachers are fairly young, most with three or so years of experience, although in social studies Small decided to go with a slightly older man of fifteen years' teaching experience. The teachers begin to meet together on establishing programs for red-headed children.

Ted Charisma is a young math teacher involved in the program. He has been teaching five years and is interested in the new teaching techniques. He also sees the project as an opportunity to advance himself. There are not so many opportunities for ambitious math teachers. In the meetings Charisma begins to emerge as the natural leader of the group. The project director, Small's friend, is a bit of a lightweight and not too involved.

The more the teachers meet the more enthusiastic they become. They write a proposal to secure money from the state. Although the money is

administered and controlled by Small, there are funds to travel to conferences and to meet teachers from around the state who are involved in
similar programs. Getting out is fun. So is the publicity among the other
teachers in the school and in the local newspapers.

As they work together the group becomes increasingly friendly and
supportive of each other. In their new cohesiveness they develop a group
morale. Charisma becomes their spokesman, representing their group interests to the administration, asking for funds, helping solve problems
caused by the new materials, helping some teachers in the group with their
personal problems. Small, the curriculum director, turns to him more and
more when he wants to communicate with the project.

About once a month university consultants who have been developing the materials visit the teachers to see how they are doing. This is an
important contact for the teachers. Charisma, through Small, arranges for
some of the more involved teachers to be released one extra period so
they can work more on the project. Thus, released time is paid for with
state funds.

After several months some of the teachers in the school who are not
involved begin to get edgy about the project. They see the project teachers
as getting special favors, such as released time and publicity, undeservedly.
At first noncommittal and neutral toward the project ideas and materials,
they begin to resist more actively the ideas and to make humorous but
derogatory remarks about the project in the teacher's lounge. They refer
to the project good-naturedly as a "rip-off," as a public relations ploy.

The principal also shows some signs of nervousness. At first, he too
had been neutral and noncommittal. Things were working smoothly for
his school and he didn't want to rock the boat and cause trouble. But he
didn't say much because the curriculum director seemed so enthusiastic, as
did the project teachers once they got into it.

Just as he suspected, however, trouble does arrive. The local John
Birch Society gets hold of some of the social studies materials in which
the word "comrade" was used. They launch a publicity campaign against
the school to drive the materials and project out. The school district
defends itself successfully but much bad publicity results.

The superintendent gets a little nervous because of this, and for another reason. The new curriculum director has expanded his project to
more teachers. He uses the money and publicity to build himself a power
base. He develops close personal contacts with school-board members.
Does the curriculum director want to be superintendent? A conflict develops between the two.

Meanwhile the project teachers become increasingly cohesive and
identified as the "project teachers." They represent a special group within
the school with which others must contend. The program for red-headed
children becomes more established within the school in spite of its enemies.
It is able to defend its own ideas and interests. Things stabilize somewhat.

After a few years, the assistant principal's job is open. Charisma is a major candidate for the job. In his favor is the way he has worked with teachers, the respect in which he is held by the faculty, and his outside contacts and publicity from the project. Small acts as his sponsor inside the administration. Against him are his general intellectual and academic interests and, in the superintendent's mind, his close association with Small.

Also a candidate for the job is the coach of the junior varsity basketball team, who is a driver education instructor. The coach is affable and gets along well with the public. The superintendent decides the school needs a disciplinarian. The coach gets the job.

The next year the head of the math department retires. This time there is little hesitation. Charisma gets the job. He continues his association with the project but becomes more and more a peripheral figure. No one fills the leadership role as well. The project continues but the enthusiasm wanes. Over a few years time it begins to look more like a regular school program and less like a revolutionary movement. Its threat diminishes, as does its promise. People routinely accept it.

Members of the original group drift away. Small leaves, taking a job as superintendent in another state. Some go back to graduate school, some move. A few new people are added. The university contacts diminish and finally cease. The program will continue as long as the state money lasts but its excitement is gone. Some residue of the program remains in the materials used, in the minds of the people involved, and in the social structure of the school. This is how change occurs.

This vignette of an innovation being implemented in a school illustrates the process of change. I have intentionally used a ridiculous innovation like programs for red-headed children in order to focus on the process of innovation rather than its content. The process is much the same for any innovation.

In the rest of this chapter I will discuss the major elements involved. The key concept is advocacy. No change occurs without someone pushing for it. Next, the discussion focuses on how ambition relates to innovation and what the ambitious person is like. This is followed by an analysis of what areas are most likely to be ripe for innovation. For the ambitious teacher, this means being in the right place at the right time.

In order to start new programs teachers must come into contact with new ideas. Where teachers get new ideas and how idea flow can be improved are the subjects of a later section. Just as important for success are the costs and rewards to the teachers engaged in innovation. The personal costs in terms of extra work are heavy and the rewards relatively few, which is why innovation is often not successful.

The discussion then moves to the dangers of overselling an innovation, a common error. Current policy toward educational innovation is analyzed and found to be woefully inadequate. More fruitful policies are proposed. Finally, the question of the limited effectiveness of any innovation is discussed.

## ADVOCACY AS THE KEY

In the little drama in District 119 are most of the elements involved in educational change. But the key element is advocacy. In order for a new program to develop there must be an advocate working inside the school who promotes the program aggressively. Originally the advocacy role may be filled by only one person, but in order to be successful it must usually involve a group of several people.

The advocacy group is the key element in promoting and defending a program's interests. Usually there is one person who acts as the spokesperson of the group and who is in effect the informal group leader. In the program for red-headed children Ted Charisma was this person. He worked to keep the group together, provide emotional and intellectual support, and informally bargain with those who held the resources.

The advocacy group essentially comprises a special interest within the social structure of the schools. They form an in-group which meets frequently. They are only one such group. Other groups promote and protect other program interests. The school district can be seen as a set of advocacy groups contending for limited resources. The success of the new program depends on its establishing itself within the competitive field of contenders. If it does not, the program will not develop or survive.

The program advocates cannot sit by passively waiting for people to recognize the advantages of their new programs. It will not happen. They must actively champion the new program, whether it be a new program for red-headed children or a new teachers' union being organized. Change occurs through active effort.

Notice that Lance Sterling's group, as well as Ted Charisma's, is an advocacy group. On a grander scale, Sterling organizes people, gets experts to justify and secures resources for the programs at the state level. The activities and the skills of the chief advocates are the same. Both orchestrate their forces.

No matter how much help comes from the state, however, the local advocacy must grow from within the district. The state authorities cannot create a program inside without local receptivity and formation of an advocacy. The state money is a powerful incentive for the local administrators to initiate a program, and the university consultants provide ideas and legitimacy, but the major activity must come from within. Without the strenuous effort of Charisma's group or one like it, there would be no program for red-headed children in District 119 or else the program would be a paper program—one not existing in actual fact.

The fact that there is strong outside sponsorship is critical, however. The program is bound to run into difficult problems eventually. Teachers become frustrated. New approaches don't work. The enemies gain ascendancy. In District 119 the Birchers would have sunk the program if it didn't have outside help. When the program runs into its inevitable troubles the outside sponsor can step in with more money, more authority, more consultant expertise. The well-sponsored program is like the son of a rich man: it gets many chances to succeed in spite of many failures. The weakly sponsored program, like a poor man's son, goes under.

Since the new program is competing for scarce funds and resources, it will inevitably have detractors and enemies. Other teachers see promotion opportunities, attention, publicity, respect and good will, as well as extra resources, going to the innovators. They naturally resent this and attack the project. The new innovation spreads only so far in the school district.

The advocacy also has a natural life cycle. Because the new program attracts attention, the chief advocate will often be promoted or leave to take a better job elsewhere—even if the innovation is not entirely successful. It is seldom possible to replace this leadership adequately. Even a successful innovation is likely to lose steam eventually. The initial fervor necessary for the hard work required to establish a program eventually fades away. So does the advocacy. Consequently, new programs have a rise and fall, an ephemeral quality, about them. That is not to say that they are worthless because they are temporary. They may do great good while alive. That depends on the nature of the innovation.

THE AMBITIOUS TEACHER

What about the teachers who get involved in innovations? What are they like and how are they different? What happens to them? Many teachers interested in innovations tend to be ambitious. That is, they see themselves as eventually becoming administrators or consultants or advancing to other positions outside teaching. They also tend to be younger than the average teacher and usually have about three or four years of experience.

Beginning teachers seem to have their hands full the first few years simply learning the ropes. Older teachers with more than ten years' experience seem to settle in and not see innovations as being very worthwhile for themselves. They don't have so much to gain.

Teachers who engage in innovation do tend to get promoted more, probably because they are noticed. Being innovative is certainly no guarantee. As discussed in the chapter on bosses, principals are usually sponsored by older men in the administration who see the potential principal as being somehow like themselves. This may mean being conservative is better for promotion into the administrative ranks, if that is one's goal. It depends on the administrators in the district. Regardless, being involved in an innovation is one of the few ways an ambitious teacher may distinguish himself or herself, since most teaching behavior is not visible to others.

What about the special leaders like Ted Charisma and Lance Sterling? They are confident about being able to influence their own futures and believe that opportunities exist for rapid upward mobility. They are able to get access to resources necessary for development and are able to concentrate their talents on one project and to maximize successful identification with it. They believe that they will be promoted somehow if they show sufficient merit. In contrast, the people who are less successful are those who do not believe they can do much to influence their futures so they do not take risks, seek visibility, or display aggressiveness.

The really effective leader displays charisma. Personal charisma is often talked about as if it were a mystical quality but it is common to all. It is a talent that can be found in varying degrees, like any other. Charisma is based on the ability to recognize the personal needs of individuals and to satisfy those needs within the scope of the advocacy one is building. One person needs attention, another needs intellectual respectability, another needs extra money.

The charismatic leader sees that these diverse needs are met within the advocacy group. He or she orchestrates these diverse needs into the overall purpose and direction of the project so that people become emotionally welded into the group. The members commit their talents to the project in return. Social organization and direction is built upon these relationships.

As the members of the group gain satisfaction from the leader's efforts, they talk to one another about him or her until they collectively build a small myth, which is reinforced by each member. The leader has charisma, a magical power to lead. In a sense charisma is a result of mutual admiration held by a group for one person. Charisma comes from being highly valued by many. This valuing may also be based on other attributes, such as one's athletic ability or simply one's celebrity.

In the local circumstances of starting a new program, charisma is related to the leader's ability to do things for the group as individuals and as a collectivity. Success leads to more charisma. This also means that some people who don't buy into the group definition, particularly those not in the advocacy group, will be puzzled by the leader's charismatic aura even while recognizing the "gift of gab" or whatever other attributes the leader's success is based on. They may even see him or her as a charlatan. He or she doesn't "do it" for them. And indeed he or she doesn't, if they are not a member of the group.

In any case, such charismatic behavior is important in social movements, large or small, because it stimulates people to make sacrifices and efforts they would not otherwise make. The feeling of success and reward is no small part. Such leadership is particularly important in situations where more tangible rewards are lacking or where personal sacrifices are required. This is true of the school setting. Ted Charisma is no Ghandi but he is closer than most people think.

Having charisma is not necessary for the ambitious teacher anxious to advance himself or herself. Ofter the administration will not appoint a particularly charismatic person to head a project because they are afraid they will lose control of it. Such was the case in District 119 when the curriculum director Small appointed a friend of his to head the project. Often projects founder because of the ineptness of such safe leadership. Someone like Ted Charisma must come along and run the project.

BEING IN THE RIGHT PLACE AT THE RIGHT TIME

Not even the most talented person can exercise his or her abilities if not given a chance. Where can one find opportunities? Opportunities vary with the school organization, the community, geographical location, and even subject matter area. Put succinctly it is easiest to make one's mark in a new school district in a wealthy suburb of a large city in a field like special education. Why?

First, it is much easier to form an advocacy group and develop a new program in a loose and fragmented organizational structure. A tight bureaucratic structure doesn't encourage and perhaps doesn't allow jockeying around by people trying to start new things. The proper atmosphere is partly dependent on the administrators. Those administrators who run a tight ship are not encouraging to innovation.

The school atmosphere should encourage risk taking and not be big on punishing failure or on finding scapegoats for things gone wrong. A newly developing school district is more likely to offer this type of loose atmosphere than an established district is. Things are less organized and more open to promotion and development. As mentioned in the chapter on bosses, a newly arrived superintendent unfreezes the school social structure and allows development and innovation, while principals tend to be rather conservative by nature. Permissiveness is perhaps the best one can except from that quarter.

Subject areas, like special education, that are expanding and developing likewise offer more opportunity than more established specialties. New specialties are unformed and ready for social organizing.

Both the size and the wealth of the school district also affect the opportunity for starting new programs. Wealthier districts obviously have more money to spend for innovation. Also wealthier districts are inhabited by parents with higher socioeconomic status, and they often demand the newest for their schools and often identify the newest with the best. Wealthy suburbs are typical of these districts.

Why larger districts also have more innovations is less clear. It may be that larger districts serve a more diverse clientele and respond by mounting many special programs. Larger districts are also able to set aside funds and are the recipients of many special funds. Special earmarked funds tend to offer entrepreneurial opportunities.

Surprisingly, geographic location is also an important determinant of where new programs are started. Innovations of all types—whether inventions, pop music, or clothing styles—begin in and are spread from the large cosmopolitan population centers. Educational innovations are no exception.

The reason is that innovations of all types follow the routes of greatest personal contact—and personal contact is greatest in the major population centers. From the major population centers the innovations spread along the major transportation routes to the next largest population centers, from there to the next largest centers, and so on. Since American cities are connected by interstate highways, regional dissemination might be expected to follow along these routes.

So one might expect to find the most opportunities to start new programs around major metropolitan areas. Wealthy suburbs around metropolitan centers offer favorable geographic location and financial conditions for innovation. Indeed suburbs often sustain a surfeit of innovation. Opportunities are greatest where innovation is heaviest. Second to these would be regional centers of transport and commerce.

## WHERE DO TEACHERS GET NEW IDEAS?

If teachers are to develop new programs, it is essential that they come in contact with new ideas. In the program for red-headed children in District 119, most of the new ideas were supplied by consultants from and materials developed at the state university. Coming into contact with new ideas is a problem because teachers are restricted to the classroom for so much of the day.

Personal contact with people who have experience with innovations is essential for a teacher trying something new. Personal contact is necessary because it enables the teacher to ask questions about things that are troublesome about the innovation. This type of information exchange can only occur in a dialogue. It cannot be gleaned from a brochure or other one-way communication.

Whereas administrators frequently go to meetings outside the school, teachers rarely have extended contact with external sources. Most teachers find new ideas among their closest friends and work associates. Within the school, teachers generally have less than an hour a day, including lunch, to talk to other teachers. This is not a situation conducive to the exchange of new ideas.

Outside the school, other teachers they know, periodicals, and college courses are in that order, the main sources of new ideas for teachers. Administrators are not significant sources. Generally, access to new ideas and innovations is very restricted, a fact that greatly limits the capability for starting new programs.

The first hearing of a new idea is not the most important however. The most credible source of information is another teacher, just as the most credible source for superintendents is another superintendent. If teachers find out about an innovation from a newsletter, a college course, or an administrator, they will turn to other teachers they know well in order to form an opinion about the innovation. The advocacy group provides this sounding-board function when it is operating.

The teacher leader who is trying to start a new program must bring his or her fellow teachers into contact with other people who have new ideas. This may be done by bringing in outside consultants who have worked on innovative ideas. However, the one-shot consultant who visits, gives a little talk, and leaves is not very effective in stimulating change.

A much better strategy, although a more expensive one, is to have the teachers travel to places where the innovation is being implemented and to talk to other teachers privately. Also effective is having an outside consultant, perhaps from a university, visit frequently. Repeated personal contact with those who have had experience with the innovation is the key.

Ultimately, however, the advocacy group must rely on itself in order to adjust the innovation to the local setting. It is the local advocacy team who must do the hard work of implementing. This means they need much time to talk to one another, changing and trying out what works or doesn't work for them.

All this puts released teacher time and travel funds at a premium. The enterprising teacher leader must bargain with the appropriate authorities to obtain such resources if the new project is to succeed. Extended personal contact is the key idea.

## COSTS AND REWARDS FOR THE INNOVATING TEACHER

One of the least understood features of the school system is its lack of tangible reward for any type of outstanding performance. A teacher is not paid more money for doing things better or differently. There are increased chances for promotion, but even here, few jobs are really available. The only tangible rewards for more teachers are perhaps released time, a better schedule, or more classroom materials.

On the other hand, the personal costs of starting a new program may be quite high. Teaching new materials or new techniques requires a great investment of personal time and personal effort. Learning new teaching skills is like learning a new job, a laborious process. Frustration is a constant companion since many things are certain to go wrong.

The lack of intrinsic rewards like money and promotion makes the advocacy group particularly important. The teacher must be rewarded with satisfaction derived from interacting with his peers, from pride in doing a good job, from a feeling that what he is doing is important, and from a feeling of power in being able to affect the school.

These satisfactions, as well as more personal gratifications and a sense of direction, are what a teacher gains as a member of the advocacy team. The increased respect of one's peers is also an important derivative. Advocacy of a particular program gives ambitious teachers who have been frustrated by a lack of opportunity in the school structure a way of channeling their energies. It increases morale and job satisfaction.

There are also teachers who simply are motivated by wanting to improve. This motive should not be overlooked. Altruism is a strong motivation for those who go into teaching, as pointed out in the chapter on what teachers are like. However, people are complex and other motivations must be looked after also. The world doesn't, even in education, run on pure motives. But pure motives are there, too.

In starting new programs the teacher leader must realize that there are limits on the types of innovations that teachers will adjust to easily. For example, teachers feel they have a need for covering so much material, for seeing that students master certain kinds of material, for generating positive student feeling toward both the teacher and the learning situation, and for maintaining sufficient control of the class so that learning can occur.

When the teacher leader has particular trouble getting teachers involved in a project to implement a new approach, he or she might step back and examine whether the approach is violating some basic premise of the teachers' world. For example, with the new approach the students might be uncontrollable, or they might dislike the materials so much that it affects their attitudes toward the teacher. By the way, if the teacher doesn't like the materials, his or her attitude will greatly affect the students' attitudes. Teachers and students are permanently keyed to each other's attitudes.

One of the most difficult problems the teacher leader has in working with fellow teachers on new programs is the feeling of most teachers that everything that goes on in the classroom is the teacher's business only. The teacher is not used to having other adults, even fellow teachers, visit the class. If something goes wrong, the teacher sees that as only his or her responsibility. Ordinarily, asking for help is out of the question. (See the chapter on what teachers are like for a fuller explanation.)

Here the teacher leader has an advantage over other people trying to implement new programs. The teacher leader can attain access to the classroom much more easily than anyone else. In fact, the ideas of teachers working with one another on actual teaching behavior, as opposed to writing curriculum guides, opens up a whole new approach to improving instruction that has not really been pursued.

Satisfaction derived from cooperatively improving one's skills in the view of one's fellow teachers offers professional rewards heretofore untapped. Movement in such a direction must be slow and gradual, however, since most teachers are habituated to complete isolation. Entry into another teacher's classroom is still considered an intrusion. Such values do not change quickly.

The new programs that will be accepted most easily are those that do not challenge basic job perceptions. Of course, the easier innovations are also less exciting and less noteworthy.

OVERSELLING

In the case of the programs for red-headed children, note that Lance Sterling, the advocate who got the program started at the state level, used a set of argumetns on why the new program was the way to go. Of course, he used his influential personal contacts to advance the ideas. But having influential contacts, though essential, was not enough. He also had to advance reasons why the new program was good.

These reasons were supported by "scientific studies," which lent them an increased air of authenticity. More important, though, they were constructed to appeal to the basic values and beliefs of the people Sterling was addressing, in this case state legislators and state officials. Sterling suggested that red-headed children were not living up to their educational potential, that they would make more money if given special training, that teachers were not handling them correctly, and even that the Russians were already mounting such programs and this would endanger national security.

If one inspects rationales given to government officials and legislators for new-program funding, one will find that the reasons given are amazingly similar. For example, the themes of full development of the child, economic benefits to the society, competition with other states or other countries, preventing waste of resources, and promoting basic job skills will appear and reappear whether the pitch is to a state legislator for a state gifted program or to the United States Congress for a computer-assisted instructional program.

Why are the reasons given the same. Is it because the educational approaches are so similar? No, it is because government officials are so similar. The arguments for the funds are constructed to appeal to the belief systems of the people providing the money. It was no accident that one of the first large-scale educational funding programs on a national level was called the National Defense Education Act, although teachers scratched their heads trying to figure out what the relevance to national defense was.

Appeals to the funder's belief system are necessary to get the initial funds but a belief system is also necessary to the program developers and the advocacy group itself. Common beliefs provide coherence within groups. Beliefs are the basis of social cooperation and social action. The advocacy group needs a belief system to hold it together and motivate it, just as legislators do.

The legislators, the developers, and the teachers all share certain beliefs. These they use to appeal to each other for aid and cooperation. If the beliefs differ, what the legislators intended for a program may be far removed from what the teachers do with it. Who is correct? That is a complex question but educationally the teachers are far closer to the students and teaching than are the legislators.

Often a dysfunction arises in the appeals to others' beliefs. This might be called overselling. The developers promise the legislators or teachers more than the program can deliver. The claims can be excessive indeed. Claims are necessary but in the long run excessive claims are damaging because they cause a reaction against the program. For example, one can see that any claims advanced for programs for red-headed children would be viewed with suspicion in many quarters. The same problem may beset advocacy groups intent on advancing its ideas within a school. Claims for a new program are always subject to the check of common sense.

THE HEAVY-HANDED APPROACH:
PUMPING IT IN FROM OUTSIDE

Is there a person in this country who has not tried to sell his or her favorite innovation to the public schools? Hardly a day passes, hardly an opportunity arises, without someone trying to slip the schools a piece of machinery, a set of materials, or a fabulous technique that will enable slow children to learn fast, satisfy all the demands placed on the school, and generally set the world right.

For their efforts the propagators of those innovations expect only fame, fortune, and gratitude. They glow with the image of national publicity, schools clamoring for the materials, teachers grateful for the help, smiling children working enthusiastically in the classroom. In spite of the great numbers of people pursuing this vision, I believe it is based on false assumptions; and I would like to suggest a sounder and more democratic approach to improving education, one which involves the classroom teachers who must put any new idea into practice.

Since the advent of the big money from the federal government about ten years ago, much policy toward innovation has been directed in accord with what has variously been called the "pipeline," the "hypodermic," or the "R, D, and D" model of change. The innovation is to be manufactured somewhere else and pumped into the schools (the "pipeline") or a solution is to be prepared by experts and injected into the body educational (the "hypodermic").

The more legitimate (and less derisive) title in the "R, D, and D" paradigm of educational change, in which research, development, and diffusion comprise the first three stages of the change process. First, basic and applied *research* is conducted by researchers, usually working in universities or specially supported government facilities. This research provides the basis for *development*. Agencies build educational products, materials, or techniques that can be used throughout the country. These products of the research and development process are then *disseminated* to the educational community where they are finally *adopted* by schools and teachers, the final stage. Thus is educational change achieved.

In my book *The Politics of Educational Innovation* (House, 1974), which examines the political and social structure of the school district, I have pointed out why such a vision of change does not work very well. It proceeds in ignorance of the way schools operate and ignores the problems people in the schools face from day to day. Put simply, it is out of tune with the way schools are structured.

A close inspection of the scheme reveals why it has been so popular with government decision makers. Note that by dividing the change process into several stages, the scheme takes the initiation of innovation activities out of the hands of the people actually in the schools. Experts will conduct the research, development, and diffusion functions; and it is they who will decide how these products will be shaped. The scheme also requires a large bureaucracy to direct these functions centrally if they are to be properly coordinated. The total process is centrally controlled by government officials who, either directly or indirectly, have the power to decide what problems shall be attacked and how.

Naturally it will take a great deal of money to operate such a scheme for all the public schools in the United States. This money is to be placed into the research, development, and dissemination functions and into the central bureaucracy itself—at the discretion of the central bureaucracy. What is the role of the people in the schools who must implement these innovations? This perspective assumes that they are passive consumers of whatever products the pipeline delivers to them. Their duty is to implement (Havelock, 1971).

Now it will come as no surprise to teachers that this scheme has not produced good results. But its failure has been a constant source of amazement and consternation to government planners at both the state and federal levels and to a large number of educational researchers and developers who are heavily invested one way or other in the approach. Beginning in the mid-sixties the federal government established and funded a set of research and development centers and a set of so-called regional educational laboratories to perform the functions delineated by the R, D, and D perspective.

For the most part the results have been disappointing. The products produced have not been very good, they have not been perceived as very useful by practitioners, and they have not been used. Several hundreds of millions of dollars have been spent on the system, but one would look in vain for any significant improvement in education as a result. It is only fair to say also that the labs and centers have not been free to operate as they might have wanted. They have been controlled largely from Washington and subject to every political wind that blows there.

The R, D, and D scheme is rational from the viewpoint of government planners and those who will control and benefit from the flow of innovations, but it is not rational from anyone else's viewpoint. The division of labor is roughly that of those who "do" and those who are "done to." The planning group initiates activities, decides what problems will be addressed, and how resources will be allocated, while the consumers are assigned the difficult and thankless task of implementing the innovation.

Initiation, control, and rewards reside at the top. Make no mistake: it is a vertical, top-down system.

It is a mistake, though, simply to use the government planners as scapegoats for the scheme, just as it is inadequate to blame only individuals for the Vietnam War. I believe that the desire to gain and maintain power is a significant and persistent factor in the top-down approach to educational change. But there is a deep fault in the conceptualization of the problem itself and even in the way in which education is conceived.

## CAN AN INNOVATION BE USEFUL IN ALL CLASSROOMS?

It is true that the R, D, and D approach to problem solving has produced impressive solutions to problems—under very particular conditions. Consider the Man-on-the-Moon program of the National Aeronautics and Space Administration. This required a decade of coordinated effort of hundreds of thousands of workers and tens of billions of dollars. When the Right-to-Read program was launched, its designers drew explicit parallels between it and the moon program. But there are significant differences between the two—and not just in the magnitude of resources available, although that is significant.

The Man-on-the-Moon program put a few men at a particular place at a specific time. The act itself could be conceived as a single event in space and time. Everything in the environment was carefully controlled, from the air the men breathed to their very movements. Millions of man-years were devoted to bringing the situation under as absolute control as possible. And, given the same conditions, the act could be replicated, albeit at great cost.

Now consider teaching children to read. If we took a few children, or even a classful, and spent ten years and millions of man-hours, and concentrated on just those children, I think we could teach every child there to read. Given enough time and money we could probably surmount almost every problem. We could try out any number of things until we found something that would work.

But the real problem is not teaching those few kids isolated at a particular point in space and time. The problem is to teach tens of millions of children, each of whom comes from a different background and whose life is open to indeterminable influences over which we have no control. I would contend that there is no single device, no technique, and no set of materials that will provide a universal solution to this problem, for it is really a host of problems.

Yet the universal single answer, a solution packaged for easy transport to any situation, is what the R, D, and D approach aims at. Underlying the R, D, and D perspective is a set of ideas I have called "the doctrine of transferability." It assumes that one can produce a technique or set of materials that can be universally useful and used, that will work with everyone. Given our highly technological society, it is not hard to see the currency of this belief; but it is based on a profound misunderstanding of education. We can no more "fix" reading than we could "fix" Vietnam. And the logic is not entirely dissimilar.

The best answer to teaching reading we all already know: provide each child with a full-time tutor. Even the sons of the American upper class can be educated by this approach. It would cost at least twenty-five times what we are now spending on education. I do not think we will see that in any foreseeable future.

Now we may recognize that the R, D, and D kind of approach is productive and possible in certain areas like national defense and space exploration while at the same time seeing that many social and educational programs require a quite different approach. Centralized goals like space exploration do require central focus, sponsorship, funding, and control. In the centralized approach the government is not only the sponsor of the project but also the client. The program must respond to Washington pressures regardless of local and regional concerns.

The most important considerations in education and in most other social programs are *local determinants*. What a child has to eat for breakfast, what his mother says to him, how the teacher handles him, which particular word he does not know—these things determine whether he learns to read. The important things are in the surrounding context, and central authorities simply cannot control and respond to these innumerable factors. You must be there.

With enough resources one might create a successful solution for a particular class of kids at one point in time. But the R, D, and D approach prohibits that. Rather than create separate solutions adjusted to each local situation, the doctrine of transferability says that one can invent a uniform, highly generalizable solution which can be materialized, mass-produced, and used in most settings. The content of the innovation will be cheap and controlled by central authority. So we produce solutions, but our problems remain.

Now it seems to be that some innovations—automobiles, computers —are transferable, but not educational programs. Why are automobiles readily transferable while most educational programs are not? A program consists of a set of personal relationships built up around the teacher, the student, and the materials. It is not the materials, not the teacher, not even the relationship between the teacher and student, though that is very important.

The actual program is much more complex. It includes the child's relationship with his parents, their relationships with other parents, their relationship with the teacher, the teacher's relationship with the principal, the teacher's relationships with other teachers, and so on. If a child is in competition with his younger brother, that will affect his learning. If a parent is offended by the materials, so will that. One can transfer a schedule of learning activities from one setting to the next, but those activities will have widely varying outcomes, depending on the contextual factors.

The more of these relationships one could duplicate the more assured one would be of transfer. The teacher plus the materials would be much better than the materials themselves. In fact, transferring people from one setting to another is one of the best ways of replicating programs. The person can work with the different variables in the new setting, remembering what the old one was like. But the program is still likely to be significantly different.

It is also a truism that every child is different. What might be called the "intrusiveness of personal experience" has a key role in learning. "If one could look at a memory and see the traces to it, most content (school offerings, learnings) would be found to be personalistic—'what it means to me when I encountered it'—more personalistic than knowledge-structure related. So each collection of memories, each knowledge-structure, has personalistic trappings. Transferable education minimizes them; personalistic education features them. The latter is more natural, probably more efficient, surely more capable of highly complex accomplishments" (Robert Stake, personal communication).

A car is much easier to transfer to a new setting. Though it is a status symbol, it affects few personal relationships, advertising notwithstanding, and is affected in turn by few of them. Overall, the car makes few demands on one's relationships with others. There is a place for it in one's life, the need being defined by the surrounding social and physical system. There is nothing to take its place.

My colleague, Bob Stake, points out that being highly transferable, a car is very difficult to personalize. There is little one can do to put one's stamp on it, in comparison to a house for example. A house is much less transferable, but it still can change hands. In order for it to do so, though, it must be stripped of all previous personal traces before the new owners really feel it is theirs.

There are educational innovations that transfer. The ubiquitous blackboard is a good example, although it cannot be called a program. It can be adjusted to a million idiosyncratic uses by the teacher. It makes few demands. A blackboard filled with writing is not transferable at all, unless it has something like the multiplication tables on it. I would predict that computer-assisted instruction that the teacher can rearrange, adjust, and input new content into will be relatively transferable, while content-determined CAI will not be. As with textbooks the teacher must be able to leave out parts, teach some sections in reverse order, and generally adjust to local circumstances.

In any case, there are transferable products that are useful and can be used, but educational programs in the fullest sense must be grown rather than replicated—even when they look the same as the one next door. We have successfully realized the concept of the kindergarten. We must think of program development as a "program-garten" in which the program is built from immediately available surroundings. The personal relationships, the personalistic trappings, the traces of memory are elements from which a program is constructed, even if the germinating idea originated elsewhere. And, of course, as the program grows it must follow the contour of the land on which it lies, as well as subsist on the elements, the personal relationships, that surround it.

## NEGOTIATING A NEW PROGRAM

Are we to have no innovation then? What are we to do? I believe we can have innovation while at the same time avoiding the impractical, impersonal, and inequitable byproducts of the R, D, and D approach. I believe we could do this through *negotiated innovation*, a more effective and democratic approach.

In negotiated innovation those to be affected by the innovation would bargain with the innovators over the terms of the implementation. How far would the innovation go? What would the teachers get out of it? What would be the rewards to the innovators? What resources are available to implement? In this scheme both the costs and rewards are distributed by a deliberate bargaining process between the concerned parties.

The differential rewards that place the burden for implementation on the lowest workers while rewarding those who run the innovation are major impediments to change since those at the bottom naturally and rightfully resent this unfair situation. Negotiation over costs, rewards, and who shall bear them should alleviate this concern considerably. Resources are likely to be more widely distributed.

The innovation may even be developed by a central organization, but each local group can bargain for those elements it deems most important. Divergent goals can be mediated through negotiation. Each local situation will be somewhat different; and the innovation, shaped by negotiation, will take on different forms. The innovation might be stimulated by an outside agency; but it would grow in the local setting, necessarily reducing centralization of control.

Innovation would cease to be a cheap, mass-produced, highly transferable commodity insofar as negotiation procedures found compliance of the innovation with local circumstances. I would presume that school staffs so oriented would insist that new skills they have to acquire would be paid for by the innovating forces. I would presume that school staffs would insist on involvement in the innovation, which should lead to higher quality in its implementation.

Negotiated innovation, then, still calls for a strong government presence but one in which local authorities, particularly those who must actually do the work, have equal power in key decisions. In fact, the government should be concerned with stimulating innovation generally but not with determining the content of the innovation.

Within the school, then, the advocacy group would be the unit negotiating the innovation. Their negotiation would be more or less informal, bargaining with the school and district administration for released time and so on. They would also negotiate with the outside sponsor of the innovation, although the larger the operation the more likely the administration and others would have to be involved.

For large and long-term operations it might be advisable that the teacher organization enter the picture. While teacher organizations typically refrain from formally negotiating on the specifics of school programs, such as what innovations should be allowed into the school, they are likely to be increasingly concerned about formal policies regulating such matters.

The smart advocate would also generally do well to inform the leadership of the teacher organization and to solicit their aid on occasion. The teacher organization could be particularly helpful in dealing with powerful outside sponsors and the administration on stickier issues. Such support also would have a beneficial effect on the other teachers in the district. Teacher organizations have certainly ruined innovations before; they could also be helpful. In the years ahead their cooperation will be essential.


BOOKS TO READ

House, Ernest R. *The Politics of Educational Innovation.* Berkeley, California: McCutchan Publishing Corporation, 1974.

Only a fantastic amount of modesty prevents me from saying that this is *the* book on how innovation takes place in the schools. Seriously, the book is written mainly for specialists and researchers in the innovation field and is not as clear as it might be for other audiences. It is, however, full of ideas about school innovation and is the basis for many of the ideas in this chapter. There are highly readable sections, and the discriminating reader is advised to skip the rest.

# 11

# Office Politics—How to Play Them

## The Informal Power Structure of the School

It is possible to be the most influential person in a school without being the principal or any administrative officer. One may not want to, but it is possible to do. This is so because of what is called the "informal power structure." The *formal* power structure consists of the legal officers of the school—the school board, the superintendent, the central office staff, the principal and his assistants. In short, the administrative hierarchy.

These positions are officially charged with running the school and are well defined, often represented in the "organization chart" that specifies the relationships between these positions. A favorite game of those in the hierarchy is to play with the organization chart, speculating as to who is "over" whom. What is not so obvious is that a significant amount of power lies elsewhere—in the *informal* power structure. There is always someone or a few people from whom everyone solicits advice on important matters.

Before even the principal makes an important move, he will consult with a few powerful and influential teachers in the school as to whether it is all right. These may include the representative of the teacher organization, the head of a particular department, a senior teacher, or just someone everyone respects. These people comprise the informal power structure.

In every organization and in every school, there are particularly powerful people who determine by advice, support, or veto, all the important changes that occur. These powerful people are usually not appointed to any formal position of authority, though they may be. Rather, their influence is achieved by other means—by particular expertise, by special personality traits, or by being in the right place at the right time.

Often the influential person is the head of an informal coalition of people. The coalition may be a new program group, an advocacy group, a friendship clique, a department, a teacher organization, a group of coaches, and so on. The influentials represent more than themselves, usually because they are extremely influential in determining the attitudes of the people with whom they are associated. The other people listen to them. If the principal wants to put through a policy change of some kind, he had better talk to this influential leader first to see whether he or she will support the change. Otherwise, the principal faces the unhappy prospect of having the informal leader convince his or her group to oppose the policy at issue. In even the most authoritarian organization, policy implementation depends to a considerable degree on the voluntary cooperation of those who must do it.

The principal or other administrators solicit the informal leader's advice on the particular issue. The principal sounds him or her out. This takes the form of the principal's asking advice of the informal leader. Having the administrators solicit advice adds to the reputation of the informal leader as a powerful person and further enhances his or her influence with other teachers. The appearance of power enhances the power itself.

Actually there are several such coalitions operating within any organization—and several informal leaders. Not all the coalitions or leaders are equally important within the organization. There is a hierarchy of influence and power among the coalitions within the school just as there is a hierarchy of influence and power within each coalition itself. For example, the math department may be the most powerful coalition operating within a high school. It may get what it wants more than anyone else and be able to veto what anyone else wants—all through its informal influence.

The head of the math department may or may not be the informal leader of the group. The real informal leader may decide he or she doesn't want to mess around with the unimportant issues of distributing books. The leader would rather concentrate on the more vital issues of politicking and working on the important decisions. On the other hand, the informal leader may decide to hold the formal position of department head. It depends on whether the department heads exercise real power. And that depends on the rest of the formal and informal power structure. Other groups may actually make the important decisions, thus circumventing the heads.

The department acting as a coalition is much more likely in a university than in a public school. At the college level, identification of the faculty member with a field of study is particularly strong. Hiring, firing, and promotion are usually handled at the departmental level. The leaders who emerge to make these important decisions see the department as the natural group. National reputation gained by publishing is one of the prime bargaining resources in the university. Again, publication prestige is limited to a particular discipline. Hence, one is likely to hear talk in a university of the physics department being especially powerful or of agricultural being very strong. Within the university as a whole, the department is likely to be the natural coalition.

This is less likely in a public school. First of all the public school is much smaller and friendships cut across departmental lines. The department does not have the hiring, firing, and promotion power so that's not where the action is. Coalitions in public schools are more likely to be based on relationships with the administration, friendships among teachers, common work within the teacher organization, or common work on particular projects and committees.

There are two ways to find out who the power people in a school are. The easiest way is to ask different people and see whose names come up most often. One will find that the same names keep popping up. This method will not establish a clear hierarchy among the informal leaders but it will tell who the top group is. The other way is to take a particular decision and to trace through what happened on it and who decided what. The more important the decision the more likely the power group will emerge. The difficulty with this approach is that the decision-making processes are rarely open to outsiders. It's not easy to find out what's happening unless one is already in the power group. Overall, though, it is not too difficult to discover the power group. There will be some surprises, as for example when you discover that the little old gray-haired lady down the hall is very tough and that the principal lives in constant terror of her.

Much of the important history and politics of the school will be the story of how the various coalitions relate to each other. On particular issues some will be in agreement and form supercoalitions to win the day and on other issues the supercoalition will break up and the groups will take different sides. The principal and the other major leaders of the school will be trying to gain coalition support for, and to prevent opposition to, the things they want to do.

No matter how authoritarian, the principal's reign will not be a happy one if the major power groups and informal leaders in the school continually oppose him. He must be sensitive to their feelings or they will eventually put him under. Machiavelli himself claims that even in the most ruthless applications of brute force by a ruler the one thing the ruler can never afford is to become generally hated. He can be generally feared and hated by some but he cannot incur the enmity of all. The principal and the informal leaders of the school *must* balance, one against the other, the power and influence of the separate coalitions within the overall organization.

How does one become an informal leader? What's the basis of their power? That not an easy question to answer. On one level, the answer is apparent. The basis of their power is influence. Other people listen to them. Why? The answer to that one is not so easy. Being an informal leader is based on a person's characteristics, but these characteristics are of value only within certain situations. So the situation matters just as much as one's own qualities.

For many years researchers tried to define what personal traits make a good administrator. They were never able to do so because the good traits vary with the situation. The same thing is true of what makes a good teacher. It varies depending on the kids, the circumstances, and so on. Likewise the base of the informal leader's power varies from situation to situation.

In the chapter "Starting New Programs and Getting Promoted," I emphasized the characteristics necessary for developing a strong advocacy —drive, aggressiveness, a sensitivity to the diverse needs of others, a way to satisfy these needs, a vision and ideology, and a belief in the ability to shape one's own future. When some of these abilities are finely honed, they begin to envelop the leader in an aura of charisma that feeds back on itself and makes him or her even more powerful. Sometimes this air of super power and unreality becomes as difficult for the leader as for the followers to handle. He or she may begin to believe his or her own stuff.

While belief in one's mission is a powerful motivation, as witnessed by George Allen's conversion of the Washington Redskins, there comes a time when the air of unreality this intense belief can produce becomes so thick that it clouds the group's vision. Then it becomes dangerous and dysfunctional rather than giving them an edge. There is a difference between dedication and fanaticism, though the line is not always easy to draw.

There are other bases of personal power that are less enigmatic. One may possess some expertise that is valuable to others. One may know more mathematics or have been around longer and hence know the ropes better than anyone else. One may have special knowledge in school law or school finance that enables one to thread the maze of the state school code or to decipher the school district budget. Expertise is highly valued in our specialist society and it lends considerable authority to those who possess it. Informal leadership is often based on its recognition.

Another basis for leadership is legal power or status. The formal power structure is defined this way. The principal automatically has it. Then again, all the important decisions may be made by the assistant principal, who combines formal with informal power. Informal power may be enhanced by an important legal position, such as being the chairman of an important committee. In the legislatures a few men will control most of the action in a particular area like education—a combination of formal and informal power. The head of the teacher organization may possess considerable influence on issues far removed from the direct surveillance of his or her organization.

Of course, there are the personal qualities that one normally associates with any kind of leadership: toughness, determination, perseverance, aggressiveness, and verbal ability. One doesn't want to send someone to represent the group who will not speak out for the group's rights. On the other hand, one doesn't want a loudmouth. All in all, there are opportunities for many different kinds of informal leadership and a number of ways to get into influential positions. The one thing that is definite is that the organization, whether an elementary school or General Motors, will be run by a small group of informal coalition leaders interacting with the formal power structure.

## Building a Personal Power Base

How is it that one gets into a position of power? And what does one do? Consider the case of Brad Tyler. Over a period of thirty years Tyler built a position of immense power for himself. Perhaps not intentionally. But things just came out that way. In a large high school of almost one hundred teachers, Tyler became second in power to the principal and perhaps in some ways more powerful than the principal. Certainly he outlasted several of them.

Tyler's career is an object lesson in faculty politics. At the beginning of his teaching career more than thirty years ago, counseling was not a very widespread field. It was new in the public schools. Tyler began by getting an advanced degree in an area related to counseling. As a young man in his twenties, he was hired by the school district to begin a counseling program—whatever that was.

In the beginning Tyler was attached to the central office of the district so he could work with several different schools. This was very important because Tyler established close personal contacts with several of the members of the central office staff, especially Webber Allen, who was a very powerful assistant superintendent for many years. In fact Allen really ran the district internally when the superintendent was preoccupied with expansion of the school district, passing referendas, and school board politics—which he was for many years.

Brad Tyler always had a line "downtown" which he could call upon when he needed help with something. And he used it often. It also enhanced his influence considerably for others to know that his personal ties with the central administration were so good. The implied threat as well as the actual use of that influence were potent bargaining chips over the years.

In addition to his contacts among the central office staff, Tyler also automatically came into contact with others outside the schools. He naturally came into contact with many parents in the district as he explained the new counseling programs to them. As different schools started up a program he would provide advice and come in to talk with groups of parents and school faculty. He became well known around the district among both the parents and teachers. He also became known as a man who would give you his time.

Perhaps Tyler's outstanding personal characteristic was his extreme likability. He genuinely seemed to like doing things for other people. And he would go to great lengths to do so. He always had time for everyone, no matter who it was. Some thought that, like Will Rogers, he never met a man he didn't like. In actuality this was not true. He developed an intense dislike for some people but it did not ordinarily show.

If he really disliked someone, Tyler made it a deliberate policy to do things for them—get them coffee, take them someplace in his car, and so on. As he did things for them, he found that he came to like them more and more. By doing favors for people he had turned many cases of dislike into friendship. If he still did not like someone after this treatment, his policy was to avoid them altogether. He did not like to be around them or to make judgments about them.

This personal touch had a tremendous effect on those who met him. His solicitude caused them to like him immediately. At first one would be put off by his personal concern. Could anyone really be that concerned about everybody? It seemed phony. But after a while one began to sense that his concern for people was nearly universal and no less sincere because of that. Which is not to say that he never played favorites when he was in a position to help someone—quite the contrary.

So he built quite a good rapport with the public, which responded well to his affable manners and direct style of communicating. He didn't try to snow them with big psychological terms. He explained the program in language as homey as possible, without talking down to people. If he had any fault at all in this regard, he was too reassuring. He made it sound as if the new counseling program would have no problems at all.

Increasingly, as counseling became a big thing, he was asked to speak at regional and even national meetings of counseling professionals. He became well known and held office in a national organization. He wrote a few papers which were well received but he never became a well-known theorist or an intellectual leader of the counseling movement. Although he knew most of the big-name people over the years, his efforts were always invested primarily in his personal relationships with others. That's where he derived his satisfaction.

As counseling became well established in the district, he saw no need to maintain the central office position. He was offered several lucrative positions, including the principalship of a new high school. He received several job offers from outside the district, including several from faraway states where he had met people. Almost all were administrative. For reasons known only to himself he turned down all the offers of administrative jobs over the years. He decided to remain in the district and elected to run the counseling program in the largest high school in the district. This enabled him to maintain both his local contacts within the district and his professional contacts within counseling.

Of course, he came to the new high school with considerable local prestige. From the beginning he was the senior faculty person, even though not so elderly. He helped organize the new school, hire the faculty, and plan the building. As the school grew he was perenially elected to the Faculty Advisory Committee (These were pre-union days). Although the committee was only advisory to the principal, its advice was taken very seriously—perhaps because Tyler was always on it.

His position as head of counseling gave him plenty of unprogrammed time to attend to faculty and school business. He was appointed by the principal or elected by the faculty to all important committees. No important issue was ever decided within the school without careful consideration of his advice. Most of the new programs in all areas of the school were begun with his support in some form or other.

In the last twenty years or so of his career he turned more and more to counseling the faculty members in both professional and personal problems. Although his own background in counseling was much more in the testing and vocational guidance area rather than psychotherapy, he was increasingly drawn into trying to resolve personal problems. At any given time his office was likely to be occupied by faculty or student explaining his or her latest personal distress while Tyler listened patiently nodding his head from time to time in sympathy.

Here was a man you could turn to in need. He was understanding and also successful in his own right. To the faculty he was nonthreatening. He had no reason to hurt them in their careers. He was past the competition age. To the students he was experienced and nonjudgmental. The old gray beard—for he had indeed grown a beard in his later years—had seen it all. Even in this therapeutic role, though, he knew his limitations. He kept a handy list of professional counselors and psychotherapists ready for reference.

He was also extremely confidential about the information he received. Although he had a few friends in whom he would occasionally confide, most of the time he kept his knowledge of drugs and divorce to himself. Keeping such information secret in a faculty is extremely difficult. The gossip network is extremely tight knit. One slip and it's all over.

Of course the administration consulted him heavily too. The balance between keeping knowledge about the faculty confidential and helping the administration solve its problems was a delicate one and he must have gone beyond the boundary more than once. He had a strong, perhaps overzealous desire to help the administration. Yet even the most ardent faculty rebels, those who were simply antiadministration in principle, came to confide in him. It would have been impossible for them not to know he was a confidant of the administration. Perhaps they believed in his integrity too much to care.

The school administration's attitude toward him was mostly favorable but often ambivalent. He could do two things with facility. He could go over their heads and talk to the administrators at the central office, to whom he was a faithful and highly credible source of information and opinions. And he could talk directly to the faculty members in the school, most of whom he knew fairly well. This made him extremely powerful in the eyes of the school administration. He could muster opinion both above and below them on a given issue. That didn't leave much. They *had* to talk to him.

The school administrators described him as being "too powerful"— not when he was around of course. They did not like having such a counterfoil to their own power. However when an issue arose on which they needed help in influencing faculty opinion, they wasted no time in soliciting his help. Usually he gave it to them. At the same time, he was a zealous defender of the prerogatives of the faculty.

His usual mode of behavior was to do personal and professional favors for other people. He helped faculty get jobs for themselves and for their spouses, lent them his car, helped them find houses, helped them with reports, entertained their families, and most anything one can think of. He was inevitably at every faculty social function, whatever it was. He performed these favors with no apparent expectation of return. Except of course one had to feel gratitude and friendship.

For the most part he never asked much for himself. He was one of the most highly paid faculty members partly because of his many years on the staff and partly because in his special position he could be paid more than a regular faculty member. The administration no doubt considered this high salary a good investment. He was not the kind to ask for more. Actually he could have made more money by doing a number of other things. He could have gone into administration or private consulting work. In the early days of counseling some of his friends had made a good deal of money by setting up private operations to sell tests and other counseling materials outside their school jobs for private profit. Tyler always disdained such operations.

Even in his later years he always put in more hours than perhaps anyone else on the faculty, arriving at his office early in the morning before school started and staying late. Working on the weekend was common. This also contributed to his reputation within the school. In the last years of his career he cut back a bit on the hours and led a more normal work week.

Although he didn't ask for much for himself, when he did he usually got it. He built a five-person counseling operation within the school. When new faculty were to be added to the school, it was not always the administration's decision to add counselors rather than other personnel. They often had no choice. Once, after dozens of requests for teachers had come in from other department heads, Tyler asked for an addition to his staff. As one of the assistant principals said, "As soon as Tyler asked, I knew it was all over. He started pulling in his IOUs and it was like an avalanche on our heads. There was no way around it." That year the high school asked for a new counseling position as top priority hiring. And got it.

Besides helping other people, Tyler used his power to build a top-rate counseling division. Like any good advocate, he acquired resources

for his people. The counseling operation received national recognition—
according to some teachers because the counselors had so much time to
develop new programs and write articles about them. The superior resources and privileges of the counseling group remained something of a
sore point over the years among the faculty. But they were never seriously
challenged. Tyler was too influential and too many people owed too much
to him.

Tyler's performance was not entirely benign however. He could on
occasion be as rough as the situation demanded. It was partly an intuition
of this inner core of steel that kept many potential enemies at bay. It was
a memorable mistake to think that Tyler was such a nice guy and that one
could simply walk over him to get what one wanted. Immediate gratification was not a desirable trait in Tyler's view. One should give one's time.
Don't reach for too much too fast. On one occasion one of the new
assistant principals made a power play trying to outfox Tyler on a hiring
issue. Tyler said, "One of these days he's going to pull that again and I'm
going to shit all over him." And he did. And he did.

Within a committee, contrary to his outward beneficent appearance,
Tyler could be exceedingly tough. If he thought a teacher was not suited
for tenure then he would fight against him or her. This was fairly rare,
however, since he thought most people would come around eventually.
His major weakness was his paternalism. He could not resist anyone who
asked him for help. He would eventually become that person's supporter.
If he identified him or her as one of his own, he would fight long and hard
for the person. Many a teacher would not have been granted tenure without
Tyler's assistance. He fit the role of the godfather well.

Tyler's longest and hardest fights were with another major faction
within the school. The other faction was centered around the vocational
education department and was led by another long-timer at the school
named Michael Calloway. The two factions and the two men differed
considerably in their approaches to education and the direction the school
should be moving. And, of course, at one level it was also simply a fight
for political supremacy. Who would control the resources? Over the years
the conflict had aroused a personal bitterness between Tyler and Calloway.
One of Calloway's favorite remarks about Tyler was, "I'm certainly glad
Tyler has grown a beard. Now I don't have to call him a barefaced liar."

Over the years Tyler's faction had won most of the battles but the
conflict continued and became more embittered. Calloway's faction thought
the school should attend more fully to vocational training, and he was able
to muster a group of several people, mostly in that department, who
agreed with him. Tyler's group was more inclined to the straight academic
subjects. Calloway and his group thought that over the years the vocational programs had been shafted in terms of getting their share of
resources and emphasis.

The last pitched battle had come in choosing the current principal,
the third in the thirty years of Tyler's career there. Tyler had been on the

faculty advisory committee presenting possible candidates to the superintendent. In fact, the man who was eventually chosen was Tyler's choice. It did not hurt either that the man was a favorite of the assistant superintendent. Calloway's faction had been in favor of a man they thought more favorable to their position. They charged duplicity in the selection process.

After the new principal was appointed, Calloway carried on a kind of guerrilla warfare for a while—mainly by getting employers outside the school to charge that the school was not paying enough attention to vocational training. After a few flaps on this, things quieted down. Calloway, who had had some emotional problems over the years, became more seriously ill and finally retired. Needless to say, he did not go to Tyler for counseling. Finally the thirty-year war was over.

Tyler has almost reached retirement age himself. He is not anxious to retire because his whole life has been wrapped up in his work. It is easier to imagine the principal leaving the school. The changes would be fewer. Tyler's departure will leave an enormous power vacuum. Perhaps the power base he has built will be passed onto someone else, although that is difficult to imagine. In a sense, building such a power base has been the work of a lifetime.

# A Conversation with Machiavelli on Power Politics

(*A man in a business suit sits in a chair ready to interview Machiavelli. The latter is resplendent in his colorful robes, the dress of medieval Florence. A gold medallion inlaid with jewels, the symbol of power, adorns his neck.*)

INTERVIEWER   Through the miracle of modern technology, we have with us today Nicolo Machiavelli, infamous author of *The Prince,* the classic of power politics.

MACHIAVELLI   I wish you wouldn't say "infamous." Notorious perhaps. I prefer "famous." Infamous sounds like I committed a crime.

I   Isn't it true that your book is regarded by many as a shocking example of politics at its most ruthless.

M   I didn't make it all up. The popularity of the book speaks for itself.

I   Fair enough. But didn't you previously write the *Discourses* lauding republican governments, then wrote *The Prince* advising the Medici how to stay in power?

M   Times change.

I   Let's get down to business, Mr. Machiavelli.

M   Suits me.

I   Do you think your advice on power politics applies to the public schools?

M   Sure. Some of it. They're people, aren't they?

I   I don't see how advice on kingdoms and the use of mercenary troops and such has much relevance to the schools.

M   Look. Let's take the use of mercenaries. I advised against that because they are unreliable. People who are helping you because you pay them or only because they get a reward are not very reliable. They may turn on you when someone else offers them a bigger reward. Or falter when the going gets rough. Ultimately you have to rely most on those who believe in you and who believe in what you're doing. See what I mean?

I   But you could apply that kind of analysis to any group of people!

M   Right. Now I think you're getting it.

I   So you're comparing any kind of leader to the "Prince."

M   Right. The analogy is not too good but it sells books. The sales have been dropping off over the last few centuries. Ever since the democracies came along.

I   It's good to know these principles apply only in nondemocratic settings.

M   Yes. I took care of the republics in my *Discourses*. Same publishers.

I   I'm glad we cleared that up. What kind of person should the leader be?

M   For one thing he should not be too generous nor too parsimonious. If he's too generous, he'll use up all his resources too fast. He's pretty dependent on those. His people won't like it if they have inadequate resources. It comes out of their own hides. Also he'll have to go back for another handout from wherever he gets his money. On the other hand, he has to hand out enough to keep his people happy. Don't be too stingy.

I   Isn't that a little mealy-mouthed? "Be neither generous nor stingy."

M   Okay, if you have to choose, be parsimonious. It looks better to everybody. With one exception—unless you're spending someone else's money.

I   Like a government grant?

M   Right. Then you want to be generous with your people. Don't be too tight in the fiscal control. But with your own resources, be careful.

I   Any other traits that are necessary?

M   Yeah. Don't be too easy or too tough.

I   Here we go again.

M   Okay. Let me put it this way, it's better to be *both* loved and feared than one or the other. But if you have to choose, go for being feared.

I   Why is that?

M   It lasts longer. If people really like you, they still may do something to hurt you for their own interest. But if they are a little afraid of you, they are much less likely to.

I   Isn't that a matter of opinion?

M   That's my opinion. Substitute "being respected" for "being feared" if you like. As I say though, it's better to be both.

I   Any other traits?

M   Yes. I've left the most important one out. The major thing in surviving as a leader is to avoid being hated and despised.

I   Why would you be hated or despised?

M   Don't kid yourself. Look at people in leadership positions. Others are envious of you. Or maybe they don't like how you behave. If you get people hating you, you're in big trouble. The biggest trouble. It's probably just a matter of time until someone brings you down. You have a lot of enemies and little support.

I   Well, how can you avoid it?

M   Some of it you can't. If you're going to put yourself up front. But a lot of it is dependent on your own behavior.

I   Like what?

M   Well, like being too greedy. Don't be so damn rapacious. Don't try to steal everything just because you're the leader—all the glory, all the honor, all the money, all the women.

I   All the women? This isn't ancient warfare!

M   Where have you been the last few centuries, son? Lots of women really turn on to men with power. *Voluntarily.* But the wise leader has to have the resolve not to take more than his share. Otherwise the other guys are going to hate his guts. It's a good way to undermine your base of support. One of the best. Same thing with other things.

I   I don't think this interview is going to pass the women's liberation front. Let's turn it around. Don't you think men are attracted to women with power?

M   I never thought of that. I guess the same rule would apply. That makes a lot of sense. In fact, I remember a story about the Queen of Naverone . . .

I   Never mind. I think the discussion is a little sticky as it is. Where are we? Not being hated . . .

M   If you're not hated by a lot of people, you only have to worry about those few with ambition, a relatively simple task. Most men will really go along with you if you don't cheat them of their honor or substance.

I   Other ways of incurring hatred?

M   Being too greedy is the main thing. Now there are also a lot of ways you can be despised.

I   How?

M   Well, anyone who is wishy-washy, variable from day to day, inconsistent over the long run, is going to be despised eventually by those around him. People expect their leaders to be resolute, determined, courageous—even if wrong. Also not too effeminate.

I   Oh, oh. Here we go again.

M   Who wants to be represented by someone with a limp wrist? Strength, manliness is consistent with our image of leadership. The same is true of a man or a woman leader.

I   Don't you think a little second-guessing is sometimes good?

M   Sure, but not too much in public. Weakens the image.

I   Anything else?

M   The whole point is that being hated or despised weakens your internal solidarity and solidifies your enemies. Your strength depends on your internal unity. Don't blow it unnecessarily. It's your greatest resource.

I   That brings us to one of the most controversial of your principles, Mr. Machiavelli. You say that it is all right to break your word if it is in your interest?

M   Ahh, yes. That has caused me some trouble.

I   Isn't that a little raw? Won't people object to that kind of unprincipled approach?

M   Bourgeois morality.

I   Aren't you borrowing someone else's terms here a few centuries in advance?

M   I can't help it if people steal my stuff.

I   Just on a practical level, won't not keeping your word cause you to be despised and hated and destroy your internal unity just as you suggest?

M   I'll have to think about that. You may have a point.

I   Any other advice for leaders of political factions?

M   Yes. If they're interested in building a big reputation, the way to do it is to undertake great enterprises. Take over another kingdom or something. Build a great building.

I   These are teachers you're talking to.

M   Okay. Take over the school board. Take over the math department. Start a new program if you're ecclesiastically minded.

I   Aren't those dangerous enterprises?

M   Yes, but esteem is based on grand undertakings.

I   But isn't failure more likely in grand undertakings?

M   If the truth were known, reputations are more likely to be built on grand failures than on modest successes. Be bold. Declare yourself openly for or against something. Neutrality is generally not good. It just means you aren't to be counted.

I   We get the message. Anything else?

M   The wise leader chooses wise advisers. He is known by the advisers he chooses and can only be as good as they are. He doesn't have to be a top intellect himself to be a good leader. He just has to be able to recognize high-quality thinking when he sees it.

I   Sometimes I think I'm talking to Benjamin Franklin.

M   Who's that?

I   Never mind. We're on advice giving.

M   Yes. The other thing is to barricade oneself against flattery. People in power draw flatterers, and it's tempting to believe what they say. One is likely to get bad advice and a distorted sense of reality. Very dangerous.

I   We call that "surrounding oneself with 'yes' men." How can you avoid it?

M   Trust only a few people to tell you everything and make sure they tell you the whole truth. Don't listen to everyone or people will not respect you. They'll say that all that matters is who talked to you last.

I   Not taking advice from everyone—isn't that a little undemocratic?

M   We aren't talking about democratic politics, remember.

I   What about taking over an organization? Do you have any advice on that?

M   Well, if you take over an organization, it's best to do it by winning the confidence of the mass of the people in it. That's better than taking over only because the elite of the organization want you to.

I   Why?

M   If the elite of the organization invite you in—any organization is run by a small elite of people—they will feel you are beholden to them. Later if your policies don't suit them, they may want to get rid of you. There's always someone in the elite who is ambitious and may want to run things himself. Now, take Alexander's conquest of Persia . . .

I   Yes, yes. What should you do?

M   You must gain the confidence and support of the mass of people in the organization, even if invited in by the elite. In order to survive real adversity, you must have the support of the people.

I   How can you do that?

M   That's not so hard as it sounds. Most people simply want not to be oppressed. If you act as their protector, you can win their confidence. They are basically honest and undemanding.

I   Those are nicely democratic sentiments.

M   Just a truth necessary for survival, my friend. No more.

I   Anything else?

M   Yes. If you come into an organization and must purge people from leadership positions, it's best to do it all at once rather than piecemeal.

I   Why?

M   Cruelty is diminished by the quickness with which it's performed. If you string out your harsh actions over time, they will seem much worse than when perpetrated together. In a purge people will begin to wonder, "Who's next?" That's a good way of building

resistance to yourself and eroding your support. If you get it over
with all at once, people will be shocked by your precipitous
action but say, "It's over," and feel secure.

I  Aren't some of these things determined by chance events or luck over
which you have no control? And may backfire on you?

M  Yes. I admit that's true. You have to be flexible and go whichever
way the wind blows. When times are cautious, you have to be
cautious. And so on. You have to adjust. Go with the times.
Most people can't manage this. They get stuck in one style
and can't get out of it when times change.

I  Aren't you being a little wishy-washy again?

M  No, I don't think so. There are some things outside one's hands.
But one must believe in his ability to affect his destiny, even in
the face of fortune. Overall, if one must choose a style, it's
better to be aggressive than cautious. To seize fortune by the
throat. But, as I say, it is better to be flexible than either of these.

I  Well, thank you, Mr. Machiavelli. I'm afraid we've run out of time.
Thank you for an interesting and provocative discussion on politics.
Naturally we do not necessarily endorse your views on all those
matters. Your opinion is your own.

M  Me, either. These aren't my opinions exactly. It's just science.
I found all this out from the scientific method. It's not my
responsibility. It belongs to science.

I  Thank you.


## Vulnerabilities of Administrators

In dealing with bosses and colleagues, what characteristics should one be
aware of? The superintendent is first. He is characterized by his career
ambition, his small-town background and respectability, his dependence
on the school board, and the fact that he has little direct control over
teachers in the classroom. His influence over teachers is limited to his
powers of persuasion and the example he sets. This is a severe limitation
on his power.

When a new superintendent takes over a district, he is dependent on
the board for his job but he is also unsure of the loyalty of all the people
around him. If he is interested in building a career in the district, assuring
him of one's loyalty is a good way of approaching him. In spite of his
limited authority, he is the most powerful person in the district. The new
superintendent needs loyal followers in the beginning. Helping him here
may have good payoff.

The career-bound superintendent is always looking down the road
towards his next job. He also needs competent people to help him polish
his reputation. People who get things started and can make visible new

programs and so on are valuable to him. This reputation is the basis on which he will eventually seek advancement.

The place-bound superintendent who comes into the job from within the school district or the superintendent who is already in power are somewhat more difficult to approach as individuals. The superintendents are already committed to power blocs within the school district so one must contend with the whole entourage rather than just the superintendent.

In most districts the superintendent is from a small-town background so certain obvious violations of sexual or social mores are likely to alienate him. As in small towns, it is not so much the acts themselves as their public exposure that the superintendent finds offensive. His natural sense of propriety is strongly reinforced by his dependence on the inevitable conservatism of the school board. While their senses of propriety and respectability may be somewhat hypocritical, both superintendents and school boards often act upon these feelings. The ambitious teacher is forewarned.

Next in power to the superintendent is the central-office staff. Their primary power rests on their ability to control access to the superintendent and the school board and on their control of discretionary funds. No ideas can receive official district support or approval or even consideration without their help. They are necessary advocates for activities within the administrative decision process. They can block most initiatives of which they disapprove. In addition, they control discretionary funds, like travel money. The funds are essential to building an advocacy group and maintaining progressive action.

The vulnerabilities of the central office staff are that they are under the direct surveillance of the superintendent, who is around them on a daily basis, and are more subject to both his wrath and rewards. Partly because of their direct status and power, they find it necessary to appear to be in control of events even when they are not.

If one has strong personal ties to the superintendent, most of one's central-office problems are solved, for the staff is not going to buck a friend of the superintendent. That is the surest way of securing their cooperation. Ordinarily, however, this is not the case and one must deal with them. Usually this means having one particular supporter, advocate, and protector within the staff. One can search around until one finds the right central-office staffer to cultivate.

As a general strategy, it is important to let the central staffer present things publicly as if he were in control of everything, even though this is probably not the case. This appearance of control is how the staffer justifies his position to himself and to others. Upstaging him is not a good idea if one wishes to maintain his support. The staffer works in his own behalf, of course, but he will also work for your benefit.

It is possible to "end-run" a central-office staffer but it will have long-range consequences for one's relationship with him. In a small district, planting bad words about him in the superintendent's ear is effective, but may also backfire. It is better to seek out another staffer more sympathetic to one's ideas. Compliments paid to the staffer through the superintendent's or supervisor's ear are bound to get back to the staffer and strengthen both his and his supervisor's allegiance. The positive strategy, if possible to implement, is the superior one.

The principal is the administrator closest to the teacher. By role he is a mediator and compromiser. He is vulnerable to pressures from outside groups and particularly sensitive about bad gossip getting back to the central office. No news is good news as far as the principal is concerned. He strives to keep things quiet. As a continuing strategy the principal tries to appease all groups. An effective tactic is to tell one group one thing and other something else.

At the same time the principal is very possessive about his school—students, teachers, building, and all. He likes to think they are one big, happy family. Lack of trouble is a sign that things are going well. Lack of attendance by teachers at faculty meetings is a disturbing indicator. In running the daily business of the school, the principal is completely absorbed in routine tasks. In spite of proclamations and admonitions, he doesn't have the time to be an instructional leader—and, perhaps in most cases, neither the inclination nor ability. His real focus is on crisis management, waiting for and taking care of whatever crises arise. Those events structure his work life.

By background and training, the principal is likely to be long-suffering and self-disciplined. He has managed his own personality and impulses in order to attain his important position and he expects others to display the same kind of control. He is often impatient with those who do not. Often coming from a nonprofessional background, he is highly conscious of his own role and status. The principal is a person very much determined by the occupational role.

The thrust of all this is that most principals are very conservative and conventional in their behavior and demeanor. They are likely to look upon new things with suspicion, yet because of their control over vital dimensions of the school like scheduling, physical space, teacher evaluation and parent contact, their cooperation is essential for any substantial undertaking.

In starting a new enterprise, it is best to assure principals that there will be no disruption or trouble resulting from it. The principal is most likely to believe this assurance from someone with whom he has had no trouble before. For most principals an appeal to personal ambition is less effective. Their career aspirations are tied up in keeping things quiet. One of the principal's great vulnerabilities is what people say about him and his school.

## Justice in the Wielding of Power

Since so much attention was paid to Machiavelli's ideas, perhaps it is appropriate to give the moral philosophers a few words about power and justice. It seems only proper to be just in the application of power when one has acquired it. This is true whether one is a leader of a group or a teacher in a class. In fact, the success one has in maintaining oneself in power is partially dependent on how just or how fair others see one as being.

The formal definition of justice requires giving the same treatment to persons or situations of the same kind. Students complaining that a teacher has favorites are essentially objecting to some students receiving special benefits from the teacher. These students are seen as undeserving of these special benefits or at least no more deserving than those who do not get them. So in the formal sense, giving the same treatment to persons of the same kind requires that persons of the "same kind" be *defined* that way. Whether the persons and situations are identical is very much a matter of social definition.

Actually, of course, persons and situations are never really identical. They always differ in innumerable ways. The application of formal justice requires that they do not differ in an essential way. For example, a teacher may grant a student certain privileges because the student "deserves" them. The idea of *merit* comes into play. People are treated unequally because some deserve to be treated better (or worse). Again, the action will be considered fair or just if the situations are commonly defined and accepted.

Consistency of action, then, is extremely important in justice. One cannot change the rules and treatment of people arbitrarily day by day. That is seen as injustice. Consistency of action is often interpreted by examples of precedence and tradition—by what has normally gone before, by what has been the case in the past. The law system is particularly dependent on such reasoning. Whether a person and situation deserves a certain treatment depends on whether the current situation can be defined as equivalent to a situation that has occurred in the past—to a past case.

In an aristocracy it is assumed that the aristocrats will have more rights than the peasants. That is seen as being fair and just. However, if an aristocrat violates the accepted set of rights and obligations, both aristocrats and peasants see that as being unjust. From a democratic viewpoint the social definition of aristocrats and peasants being politically different from one another makes no sense at all. The entire aristocratic social structure seems unjust. If the peasants come to believe this, the ballgame is over for the aristocrats. The social structure depends on the peasants' accepting it as basically fair.

Moral rules like "Do unto others as you would have them do unto you" are based on the idea that since we are both persons, we should treat each other the same way. Someone who has more prestige is not to be treated better than someone who has less. Humanistic ethics tend to be based on there being no privileged persons outside of the bounds of behavior required for all people.

Yet people do differ and, whatever the theory, it is not always possible or desirable to treat them the same way. In class different children may need strikingly different things. One child needs more attention, another more help. Is it fair to spend more time with one than with another? The implicit commonly accepted belief seems to be to treat children differently insofar as their "needs" differ. Yet what are needs and how does one determine them?

In leading a group of adults the problem is also difficult. We have said that effective leadership often consists of treating people differently. Yet what about justice? One approach is to define what is meritorious to a group and to reward that behavior. In a sense utilitarian ethics do this. On a social basis the utilitarians propose that there is a total net satisfaction that can be defined by adding up all the wants and desires of individual members of the society. Any action that maximizes the net satisfaction by satisfying the most wants and desires is the proper action.

Much Western moral reasoning is based on this idea of maximizing the net utility. But there are some problems with it. For one thing, it often sacrifices the welfare of the few and of minorities for that of the many. For example, if a new expressway is to run through and destroy an old section of town, the utilitarian would merely shrug his shoulders and say, "That's progress." The welfare of the people in the neighborhood would be sacrificed to the good of the total society.

Much of our economics is based on this form of reasoning. For example, the traditional way of decreasing the inflation rate is to deliberately make money hard to get, which in turn stops business expansion and results in millions of workers being laid off. The workers laid off are always those at the bottom of the social ladder. The ones who make the policy never get laid off. So assuming the inflation rate does come down, everyone benefits from the policy, but those at the bottom of the economic system are the ones who pay for it heavily. Everyone is not treated the same, but rather treated on the basis of what will maximize total satisfaction.

Likewise, in leading a group one can sacrifice the interests of individual members of the group to the interest of the group as a whole. But there seems to be something that intuitively seems unfair and even ruthless in such leadership. Partly it violates the idea of all persons being treated equally, though of course that is a matter of defintion.

A moral philosopher named John Rawls has recently proposed a new theory of justice which has received much acclaim (Rawls, 1971). He has proposed that it is all right to treat people unequally under certain conditions. First of all, everyone is entitled to basic liberties similar to those in the Bill of Rights. Those cannot be sacrificed even if the person wants to. Secondly, some social and economic inequalities are allowable under only one condition: that they benefit the *least* advantaged people. Otherwise, everyone is to receive equal treatment. So Rawls has substituted "benefit to the least advantaged" for "benefit to the whole."

For example, Rawls would disapprove of a common policy that sacrificed the interests of the least advantaged so that everyone else might profit. On the other hand, he would approve of a policy that allowed doctors more pay if it attracted them into training. Presumably this policy would benefit the least advantaged. If it benefits the more advantaged in addition, that would be all right. The Rawlsian theory of justice permits social and economic inequalities, but at the same time is strongly egalitarian in that the welfare of the least advantaged people is paramount once basic liberties have been attained for everyone.

Leadership of a class, an advocacy group, or a teachers' union is not quite identical to setting social policy and yet the issues are very similar. How does the group leader allocate costs and rewards so that it seems fair to everyone? How does one balance off the welfare of the active members of the group versus that of those who are inactive and perhaps less fortunate in ability? How does one handle people of obviously differing abilities?

The answers are not easy. For example, in our meritocratic society it is commonly accepted that someone with more ability is entitled to more social and economic rewards. Someone like Rawls would challenge that idea. Why, he would say, should someone of more ability be entitled to more? Inheritance of intelligence or athletic ability is in large part a roll of the genetic dice and no more the fault of the person than is the color of his hair. Because people differ in ability doesn't mean that rewards should be allocated in proportion to accident of birth. People may deliberately choose to share their fortunes and misfortunes with one another through social arrangements.

There is another important factor Rawls does not consider. People feel an action is much more fair when they have a hand in it. Participation in the decision is particularly important in the American ideology, and Americans become politically alienated when they feel their ideas have no influence in the operation of an organization. This is true even when decisions are made in their interest. Needless to say, organizations cannot stop to take a vote on every issue. They would become bogged down in procedural matters. Indeed, in most organizations the members will not even show up to vote unless the issue is a particularly hot one. So there has to be a balance between effectively running the organization and giving people a chance to have their say at it.

There is also the "iron law of oligarchy." In any organization, even in democratic ones, there is a strong tendency for the small group running the organization gradually to start running it more for their own interests. Since most of the work and responsibility falls on them, they gradually come to see this as being only "fair." Naturally the membership, even though reluctant to do the work, does not see it the same way. This tendency is strong in any organization—whether a country, a school district, or a union—and the leadership must constantly be on guard against it.

Where does all this leave us? In the practical world of action no leader can afford to operate exclusively on one theory to the exclusion of all the others. By their nature pure theories are not good descriptions of reality.

What the leader must do is weigh together and balance the various considerations of justice as the situation demands. Equal treatment, merit, the welfare of the total group, the welfare of the least advantaged, participation in decision making, consistency of action, keeping privileged actions to a minimum—all these and other ideas of justice and fairness deserve consideration at different times. Sometimes one will dominate, sometimes another.

Deciding which criterion of justice is most suitable at a given time is necessarily an intuitive judgment of the leader. The leader may talk to his chief aides and to the membership but there is no escaping leadership decisions which set the tone for the rest of the group. A book may point out the relevant factors but it cannot resolve them in a particular setting with a particular group of people. One thing is for certain: there are few tasks more important for the health of the group than setting the standards for justice and fairness.

# part four

# The Profession

# 12

## *Getting a Job*

We all know that teaching positions are very scarce these days, but competing for a teaching job in any kind of market can be painstakingly difficult. Whether you are just graduating and looking for your first job or have been teaching for a while, obtaining a position for which you feel qualified requires work and perseverance. It helps to have patience as well.

Searching out and applying for teaching positions is like a job in and of itself. It requires hours of writing and rewriting letters to obtain application forms, completing those forms, and various follow-up activities to help insure that you will be one of the few to get called for an interview. And, too, preparing for that all-important interview is an emotionally draining and sometimes unconsciously ignored task not to be taken lightly.

But how do you improve your chances for getting the job, anyway? It has been said many times (and there is a ring of truth to it) that it's who you know that counts, not what you know. Now, while it is usually true that knowing someone inside the school system can help, most of us do not possess this special advantage and must achieve our goal in other ways. It is also generally the case that being in the right place at the right time can produce wonders for those seeking employment. An example that comes to mind is the teacher who happened by the administration building to pick up an application and was informed that a teacher had just resigned unexpectedly. Also, I know of a case recently where a graduating senior dropped by the local Dairy Queen for a snack (perhaps to soothe her job-hunting frustrations) and was informed through casual conversation that a position had opened up that very morning.

Well, knowing someone, being in the right place, or even managing to make face-to-face contact with a hiring officer are fortuitous examples of how some get the jobs they are looking for—but most of us have to settle for a much more rigorous approach. One should not ignore any chance to take advantage of the above possibilities, but while waiting for that payload to arrive, you can increase your chances by following some helpful job-getting procedures.

Perhaps the first important rule of thumb in setting out to find the teaching position you want is to be very serious about getting yourself organized and preparing yourself for what could be a very long ordeal. This is not intended as some kind of ethical high-road-to-success axiom. Instead, it boils down to getting your act together for a concentrated effort—one that could be fraught with disappointments and endless hours of completing forms of all sizes, shapes, and formats. But get yourself ready to expect these frustrations as they come and you'll be much more able to handle them when they do.

All right! Let's get started on this treacherous trip through job-hunting land.

### What To Do First

Make certain that your credentials at the college placement office are up to date. This may seem obvious, but there are a few important aspects you may not have thought of. For example, if you have been teaching for a while, do you have any recent written recommendations included in your file? A work record of your most recent teaching experience is very important to school hiring officers. Consider this quote from a college placement guide:

> The best prediction of success is previous successful experience. School personnel, in evaluating candidates for employment . . . are going to look at the type of previous student teaching or regular teaching experience, in addition to their overall educational background. (Hill, 1975, p. 27)

One solution to getting this important information is, of course, to ask your principal and/or department head to write a recommendation to include the specific duties you have performed. An interesting additional idea is to request a trusted colleague to observe your teaching a few times and then put together a written explanation of how you operate with the students. (This is an alternative not recommended for the faint of heart.)

Finally, in checking to ensure that everything is accounted for and up to date in your credentials, see if it is possible for you to update your teaching experience including references to more recent recommendations. This could also include any other work you have done with people and especially with children, education-related or not. You see, school personnel tend to hire teachers who can document experience or demonstrate in some other way that they not only like to work with people, but are fairly good at it. So—emphasize this kind of information when and where you can.

**Pregraduate Experience.**    While important to all job-seeking teachers, this should be especially helpful to those who are still preparing for the teaching field. Because of the importance of reporting past experience in your credential file, any undergraduate experiences working directly with people and especially with children are important to include for the hiring agent to see. Undergraduates should take every advantage of any summer work with kids and certainly should explore any programs involving field experience that might be offered at their institution.

Some colleges provide laboratory credit or various forms of internships where undergraduates can get early experience in working directly with students in a classroom setting. Such programs, like the Teacher Centers Program at Northeastern Illinois University in Chicago, provide opportunity for students to earn credit hours and/or stipends while they work directly with school children. In the case of Northeastern, students start as early as their sophomore year in college and spend between five and twenty hours a week working in the intern role.

Be certain that you explore any such programs available at your institution, and, above all, report these experiences in your credential file. Hiring agents in these financially lean times find it very helpful in their budgeting to hire teachers with one or two years' experience at a first-year salary.

**A Final Note on Credentials.**    Dealing with college placement offices is not always a pleasant experience, as I am sure many of you know. Despite recent legislation (the Buckley Amendment), making certain persons' credentials available to them for examination, placement people do not always encourage such inspections. Indeed, in some cases they have been known to employ rules of their own or in other ways make it very difficult to get at those records. But remember, whatever is contained in your credentials will be used in some way to decide whether or not you are a hirable candidate. Thus you should persevere in making every effort to get a look at your records so that you are able to remove anything that you consider incorrect, unfair, or damaging.

Most placement offices will, with enough prodding, let you perform this necessary surgical work on your records. However, if they do not— whether or not you enjoy the heat of battle—you must persist until they comply. One approach to gaining an advantage in this kind of situation is to know your rights, which consists in part of knowing the letter of the law in the General Education Provisions Act, better known as the Buckley Amendment. Among other provisions, this piece of legislation assures:

> . . . parents and students aged 18 or enrolled in college . . . access to the students' education records—the files, documents, and materials, including those of a photographic nature, such as those

in microfilm, that contain information directly related to the students . . . [and it] also gives parents or eligible students the right to challenge any portion of the educational record that they consider "inaccurate, misleading, or otherwise inappropriate." (Davis, 1975, p. 11)

. . . Parents [or students] not only have the right to know, review, and challenge any part of the data, they also may add information to the files of a corrective or clarifying nature. . . . (p. 13)

While the law lends itself to enough interpretation by placement personnel that they could devise ways of putting you off, knowing the law and demanding your rights should get you the necessary access to your credentials. Also, although the Buckley Amendment does not directly apply to persons other than students and parents, institutions have moved toward making such records more accessible to all. The important factor here is to know your rights in this situation by investigating all existing state and federal laws if a placement office persists in denying you access.

One way or another, get a look at those credentials. Even small errors in tabulation or judgment could cost you a necessary advantage in the job market. An incorrectly recorded grade in student teaching or a recommendation that emphasizes your weaknesses while glossing over your strengths might very well be that extra minus that could knock you out of the running. So—examine those credentials, if for no other reason than to put your mind at ease. The added advantage, of course, is that you know what school hiring personnel are responding to when they are considering you for a position.

If all else fails, one sneaky suggestion I have is to find a friend, a very good friend who is willing to request your credentials as though you were seeking a position in his or her organization. Examine the credentials and inform the placement office of the changes that you want made. While this may appear to be an unethical approach, it seems no more unethical than school personnel having personal information about you that you know nothing about. And after all, survival in the job market is the essential key to the ethics question anyway. If you're competent at what you do, it would be unjust for you to be refused a position because of something misrepresenting you in your files.

Perhaps the most important reason for examining your placement credentials is that you are legally allowed to request removal of recommendations or other material that you consider unacceptable. Thus, when you examine your credentials, it will be important for you to know what to look for, what you may want to rearrange or delete. First, the written recommendations are fairly important from the standpoint that they really can't appear negative in your behalf. If you find one that tends to emphasize your weak points while underplaying your good ones, throw it out. The exception to this rule is when the recommendation is the only one of its kind (e.g., cooperating teacher in student teaching). These have to stay; it just looks fishy if something as vital as that is missing. Also, think of the recommendation in terms of its importance to the school hiring agent. Principals and other administrators consider cooperating teacher recommendations of some importance, but really zero in on recommendations from their own kind. Specifically, principals will closely scrutinize recommendations from other principals or department heads. University supervisor recommendations hold very little weight with local school people, and college instructor recommendations hardly count at all. School personnel can see by your grades how you fared in courses, but what they want to know is: can you teach? And they judge this by looking at what other public school people have written about your practical qualities on the job. These people also want to know how you get along with others in school settings as well as any other work situations.

In his survey work at Northwestern University, Frank S. Endicott (1975) has discovered the following priority listing of hiring factors according to how school district superintendents rate their importance:*

1. Personality. Ability to relate and get along with others and ". . . able to relate in an understanding and sympathetic way to students."
2. Professional education courses. These were especially important for elementary superintendents whose teachers must be competent in many areas.
3. Teaching field. These are represented by the liberal arts courses or specializations in content areas.
4. Grade point average. This is in fourth place, but this ". . . does not mean that superintendents consider grades to be unimportant."
5. Extracurricular activities. While not as important, these represent a different side to the candidate, again related to dealing with people.
6. Other liberal arts courses. Perhaps rated last because they don't seem to relate directly to the practical aspects of classroom teaching.

## What Next

Once your credentials are in order and you are specifically aware of what they contain, the next logical step is to decide where it is generally that you want to teach. Here it is paramount that you identify the extent to which you are willing to be flexible. Those teachers, old and new, who really want a position because they really want to teach find themselves a much more marketable commodity than those who must limit themselves to one area of the country, state, or metropolitan scene. These geographically place-bound teachers will have to be lucky, good, know someone, or perhaps all three if they expect to get a position.

However, the career-bound teacher can go where the action is. In the greater Chicago area, for example, some suburban school districts near

* After Endicott, 1975, pp. 13–14.

the Chicago city limits are actually letting nontenured teachers go and certainly aren't hiring anyone. But if you are willing to travel thirty to forty-five miles south, west, or north, the student population is growing and in some cases the school districts are even building new schools. Career-bound teachers will be willing either to drive that far each day or to move to accommodate their strong motivation to teach.

Start by getting out the map and drawing a circle defining the boundaries outside of which you are unwilling to go in order to obtain a teaching position. Then make a list of all the municipalities within the circle to give yourself a target group of schools that you will be shooting for. Following this, request from each area or county or the state school agency a listing of public schools that will contain names and addresses of the schools within your target area. You may also want to request from either the regional or local archdiocese a list of private schools as well.

Your next move should be to take your list of schools and their addresses and trot over to the placement office at the nearest college or university. In comparing any openings they may have with your list, you will be able to identify three sets of school names: one list containing those in your target area that have openings, a second list of the remaining target schools not reporting openings, and a third list representing schools not in your target area but reporting openings. I would certainly recommend that you contact all of the schools that report openings, since you may be willing to go even farther than you planned to get a job.

While you are wandering around the local halls of higher education you should try to talk with the department heads in early childhood, elementary, or secondary education as well as someone in the student-teaching office, if they have one. Not too much can be hoped for from these somewhat out-of-touch creatures, but you could get lucky. Every so often a memo will be sent or a handwritten note passed around to various departments saying something akin to: "There is an opening for a teacher in the sixth grade at Lyon School in Glenview. Can you recommend anyone?" Usually when such notes are received they are filed or posted in some out-of-the-way place, soon forgotten by the irrelevantly busy inhabitants of academic city.

Above all, remember to play all the angles you can in seeking out possible openings. If you have any relatives, friends, or even friends of friends who might be in touch with such information, don't be shy. Don't be rude, but remind them every once in a while that you are still looking. Whatever you do, play the odds. The more people you check with, the more placement bulletins you examine, and the more letters requesting applications that you send, the better your chances are of stumbling into the position you're looking for.

Finally, if you are looking for work in another state, get a map and go through the procedure just described. Any state office of education should be able to provide you with the needed school names and addresses, but try county or regional offices, too.

## Building Your Résumé (and Other Fun Tasks)

Most school districts prefer to have a completed application and a summary (résumé) of your work experience and academic background attached to the application form. The résumé is your opportunity to identify important aspects of yourself that were not necessarily asked for on the application form. This makes the résumé an important door opener for you in that it provides you the opportunity to demonstrate more of what you really are. Applications provide information, but you are generally filling in blanks. In the résumé you can show your ability to organize your thoughts, as well as your ability to write. Done well, this can impress a school administrator enough to help you get your foot in the door.

The basic rule of thumb is to try to express who you really are professionally and personally, and express it in a way that will gain the attention of those who will read it. You can be relatively informal to the extent that you need not use educational jargon or 250-dollar words, but don't be careless or provocative. And don't get cute. I know of one instance where an applicant sent a résumé with a coin cellophane-taped to it and a note saying, "Take this and buy a cup of coffee at your leisure as you read through my application."* Now that's a bit too cute.

The résumé should be checked over carefully for spelling or typing errors and any other spacing or indenting inconsistencies. And it pays to invest in having the résumé commercially printed (and typed also if you aren't so good at it) on reasonably good paper. While this may not impress the hiring agent, he or she will be noticeably unimpressed if it is not of good quality. These are all minor issues and make one wonder what is going on in these people's heads to make them pick at such things. But remember, they may get ten or twenty of these a day, and anything that will help them weed out some quickly they will consciously or unconsciously use. One school administrator even admitted that candidates for positions in his school district had a far better chance if their last names started with the first six or seven letters of the alphabet. "It may not be right," he said, "but it sure is a helluva lot easier than going through the entire stack." I think it is safe to say that most administrators do not share this cavalier attitude, but keep in mind that the little things can count.

In their article entitled "Preparing for and Getting That Teaching Job," Gibson, Marshall, and Burd (1975) provide a helpful and comprehensive outline of the application process.†

> We consider four things necessary to complete the application process. Three of these can be done by you at the same time. They include:
>
> 1. Obtain an application form from each district in which you are interested. You may do this by letter, phone or stopping by to pick one up. Type it neatly.

* Ronald Glovetski, personal communication.
† Quoted from ASCUS Teaching Opportunities for You; permission granted by ASCUS, Box 4411, Madison, Wisconsin 53711.

2. Return the completed application form as soon as possible. Include a picture of yourself.* The importance of that is that after you have left an interview, the picture will help to recall your candidacy. Human nature is such that we tend to forget names, but remember faces.

3. Include a résumé and a xerox copy of your transcript from college with the application. Your résumé** should include personal information—age, height, weight, marital status, address, telephone, etc.; Academic background—high school attended, college attended and education major; Any honors received—Personal and educational references—character references and those knowing of your teaching interest and abilities.

You might include a personal statement in your résumé regarding your interest in working with children in after school activities, lunchroom supervision, assisting with musical productions, and extra-curricular areas. Anything that might indicate a willingness to serve kids*** that would show a sincere personal desire to become a part of the total school program could be helpful. The reason you should send a transcript is to point out your academic abilities. Some districts require it and some do not. Acquire one official transcript for your records and have a copy run off to send with your application. Do not bother sending official transcripts as it is just an added expense to you.

4. Contact the Educational Placement Office immediately and request that your credentials be sent to each district in which you are interested. Give them specific addresses each time to assure expediency. (pp. 7-8)

Number four on the Gibson, Marshall, and Burd listing may be sage advice in some cases, but a few problems can arise by using this procedure. First is the fact that not all school districts want credentials until they have sifted through mounds of application forms in a preliminary way, and they could be offended or at least find it unnecessarily bothersome to have unrequested credentials flying in from all over the country. These administrators generally sort out the applications using the information in them to judge which candidate's credentials they would like to see. You may want yours there so that they won't have to take the trouble to request them, but you are risking their finding such pushy behavior a minus.

A second problem arises out of the fact that you could be sending out 50, 150, or even more applications in an attempt to play the odds as

---

* I'm not altogether sure I agree with this idea, but I'll leave that up to you.

** You should consider making up two or three different résumés, each indicating a slightly different kind of position for which you are qualified. This is especially important when you have been able to ascertain which job is open. That is where you want to focus.

*** Emphasize this including any special experiences you have had working with kids and adults in and out of school. Administrators consider this almost as important as direct teaching experience and even a part of overall personality.

I mentioned earlier. Can you imagine a college placement office complying with that many requests in a month to six weeks time? I think not. And depending on the policy of each placement office, it could run into a lot of dough. In addition, some placement offices will charge you if *you* request the credentials, but do not if the potential employer makes the request.

Because of these potential difficulties, I recommend a procedure which includes some cost to you but could serve your purpose very well. If you like, go ahead and send credentials to school districts where you think your chances are very good or where you have been requested to do so by that district. However, with the remaining school districts, attach a stamped post card with the college placement address typed on it and a request for credentials indicated on the other side. The school district's mailing address will have to be included by you or a space indicated for the school district to fill it in. Most important, make it very, very easy for the hiring agent to send. It will take you more time to type in each hiring agent's name and address, but it makes it much easier for them.*

## Between Application and Interview

This is the hard part and the most important part as well. Getting all of the forms completed and mailed may seem pure drudgery, but they can't mean very much unless you get inside the door for that all-important interview. Therefore, following up your applications by checking with the various school districts is an absolute necessity. All of the words on paper have introduced you, but no school administrator is going to be thinking of hiring you unless he or she has seen you and talked with you.

Contacting school districts after they have your application in hand is a very delicate matter. In fact, many teacher candidates will not do it, even by telephone, because it seems pushy, egotistic, and generally too openly aggressive for their tastes. However, it is really necessary to make telephone and/or personal contact once you know that all of your papers are in** and they have had ample opportunity to appraise them. You are, after all, competing with a large number of other candidates for any position which might be open. So like it or not, it is part of the territory. In providing a description of how this follow-up procedure should be handled, I once again turn to the practical advice of Gibson, Marshall, and Burd.

---

* Incidentally, it has been found that some placement offices will send credentials much more quickly when they are requested by school districts. It seems that they don't mind dragging their feet when you ask for them, but would not dare to offend the schools.

** It is important to check periodically with your placement office to see which credentials have been mailed and to whom.

. . . hit the road and try the following which are intended to be suggestions.

1. Call a district and indicate that you are going to be in their area on a certain day. Indicate that you have a completed application on file and you would appreciate an opportunity to discuss teaching, substitute teaching, or aide work. Indicate that even if they should not have an opening at this time, you certainly would appreciate the opportunity to discuss your candidacy in the event something might become available in the near future.
2. Stop by a district and politely ask if you might discuss your application status. Indicate that your application is on file and it is complete. Try the same line and indicate that you would like to have just a second to introduce yourself to the hiring official.
3. If you have met or know of any administrators in a district, go to see them personally. Indicate to them what you are attempting to accomplish and maybe they will refer you to somebody who is involved in the hiring process.

Your taking the initiative for a personal meeting will not appeal to you, I am sure. We do consider it a necessary evil, however, due to the supply and demand situation. You get hired on your personal attributes and your desire to use your talents. You, therefore, have to make every attempt to get that personal contact. The difficult part is to do it tactfully and appear to be eager while not being pushy. You will feel more comfortable after trying it. (p. 8)

An additional piece of advice seems appropriate at this juncture. Like the sentry outside the forts of the Old West, central office and local school secretaries often perform protective functions far beyond the call of duty. When it comes to responding to job-seeking applicants these secretaries are especially vigilant in warding off an attack. In too many cases, they may keep you from making necessary contact with either the district hiring official or a school principal who does his or her own hiring. You must persist without being belligerent, asking the secretary if you might speak with the person in charge of hiring or perhaps dropping by when he or she might be available. Keep in mind that these secretaries will usually attempt to put you off, with or without the consent of the hiring official, because of the large number of applicants they hear from each day.

One particular case comes to mind that exemplifies how secretaries can give a job applicant the deep-six. A very well-qualified former student of mine had telephoned me asking if I knew of any positions available in the area. Although I knew of no positions at the time, I said I would certainly let her know if any came up. Soon after that a superintendent informed our office that two positions were open in his district and if we had someone in mind, the person should contact his secretary and mention that we had recommended that they call. My former student called the district secretary three or four times, attempting to get through to a principal who was doing the hiring. Although she mentioned our names each time she called, the district secretary was apparently unimpressed and continually put her off. By the time my former student finally got through to the principal ten days later the position had been filled. She was qualified, she was available, and she probably would have been hired; but the secretary felt *she* was doing her duty keeping people out of the principal's hair. *Don't* let them do that! It can cost you a job! If you must, drop by the school or central office unannounced and request to spend just a few minutes with anyone available. This approach can sometimes be surprisingly effective.

In any event, it is hoped that at this point you will have been able to secure a few job interviews with districts that have openings. If such is the case, you should be prepared for what is yet ahead.

## Interviewing for the Job

Preparing for a job interview is a tricky process. Do you try to guess what the questions will be? Do you memorize the notes from your last course on open education? Perhaps a stiff drink would do the trick. Quite frankly, any attempts to guess at questions or "psych out" the interviewer are relatively fruitless and only serve to drive your blood pressure over the top.

Instead, you should explore three issues which can make you as ready as you will ever be by the time that interview rolls around. These are:

(1) learning about the school district,
(2) knowing what interviewers look for, and
(3) practicing areas that might be discussed.

**Get to Know the District.**   Use any means possible to find out about the school district in which the interview is taking place. You can ask the district for pamphlets, newsletters, or any other source material that could help you become familiar with the schools. Your goal is to familiarize yourself with the school system to the extent that you can intelligently discuss or ask questions about it. Some important areas would include:

1. Population of the area serving the school, total school population, average building population.
2. Is school population rising or falling?
3. Grade levels served, special educational services, and other supportive services.
4. Any new or innovative programs that have been recently implemented.
5. Any specially funded programs that receive district support.
6. Textbook usage standardized for district, for school, or up to departments or individual teachers?
7. Any difference in what the various schools offer in the way of classroom styles, e.g., open education, self-contained, departmentalized?
8. Anything on administration and teacher turnover in the district.

Knowing these and other details about the district makes you feel much more at ease when the district's programs and policies are discussed.

It also enables you to develop one or two relevant questions to ask at times when your mind has gone blank or when the interviewer provides the opportunity. If this data cannot be obtained from the school itself, the public library, city government, or the Chamber of Commerce should be able to meet your needs.

**What Interviewers Look For.** There are many things, of course, that one could never predict about how school district personnel judge teacher candidates because of differences in personality, interview competency, and school district philosophy, among others. But hiring agents tend to agree on some basic discriminators that they value, and most will use these to judge your suitability for the position.

As mentioned before, overall personality is an important factor to school hiring personnel and they will attempt to assess this before, during, and after the interview. For this reason it is important that without going overboard you should give them ample opportunity to find out what you believe are the important aspects of your personality that lend themselves to working with children. Don't get carried away with long, intense self-appraisals but be sure to describe succinctly your interests, experience, and abilities in working with people, especially children. Point out characteristics that cannot be found anywhere in your credentials. In addition to this, take every opportunity to verify your commitment to teaching, your interest and concern for working with individual children as well as groups, and how important you feel getting to know each child is in the overall teaching process.

Beyond this, interviewers tend to react positively or negatively to some very specific attributes or characteristics of candidates. For example, in their study of college graduates seeking various kinds of jobs, Anton and Russell (1975) found these areas to be important:

- Males created a mildly positive impression if they wore a sport coat and tie, but a much better impression if they wore a suit.
- Males who had shorter, more neatly trimmed hair and beards made a positive impression.
- Females created negative impressions if they wore casual outfits such as jeans, sandals, etc.
- Failure to maintain eye contact by the candidate was considered negative.
- Fiddling with objects on the desk or something brought along was judged to cause a negative impression.
- A candidate's use of speech that was heavily loaded with jargon was considered negative.

Anton and Russell also discovered that applicant characteristics that affected their job chances were judged this way:

- Assertive, intelligent, independent, and inquisitive candidates were received as mildly positive.

- Grateful and jocular candidates were received in a neutral way.
- Composed, cordial, cooperative, enthusiastic, and sincere candidates were received with very strong positive feelings.

While this study dealt with applicants for positions in industry, it has been shown that such perceptions by potential employers are very similar to those in schools (Endicott, 1975).

Another report (source unknown) indicated that there were fifty different negative factors evaluated during employment interviews and that these frequently lead to rejection of the applicant. This data was collected from 153 companies and schools and is not listed in any order of importance.

1. Poor personal appearance.
2. Overbearing—overaggressive—conceited—"superiority complex"—know-it-all.
3. Inability to express himself clearly—poor voice, diction, grammar.
4. Lack of planning for career—no purposes and goals.
5. Lack of interest and enthusiasm—passive, indifferent.
6. Lack of confidence and poise—nervousness—ill-at-ease.
7. Failure to participate in activities.
8. Overemphasis on money—interested only in best dollar offer.
9. Poor scholastic record—just got by.
10. Unwilling to start at the bottom—expects too much too soon.
11. Makes excuses—evasiveness—hedges on unfavorable factors in record.
12. Lack of tact.
13. Lack of maturity.
14. Lack of courtesy—ill-mannered.
15. Condemnation of past employers.
16. Lack of social understanding.
17. Marked dislike for school work.
18. Lack of vitality.
19. Fails to look interviewer in the eye.
20. Friction with parents.
21. Indecision.
22. Loafs during vacation—lakeside pleasures.
23. Unhappy married life.
24. Limp, fishy hand-shake.
25. Sloppy application blank.
26. Merely shopping around.
27. Wants job only for short time.
28. Little sense of humor.
29. Lack of knowledge of field of specialization.
30. Parents make decisions for him.
31. No interest in school, company, or industry.
32. Emphasis on whom he knows.
33. Unwillingness to go where we send him.

34. Cynical.
35. Low moral standards.
36. Lazy.
37. Intolerant—strong prejudices.
38. Narrow interests.
39. Spends much time in movies.
40. Poor handling of personal finances.
41. No interest in community activities.
42. Inability to take criticism.
43. Lack of appreciation of the value of experience.
44. Radical ideas.
45. Late to interview without good reason.
46. Never heard of school or company.
47. Failure to express appreciation for interviewer's time.
48. Asks no questions about the job.
49. High pressure type.
50. Indefinite response to questions.

Certainly there are some items on this list that seem inappropriate to apply regarding job capabilities. But according to the best evidence available, they are applied nonetheless. Thus, while it is nearly impossible to change your personality, certain surface behaviors can be altered or emphasized to improve your chances for a job. If it's a job you want, you have to play their game.

**The Strategy of Interview Practice.**    One never really knows what a school administrator might ask in an interview. The person could be the interviewer-lecturer type who has some great need to provide you with a story of his or her life, in which case you must listen and pick your spots to jump in with the important stuff; or he may be suffering from a severe case of protracted adolescence (a malady commonly found among school administrators and male university professors) and try to put the make on you before you can get out of the office. But there are some relatively competent interviewers out there who know how to ask questions, listen intently, and follow up with even more penetrating questions.

Thus you need to be ready for the best as well as the worst, and one very trustable preparatory method is to practice. Get a friend, your spouse, even one of your children and provide them with a list of questions to ask you. Run through them a few times to get used to the whole idea of being interviewed.

There are really two separate phenomena going on in the job interview setting. There are the specific questions that you must try to answer as succinctly and smoothly as possible and there is the aura, or experience if you will, of being interviewed—the interview process itself. You see, few of us experience being interviewed enough times in our lives to become practiced at it, and practice is exactly what you need. The questions are one thing, and much there depends on your experience and ability to communicate; but being in that situation where someone is asking you one question after another is something else again. Far too many people simply "blow" job opportunities, not because they are incompetent but because they "break" in the interview situation.

This practice effect you obtain by going through mock interview simulations can prepare you for the style, the rhythm, the pattern that interviews take on. It prepares you in much the same way as practicing analogies gets your mind set at the proper angle for taking the Miller Analogy Test. It doesn't have to be the same questions, it's just the same kind of experience that counts.

There are generally two kinds of interview patterns utilized by school personnel. One pattern consists of several somewhat unrelated questions, used mainly to get specific answers in the same way a questionnaire would, only it's done verbally. Usually the interviewer is getting data about you that he or she may or may not already have and learning something about you as a person in the process.

Just to give you an idea of how this "hedge-hopping" interview approach might go, I have provided here a list of ninety relatively unrelated questions. Providing this list for someone to use in helping you practice gives him or her a wide range of choices and gives you the opportunity to wrestle with this kind of pattern. Also, as you no doubt have surmised, it helps you to think how you would actually answer these questions as well.

### Hedge-Hopping Approach*

1. What are your future vocational plans?
2. In what school activities have you participated? Why? Which did you enjoy the most?
3. How do you spend your spare time? What are your hobbies?
4. In what type of position are you most interested?
5. Why do you think you might like to work for our school or company?
6. What jobs have you held? How were they obtained and why did you leave?
7. What courses did you like best? Least? Why?
8. Why did you choose your particular field of work?
9. What percentage of your college expenses did you earn? How?
10. How did you spend your vacations while in school?
11. What do you know about our school or company?
12. Do you feel that you have a good general training?
13. What qualifications do you have that make you feel that you will be successful in your field?
14. What extracurricular offices have you held?
15. What are your ideas on salary?
16. How do you feel about your family?
17. How interested are you in sports?
18. If you were starting college all over again, what courses would you take?

* Source unknown.

19. Can you forget your education and start from scratch?
20. Do you prefer any specific geographic location? Why?
21. Do you have a girl friend or boy friend? Is it serious?
22. How much money do you hope to earn at thirty? Thirty-five?
23. Why did you decide to go to this particular school?
24. How did you rank in your graduation class in high school? Where will you probably rank in college?
25. Do you think that your extracurricular activities were worth the time you devoted to them? Why?
26. What do you think determines a man's or woman's progress in a good school?
27. What personal characteristics are necessary for success in your chosen field?
28. Why do you think you would like this particular type of job?
29. What is your father's occupation?
30. Tell me about your home life during the time you were growing up.
31. Are you looking for a permanent or temporary job?
32. Do you prefer working with others or by yourself?
33. Who are your best friends?
34. What kind of boss do you prefer?
35. Are you primarily interested in making money or do you feel that service to your fellow man is a satisfactory accomplishment?
36. Can you take instructions without feeling upset?
37. Tell me a story!
38. Do you live with your parents? Which of your parents has had a more profound influence on you?
39. How did previous employers treat you?
40. What have you learned from some of the jobs you have held?
41. What have you done which shows initiative and willingness to work?
42. Can you get recommendations from previous employers?
43. What was your record in military service?
44. Have you ever changed your major field of interest while in college? Why?
45. When did you choose your college major?
46. How do your college grades after military service compare with those previously earned?
47. Do you feel you have done the best scholastic work of which you are capable?
48. How did you happen to go to college?
49. What do you know about opportunities in the field in which you are trained?
50. How long do you expect to work?
51. Have you ever had any difficulty getting along with fellow students and faculty?
52. Which of your college years was the most difficult?
53. What is the source of your spending money?
54. Have you saved any money?
55. Do you have any debts?
56. How old were you when you became self-supporting?
57. Do you attend church?
58. Did you enjoy your years at this university?

59. Do you like routine work?
60. Do you like regular hours?
61. What size city do you prefer?
62. When did you first contribute to family income?
63. What is your major weakness?
64. Define cooperation.
65. Will you fight to get ahead?
66. Do you demand attention?
67. Do you have an analytical mind?
68. Are you eager to please?
69. What do you do to keep in good physical condition?
70. How do you usually spend Sunday?
71. Have you had any serious illness or injury?
72. Are you willing to go where the school sends you?
73. What job in our school would you choose if you were entirely free to do so?
74. Is it an effort for you to be tolerant of persons with a background and interests different from your own?
75. What types of books have you read?
76. Have you plans for graduate work?
77. What types of people seem to rub you the wrong way?
78. Do you enjoy sports as a participant? As an observer?
79. Have you ever tutored an underclassmate?
80. What jobs have you enjoyed the most? The least? Why?
81. What are your own special abilities?
82. What job in our school do you want to work toward?
83. Would you prefer a large or a small school? Why?
84. What is your idea of how schools operate today?
85. Do you like travel?
86. How about overtime work?
87. What kind of work interests you?
88. What are the disadvantages of your chosen field?
89. Do you think that grades should be considered by employers? Why or why not?
90. Are you interested in research?

But there is another species out there who is not satisfied with the hedge-hopping approach to interviewing. These are the unusually bright ones, some of whom have been trained in interview techniques and/or utilize prepared interview formats which allow them to penetrate more deeply into your strengths and weaknesses. This approach might be dubbed the "in-depth theme" interview.

The in-depth theme interviewer chooses an area such as discipline, for example, and will ask a general question followed by a slightly more specific question built on your answer, and perhaps follow that with even more specific questions. In this way the interviewer gets closer to what you really believe, think, and do about things. I think you'll get the idea by examining this set of interview questions below.

## *In-Depth Theme Approach*

1. Do you think it is important to be popular with your students?
2. Is it important for the students to like you?
3. Why is it important to you how your students would view you?
4. So you're saying that you wouldn't be disturbed if students didn't like you?
5. Would you actually have a plan for developing good relationships with your students?
6. Could you describe some techniques that you would use or have used?
7. You mentioned getting to know how the students perceive you. How would you go about this?
8. Is getting student perceptions the way you would develop good relations with your students?
9. You mentioned being a good listener. Would you describe some characteristics of a good listener?
10. Why do you think it is important for a teacher to be a good listener?
11. What kind of school would you prefer to work in?
12. What about you makes that type of school more to your liking?
13. Would it be difficult for you to get along in a more conventional school?
14. Is what the principal is like of any importance to you?
15. How would you describe a principal whom you simply wouldn't work for?
16. Can you describe the characteristics of a good principal?
17. In your student teaching or past teaching experience can you think of a favorite student, one you really liked?
18. You like students who exhibit imagination then?
19. Would you find it difficult to work with students who didn't have much imagination?
20. What kind of student do you find the most difficulty in working with?
21. If I came to visit your class, what would it look like?
22. What new ideas would you like to initiate in your classroom?
23. What do you like best about teaching?
24. Do you like to work with people in situations other than the classroom?
25. Do you think it is possible to reward students too much?
26. Do you think it is important that students be rewarded for their work?
27. What kinds of rewards do you think you would provide for your students?
28. Is it important for you to communicate with parents?
29. In what way would you set about to communicate with parents?
30. What kind of information would you want to share with parents?
31. Do you think there are some things that parents really shouldn't know?
32. What specific information would you not share with parents?
33. Do you have a favorite teacher, someone you would model your teaching after?
34. What are some of the things this teacher does that you would emulate?

As you can see, the first ten questions dealt exclusively with teacher-student relationships, the first question being very general and the other nine questions building on what the interviewee said and probing for more specificity. I strongly recommend practice using this approach. It really helps you get your act together and forces you to be very concrete and situation-oriented in your responses. Once you are fairly used to this in-depth pattern, the real interview will seem much easier, I assure you.

The practice effect has its advantages at the other end of the real interview experience as well. After two or three job interviews, you will probably have experienced enough interview patterns and actual questions to become quite proficient at it.

## SOME FINAL JOB-SEEKING HINTS

In general, for the interview you will be asked questions that fall into four categories: (1) content, methodology, material, subject matter; (2) classroom organization, management, discipline, control; (3) teacher-student relations, feelings towards students, humanistic orientation, concern for the individual child; and (4) interpersonal relations, faculty and staff relations, willingness to work cooperatively, ability to get along. These are the content areas to remember, practice on, and be prepared to answer questions about.

Also, make every attempt to find out your interviewer's name and position in the district. This allows you to be more cordial and personal in your conversation. And, above all, try to relax, keeping in mind that this is not the only position on the face of the earth—so don't take it too seriously and become so tense that your mind becomes preoccupied with your nervous condition. If you know your stuff and can provide succinct explanations of how you teach using specific examples from your past experience, you'll be as competitive as anyone trying for the position.

Once the interview is completed and you have asked one or two appropriate questions to show your interest in the school district, be sure to request politely a specified date when you will know if you are being considered for the position. You will also want to know what follow-up procedures are used, such as visits to schools or interviews with principals, teachers, or students.

After leaving the interview setting there is the additional important task of following up with the school district. By phoning and dropping by the office a few times* you will be able to know: (1) if the job has been filled or if you are still being considered; (2) if there is additional information you can provide; and (3) if there are other openings for which you might interview. This approach should be handled as delicately as the pre-interview procedure, but is necessary so that you are visible to the hiring officials and clearly available for the job. As before, don't be pushy but be around, and remember that secretaries will attempt to put you off to protect their bosses. Be nice, but don't let them run you off easily.

It is also a good idea to send a thank-you note to the person(s) with whom you interviewed including an indication of your interest in the

---

* Wait about two weeks before you begin this procedure.

position. You might also note that you would be available for additional interviews or can provide additional information if need be. Remember, all of these things increase your possibility of being in the right place at the right time.

Finally, if getting that teaching job is of long-term importance to you, your approach to job hunting should include a willingness to engage in substitute teaching or even part-time teaching for a while. Some have found that accepting a teacher's aide position has paid off as well. The goal is to get inside the school district in one way or another, establish a reputation with the administration, staff, and students so that when a position does open up you'll be the known quantity they'll want to hire.

Remember, there will always be teaching positions open somewhere. Many people I know (myself included) have found and have been hired for positions during the last week in August. So hang in there and don't despair. If you really want to teach you must keep at the job-seeking routine. Persons who have resigned themselves to clerk, secretarial or other noneducational positions effectively remove themselves from the teaching job market. After a year or more of lost contact it is nearly impossible to reestablish that needed connection with the education market.

# 13

# Teacher and Student Rights

## The Legal Perspective

As with any set of beliefs, rules, and principles dealing with interaction among humans, individual and group rights have many different sides and angles to consider. We all believe that certain things are due us just as a matter of developed cultural expectations, but these beliefs vary and in some cases cause debates or fiery arguments that usually produce a great deal more heat than light on a given issue. One somewhat settling thought is that there are certain rights that all of us may enjoy because of legal precedent and written laws.

Focusing on the strictly legal aspects of teacher and student rights at least provides you with a base from which to operate as you go about your daily activities at the schoolhouse. These legal protections were not necessarily developed specifically with teachers and kids in mind, but in many cases come from the United States Constitution. However, such rights have had to be reaffirmed on occasion by obtaining court rulings. Ballantine, Ballantine, and Cargan (1976) provided a frame of reference for these basic constitutional rights when they explained that:

> A panel of six experts active in student rights identified a list of rights accorded to adults which are key issues in schools as well: freedoms of speech and press, due process of law, right of assembly, freedom from unreasonable search and seizure, and freedom from cruel and unusual punishment. (p. 207)

These rights extend also to the provision of not only the due process clause but the equal protection clause encompassed in the Fourteenth Amendment. Rubin (1972) has further defined rights especially due teachers by indicating that:

The Constitution, of course, is not the only source of a teacher's rights. These rights are further defined by his individual contract, any relevant collective agreement, policies of his state and local boards of education, state and federal statutes, and state constitutional provisions. (p. 11)

And for students, these and other rights are protected. The important U.S. Supreme Court ruling in *Tinker* (1969) solidly planted this position in the minds of many educators and was reaffirmed in another court ruling (*Dunham* v. *Pulsifer,* 1970). Levine (1973) referring to this situation said:

> . . . in the last few years, courts have begun to recognize that injustice in schools should not be tolerated no more than in any place else in the society. The words of one federal court sum up this trend: "The Constitution does not stop at the public school doors like a puppy waiting for his master, but instead it follows the student through the corridors, into the classroom, and onto the athletic field." (p. 12)*

This, then, provides the legal backdrop for what teachers and students can look for in terms of protection under the law. There are specific and/or unique situational decisions to be made, of course, wherever an individual or group of teachers or students judge that their rights have been abridged. Knowing or seeking out information regarding how the various federal, state, and local laws interact can help the individual identify whether or not any of these rights have been denied. Some of the best sources to tap to get the answers needed are described below.

Rubin, David. *The Rights of Teachers: The Basic ACLU Guide To a Teacher's Constitutional Rights.* New York: Avon Books, 1972.

This 176-page paperback "handbook" is a very inexpensive and readable source set up in a question and answer format. The areas explored and legally explained include: "Freedom to Teach," "Freedom in Private Life," and "Freedom from Arbitrary or Discriminatory Action by School Officials." Questions are answered utilizing both the U.S. Constitution and specific courtroom cases to establish your legal standing as a teacher. The relevant questions that are answered include: "Do social studies teachers have any constitutional protection from retaliation by school authorities for controversial discussions in the classroom?" (p. 34) and "Is a teacher constitutionally protected in going over heads of his superiors to bring injustices or problems in his school system to the attention of higher authorities outside the system?" (p. 60)

Flygare, Thomas. *The Legal Rights of Teachers.* Bloomington, Indiana: The Phi Delta Kappa Educational Foundation, Fastback 83, 1976.

---

* *Dunham* v. *Pulsifer,* 312 F. Supp. 411 (D.Vt. 1970) as found in Levine (1973).

This 45-page, inexpensive booklet provides the teacher with descriptions of legal rights emphasizing contemporary court cases that lend support to the teacher's protection. This source is written in an expository rather than a question-and-answer format, but remains easy to read, covering such issues as "Academic Freedom," "Teachers' Private Lives," and "Issues in Employment." Some specific items explained include: "Criticism of School Officials" (p. 14), "Unconventional Sexual Behavior" (p. 25), and "Maternity Leave" (p. 39).

Levine, Alan H. *The Rights of Students: The Basic ACLU Guide To a Public School Student's Rights.* New York: Avon Books, 1973.

Similar in format, size and cost to the teachers' version, this book examines in the question-and-answer approach issues specific to student needs such as "Personal Appearance," "Corporal Punishment," and "School Records,"* providing answers to questions such as "Can a student publication be banned because the principal thinks particular words are obscene?" (p. 38), "Can a student be punished for violating a rule he didn't know existed?" (p. 62), and "Can a school official or policeman search a student's person?" (p. 85)

Flygare, Thomas. *The Legal Rights of Students.* Bloomington, Indiana: The Phi Delta Kappa Educational Foundation, Fastback 59, 1975.

Similar in format, size, and cost to the teachers' version, this examines essentially the same issues that are covered in Levine. Again court cases and specific examples are used to explain where students stand in terms of their rights.

**For Teachers Only.**   In the jargon of the legal world the local school board is the duly elected representative of the community, with the delegated authority (from the state legislature) to hire and fire teachers, make rules and policy, and create other guidelines that teachers are expected to follow. To the extent that these board decisions do not abridge the constitutional rights of a teacher or run counter to state or federal laws, courts have been supportive of school boards when cases come before them. What, then, can teachers do if they feel that their rights are being tampered with in some way?

First, and perhaps most importantly, teachers should focus on protecting their rights from the beginning of their contract period with a school district. This rather defensive posture demands that you examine your written contract carefully looking for things that are spelled out,

---

* Because of the publishing date of this book, the issue of access to and protection of school records does not include the legal implications of the General Education Provisions Act (known as the Buckley Amendment).

such as reasons for dismissal, duties you are expected to perform, and any other specified agreements that you are making by putting your name on the dotted line. You will have to meet these requirements since you have entered into an agreement (contract) to do so.

Let us suppose, for example, that you were hired to teach French and told that you will be teaching French full time, but during the year are told to take on an extra class of English. Can you say no? It depends. If the contract said French, then that is all you can be required to teach. However, if the contract said something to the effect that you were to "teach French classes and perform any other teaching duties requested by superiors," then you have left yourself open. Therefore, contracts and other negotiated agreements between boards and teachers take on a very important role with regard to the rights of teachers. The lesson in all of this is to review carefully any agreements before you sign and work with your colleagues to obtain further rights through negotiation. As Flygare (1976) has described the position of teachers in relation to their boards*:

> . . . if local school boards operate within the provision of their delegated authority and do not violate the rights of any individual or group, their decisions are generally not reversible under the present legal structure. That is, merely because a teacher or a group of teachers dislikes a local school board policy does not mean that the policy can be reversed by some state or federal authority. Rather, the burden is on the teacher to demonstrate that the policy or decision in question falls outside the scope of the local board's authority or that it violates a particular state or federal legal principle. (p. 5)

Beyond that which is contracted or negotiated for, there is still the case where school boards or administrators as agents of their boards have violated the right of teachers, rights which are guaranteed by the U.S. Constitution or other federal or state statutes. It is at this point that the teacher or teacher group attempts to negotiate with the board from the strength of knowing what these rights are. Bringing such solid information to the attention of the local board could win the case without litigation or legal hassle. Flygare made this point when he said that ". . . many rights which would have taken years to establish in the legislature or through the courts have been won in a few minutes at the bargaining table." (p. 44)

However, if all else fails, the teacher or teacher group must have some way of knowing what they can expect outside of the school in terms of appeal or litigation. While the purpose here is not to outline all teachers' rights, since these listings are available in the sources cited earlier, some important teacher rights will be explained.

---

* Thomas Flygare, *The Legal Rights of Teachers*, © 1976 by The Phi Delta Kappa Educational Foundation, Bloomington, Indiana.

*Some Salient Rights Issues*

QUESTION    Does a teacher have the right to say anything or use any
    words he or she wants to in the process of teaching a class or course?
ANSWER    Not really. There are situations where courts have found in
    favor of teachers mainly because they judged that even when
    "dirty" words were used or presented by the teacher, they were
    a legitimate part of the instruction and relevant to the type of
    subject being taught. The age and therefore the sophistication
    of the students is also taken into account in these cases. In
    such cases, teachers have a much better chance of winning if the
    school district guidelines are not specific on such issues. However,
    teachers should be warned regarding the finding of a recent case
    that Flygare reported when ". . . even in the absence of
    guidelines teachers could be discharged for employing unconventional
    teaching methods, particularly when more competent teachers
    are available. . . ." (p. 11)

Beyond these findings Flygare also provides advice to administrators
and school boards and at the same time gives a convincing argument for
teachers to use when he notes that*:

> . . . I believe it is fair to conclude that official acts to keep foul
> language and strange ideas from the ears of students are largely
> futile; they hear everything imaginable from their peers. This is not
> to suggest that there are no instances where a teacher's dismissal is
> warranted because of a classroom utterance. It is only to question
> whether the dismissal accomplishes the objective. (p. 13)

QUESTION    What rights can teachers expect if they are dismissed either
    in the middle or at the end of a school year?
ANSWER    Courts have found that schools must provide proper
    procedures in cases where tenured teachers are concerned.
    These procedures must include a hearing where reasons for
    dismissal are specified and where the teacher is allowed to respond
    to allegations made. Rubin (1972) provided a list of what
    should be considered "minimum procedural safeguards."

    (1) the opportunity to be heard "at a meaningful time and in a
    meaningful manner";
    (2) "timely and adequate notice detailing the reasons for a proposed
    termination";
    (3) the opportunity to confront and cross-examine witnesses;
    (4) the opportunity to present arguments and evidence orally, as
    well as in writing;
    (5) the right to retain an attorney;

---

* Copyright © 1975, Flygare.

(6) a determination resting "solely on the legal rules and evidence adduced at the hearing";

(7) a statement by the decision maker of the reasons for the determination and of the evidence relied on; and

(8) an impartial decision maker. (p. 162)*

In the case of untenured teachers, only, those who have been dismissed in the middle of a school year have a right to a hearing, but any untenured teacher has that right if he or she has been accused of "dishonesty" or "immorality." And Flygare further defines this issue by explaining†:

> . . . that whether or not a teacher enjoys the right to notice and hearing before termination, he or she still can challenge the termination in court on the grounds, for example, that the school board exceeded its authority, discriminated against the teacher on the grounds of race, sex, or religion, or punished the teacher for constitutionally protected behavior, such as free speech. (p. 20)

In addition to the rights already described, a terminated teacher should also examine his or her contract as well as state law to see if the school district is violating established agreements or rules.

QUESTION   Can a school board or its agents dismiss a teacher or group of teachers for making statements that are critical of school officials or their policies?

ANSWER   While teachers have the right to freedom of speech like any other member of society, certain limits have been placed on them by the courts regarding their "outside utterances." In a Supreme Court case, *Pickering* v. *Board of Education* (1968) the court noted that teachers have a right to speak their opinions, but that their opinions must not be "knowingly or recklessly" false nor could such statements interfere with personal loyalty or close working relationships (Rubin, p. 51).

When teachers make statements that are critical of school operations, they should have evidence that attempts were made to resolve these issues within the school structure. Flygare noted that Pickering might not have won his case.

> . . . if the school system had "narrowly drawn grievance procedures" by which teachers could submit complaints about the operation of the schools to their superior for action thereon prior to bringing the complaints before the public.‡ (p. 16)

---

* *Goldberg* v. *Kelly,* 397 U.S. 254 (1970) as found in Rubin (1972).

† Copyright © 1975, Flygare.

‡ Copyright © 1975, Flygare.

QUESTION   Can a school district dismiss teachers because of hair style, grooming, or mode of dress?

ANSWER   The consensus on this question is generally that school districts may not dismiss a teacher for these reasons. The courts are especially solid in noting that "grooming" is not within the provision of the school board's authority and making such decisions for teachers violates their right to symbolic expression as well as their right to privacy.

"Modes of dress" cases are usually handled on the merits of each case; for a school district to win they must be able to prove that such dress disrupts the educational process (Rubin).

In general, courts have ruled in favor of teachers because they viewed both grooming and mode of dress as matters of personal taste and therefore not relevant to the operation of an institution.

QUESTION   Can a school district discriminate against teachers on the basis of race, sex, religion, age, ancestry, or national origin?

ANSWER   One would think that the answer would obviously be no, and in most cases this is true. However, there are exceptional circumstances involving attempts to improve racial balances. Also, in the case of sex-based discrimination, school districts must provide proof that such discrimination is ". . . not arbitrary, and is rationally related to a legitimate goal of the school system."* It is very difficult for school districts to justify such action normally.

Basically, discrimination must be considered a very strong case in favor of the teacher and is usually handled very gingerly by school officials.

QUESTION   Do teachers have the right to join associations or unions, negotiate with school boards, and strike if need be?

ANSWER   The whole issue of teacher organization activities is still unfolding as teachers work for more rights and organize for better working conditions. Court decisions have supported teachers' rights to organize and/or join associations and to serve as active members or leaders of these organizations. Such teachers cannot be reprimanded or disciplined for these activities in teacher organizations so long as these activities do not prevent them from performing their classroom duties.

Collective bargaining with boards of education is another matter. Collective teacher negotiations is a state-by-state matter since government employees are exempt from the National Labor

* From *Reed* v. *Reed*, 404 U.S. 71, 75–76 (1971) as found in Rubin (1973), p. 125.

Relations Act (Flygare). In states where there are no state collective bargaining laws, local boards are free to negotiate with teachers, but are not required to do so. In states where collective bargaining laws have been established, boards must follow those guidelines, which sometimes state specifically what can and cannot be bargained for. Flygare (1976) has summarized the present state of things in this way.*

> Even though teachers may have the right to organize and bargain with the school board, it is settled law that the board retains full authority to make the final decision on any topic raised at the bargaining session. (pp. 36–37)

Teacher strikes are illegal in most states, and there is little evidence to suggest that courts will support teacher strikes. Recently, however, rather than finding the teachers at fault for striking, some courts have enjoined school boards to meet their obligations in the collective bargaining process. In any event, strikes are presently among the most untenable approaches for teachers to utilize as a tool in seeking their legal rights.

Many other teacher rights can be found in the two sources utilized here, and the books should be used to answer the specific questions you might have. In many instances rights must be defined out of the circumstances from which their possible abridgment comes. For this reason, if after reading this and the two sources suggested you still cannot ascertain whether or not your rights have been illegally violated, get a lawyer. Especially in cases of job termination, financial hardship, or social injustice, a few dollars for legal advice may be more than worth the money. Free legal assistance or advice from the local ACLU office are other alternatives to consider if available in your area.

**For Students Only.**  Although the specific issues are quite different, basic student rights fall under the same general constitutional guidelines as do those of teachers and other adults. With teachers it might be suspension or termination of a contract, and with students it might be suspension or expulsion from school. The same rights of due process apply and students, like teachers, should expect that their constitutional rights will be protected. The rights of assembly and freedom of speech are two other rights areas that teachers and students have in common.

However, there are other areas of protection under the law that hold greater value where the student is concerned. These rights range from the right to go to school (which some students may view as a responsibility) to specific issues such as the right to express opinions openly while in school and the right to continue schooling after marriage. While it is important for the students to understand the ways they are legally protected,

---

* Copyright © 1975, Flygare.

it is just as important that teachers understand these issues as well—first, because teachers could be unknowing parties in violating the rights of students and second, because teachers usually see their role as helping students when possible.

## A Short Interview With A Teacher

INTERVIEWER   Are you familiar with the legal rights that your students enjoy?

TEACHER   I don't know what you mean!

I   Oh, things that are protected under the U.S. Constitution and federal, state, and local laws.

T   Well, I guess I know some of them . . . like students can see their records with their parents' permission.

I   Any others that you know?

T   I don't think I have the right to search students or their lockers.

I   Are you sure that you don't?

T   Well, some of the other teachers think I'm wrong.

I   Do you think it's important that teachers know the students' rights?

T   Ya . . . so you don't violate them.

I   Do you think many teachers know those rights?

T   No. I don't really know them myself.

I   If it's so important to know, why don't teachers know them then?

T   I don't know . . . don't know where to find them out, I guess. They're not readily accessible.

I   Do you depend on the principal for such things?

T   Are you kidding?

I   Do you think the superintendent's office should make these student rights known to teachers then?

T   Maybe they should, but I wouldn't recommend waiting for them to do it.

I   I would think teachers would be concerned about their own legal vulnerability . . . that they might be taking a chance getting sued.

T   It just doesn't seem that pressing. We have day-to-day things that keep us busier than we want to be anyway.

I   Have you ever known any teachers who were sued because they violated students' rights?

T   No. But that doesn't mean it doesn't happen. Anyway, a lot of times students really don't know their rights.

I   So you think part of the teacher's job should be to help students understand their rights?

T   Sure . . . but there is so much to do, so much to think about . . .

Whatever the feeling of teachers or the responsibilities not met by administrators, students do have rights that need to be spelled out. The following questions and answers should provide the interested teacher with a brief review of student rights.

## Salient Student Rights Issues

QUESTION   Can students rightfully picket, demonstrate, or rally for a cause inside or outside the school building?

ANSWER   Students are protected by the First Amendment to peaceably assemble, but courts have found different interpretations depending on the circumstances. Students may assemble inside a school only if it does not disrupt the normal routine of the school by interrupting classes or keeping employees from their normal duties. Students may not be denied use of bulletin boards to provide information about their cause if other school groups are allowed to use such displays.

Students are allowed to assemble on school grounds to picket or march, again as long as the school routine is not materially disrupted. But in no case can students rightfully conduct such demonstrations if they miss classes or disrupt them in some way. Levine summarizes the issue in this way.*

Whether your demonstration is inside a building or out on the campus, a court is more likely to find the action legal if it concerns school policies rather than nonschool issues. . . . You should be warned however, that anyone who demonstrates on school property runs a serious risk of being arrested. (pp. 28–29)

The major court case on which most other court rulings have been based is *Tinker* v. *Des Moines Independent School District* (1969)** where it was found that students had the right to free expression. To quote Levine as to the significance of the *Tinker* decision,

. . . it is a clear-cut statement, applying to all schools in the country, of a student's right to constitutional guarantees in the school. (p. 22)

The *Tinker* decision by the United States Supreme Court can be found in its entirety on pages 149–160 of Levine.

* Reprinted from *The Rights of Students: The Basic ACLU Guide to a Public School Student's Rights*, by Alan Levine with Eve Cary and Diane Divoky. Copyright © 1973 by the American Civil Liberties Union, Inc. Reprinted by permission of Avon Books.
** Levine, 1973.

QUESTION    Do students have the right to distribute literature on school
    property or inside the school?

ANSWER    Students do have the right to hand out literature and even
    underground newspapers on school property unless ". . . its
    distribution materially and substantially interferes with school
    activities." (Levine, p. 29)* Minor disturbances, say the courts,
    are worth the right of students to exhibit their free expression.
    The courts usually protect such expression within the school building
    as well, but with important exceptions. Levine describes the
    exceptions this way.**

> (1) *Leaflets in the Classroom.* Certainly not legally protected while
> class is in session, and probably not before class either, since this
> activity would be likely to interfere.
> (2) *Leaflets in the halls.* Although this would not directly interfere
> with the classes, you might substantially interfere with traffic in the
> halls. . . . On the other hand, a blanket rule against handing out
> literature anywhere inside a school has been declared illegal by some
> courts. (pp. 30–31)

It should be added that school administrators may not
require that students submit literature to them for approval
(Levine) unless a quick decision can be made by the principal
or other staff personnel.

QUESTION    Do students have the right to defy regulations of hair length
    or dress codes established by school authority or student bodies?

ANSWER    Generally, students are on relatively firm ground in all of
    these circumstances since many court decisions have favored the
    students in such litigation. In approximately half of the states, state
    school rules indicate that it is *unconstitutional* to regulate student
    hair length unless ". . . the hair length causes substantial
    disruption . . . or there is a rational relationship between the
    rule and a legitimate educational purpose." (Levine, p. 47)
    However, in the other half of the states, schools, while not required
    to, are permitted to establish hair length rules. School districts
    are therefore able to decide on this matter, although some
    have chosen not to establish such rules.

    Levine has listed the reasons given by school officials for
    their attempts to regulate hair length. Among them are the belief
    long hair causes distraction, produces lower grades, and causes
    other students to attack, the need for sanitation and safety,
    and the need for respect for rules (pp. 48–51). Courts have shown

---

* *Eisner* v. *Stanford Board of Education,* 440 F.2d 54 (4th Cir. 1971), and other
cases, as found in Levine (1973).
** Copyright © 1973, Levine.

that all of these arguments are not sound, but some school districts are still enforcing hair length regulations based on one or more of these reasons.

Dress codes seem to fall in line with the hair length issue, although some court decisions have supported dress codes without supporting hair length regulations. In general, the principle of "substantial disruption" can once again be applied here. If schools can show that certain wearing apparel would cause such disturbances, they could win the case.

Whichever way courts decide with regard to administrative hair length and dress code regulations, they decide the same way when the study body makes these regulations. The same arguments hold no matter who set up the rules.

QUESTION   When do students have a right to a hearing?
ANSWER   It is a general rule of thumb that only for serious infractions or alleged infractions of school rules do students have a right to a hearing. In other cases of lesser "crimes" school officials may choose to provide a hearing, but are not required to do so by state or federal regulations.

When considering more serious action by the school against the student where suspension or expulsion could result, hearings are almost always required, though in some states they are not required for a short suspension. However, any time that the decision is made that a student is to be suspended or expelled, that student should receive a hearing where the issues of the case can be examined openly. Actually, if suspension or expulsion has already been decided upon without a hearing, the student's right to due process considerations has probably been violated. At the very least, schools must follow certain procedures normally established by state school codes, or parents have grounds for a suit. Levine described this student right.*

Your principal, your teachers, the coaches, school security guards, and all other employees of the school are employees of the government, and therefore under the Fourteenth Amendment have a legal duty to treat you fairly. This means that they may not impose any serious punishment for alleged misconduct without first having followed certain established procedures to determine whether or not you are in fact guilty. (p. 55)

Since most states do have such student rights to due process regulations, if the student feels that he or she is being wrongly charged and/or punished, he or she should check the state laws or local school district bylaws to see if the school authorities

* Levine, 1973.

followed the proper procedures. In Illinois, for example, in the School Code,

> ... Chapter 122, Section 10–22.6 (Ill. Rev. Stats., 1973) requires that immediately after a suspension is imposed, the parents of the student be notified of the reason(s) for the suspension, the length of the suspension and their right to appeal the decision to the local school board.*

The student's right to a hearing was most strongly substantiated by the *Goss* v. *Lopez* (1975) decision in which the U.S. Supreme Court established that school officials must not only inform the student of the charges being brought against him or her, but must also allow that student a chance either to explain or to deny the charges prior to imposing a suspension. (DeCecco and Richards, 1975)

In the case of expulsions, of course, the rights suggested before apply. And further, schools must be very careful in considering expulsion in the first place. In many states it is illegal to expel students, and where it is legal, it normally must be for a fixed period of time (Levine).

QUESTION   Must students, while in school, submit to police interviews or searches of desk, locker, or person by police or school officials?
ANSWER   Like any citizen in the U.S., a student has the right to remain silent when confronted by law officials, and should do so unless there is sufficient reason to talk. The student has a right to have a lawyer present and the right to contact his or her parents before being questioned. In most cases silence, beyond providing your name and address, is the best approach. As the saying goes, "Anything you say may be held against you."

In the case of desk, locker, and personal searches, on the other hand, students have very few rights. While on school property students do not have the Fourth Amendment protections that the normal citizen enjoys. It is a mystery why the courts have held to this direction, but it is hoped that changes will occur even by the time this book reaches the public.

Some states, school districts, and educational organizations have made strong recommendations against searches of this type; for example, the National Educational Association came out flatly against these student rights violators. Be that as it may, students beware. Do not keep anything in your desk, locker, or on your person that you would not want a police officer or school official to find. In fact, Levine recommends that**:

* From Committee on Rights of Minors: Illinois Commission on Children, February, 1976, p. iv.
** Levine, 1973.

(1) Your best protection is never to carry on you or keep in school anything that you wouldn't want the police or school officials to know about for any reason.

(2) Never consent to any search. Say in a loud, clear voice, so that witnesses can hear, that you do not consent. *But do not resist* if a policeman or school official goes ahead with the search. If you don't consent to the search, there's a possibility that anything found on you will not be able to be used against you. . . . If you consent, it may be used. (p. 88)

For those vitally interested in the specific rights of students on all counts, the two major sources used here—Levine, 1973, and Flygare, 1975—provide a much more detailed and legally substantiated rendition of the facts. While there are not always clear-cut answers even when numerous cases have been tried, knowing the legal trend on various rights issues can provide you with a definite advantage.

## The Classroom Perspective

Despite the many laws, statutes and court cases that provide the legal basis for teacher and student rights, there are those who envision that we should not wait for outside authorities to lead us in the directions we need to go. Affirmative behavior is recommended by these thinkers, who suggest that as educators we should establish guidelines and principles in the rights areas to meet the demands of a democratic society. Henning (1974) and DeCecco and Richards (1975), for example, strongly recommend that the concepts of civil liberties, rights, and responsibilities should be hammered out in the classroom so that students and teachers are not only aware of human rights issues, but are in fact developing new ways to apply them.

Henning suggests that classroom rules, school problems, and other real life issues should be used as topics for debates, discussions, and lesson planning. DeCecco and Richards, on the other hand, advocate that teachers resolve conflicts either among students or between the teacher and the students by utilizing a model of negotiation. This, they say, will not only resolve problems that occur but, at the same time teach the students through experience how the democratic principle of negotiated settlement works. They describe the procedure for resolving conflict in this way.

The first step of the model consists of each party to the conflict making a statement of issues to the other parties with the appropriate expressions of anger. The second step consists of all parties agreeing to a common statement of what the issues are. The third step is bargaining, with all sides making gains and concessions. (p. 24)

Others suggest establishing human rights codes that might apply to school personnel and students alike. These codes would be seen as far outreaching what the courts and laws have established, thus giving teachers and students more control over their destiny within the system. Further, some groups have recommended specific student codes* which would emphasize the human rights of students as *people* rather than "kids," thus reducing the need to go outside the system for legal direction. These ideas could be expanded to include the rights of parents and administrators as well.

The important issue revealed by all of these concerns is that students and teachers should take a more active role in developing how the system should work in the best interests of those involved. In talking with teachers, I have found that they have many good ideas about rights as well as responsibilities that will probably never reach administrator ears, let alone the courts. But this does not mean that their ideas should die a slow death wallowing in the moans and gripes of the lounge. To get things started, teacher groups or student and teacher groups might introduce topics for discussion by asking for reactions to questions like these.**

- Who should make the rules about how the classroom is run?
- What shall we do when the principal interrupts our class?
- What shall we do when visitors come into our class uninvited?
- What should students be able to say or do when a principal is observing their teacher?
- If a student gets into trouble with the principal, what should the teacher do?
- If a group of students want to protest against a school rule, what should the teacher do?
- If a group of students wants to publish an underground newspaper, should the teacher be involved?
- If a student or group of students want to protest the way another teacher teaches, what should their teacher do?
- If the teachers want to go on strike, should the students have any say in it?
- If the students want to demonstrate for a social issue, should the teachers be involved?
- Should the principal or teachers be allowed to search students' desks, lockers, or persons?
- Should teachers protect the students or the other teachers when students have a grievance against those other teachers?
- What should teachers do when other teachers treat their job as an 8:30 A.M. to 3:00 P.M. stint and that's it?

* See, for example, "A Sample Student Code," *Phi Delta Kappan*, December, 1974, pp. 236–242.
** My thanks for some of these ideas to Mr. James Andrésen, Ms. Pat Hays-Lapan, and Mr. David Sugar, as well as many other teachers with whom I've talked.

- What should teachers do when they know the principal is wrong?
- What should students do when they know the principal is wrong?
- Should students be allowed to evaluate teachers?
- Should students be allowed to evaluate the principal?
- What should teachers and students have a right to expect from each other?
- What should teachers and students have a right to expect from the principal or other administrators?

These are just a few of the many possible rights issues that apply to the central function of the classroom and the school. Whether they have legal implication is of only secondary importance. What is important is that these and other concerns exist in the reality of human interactions between everyone in the school, and they are therefore legitimate issues that should be confronted. They are the stuff of gossip, rumors, and hidden rationale for decision making—they shouldn't be. The respect for the dignity of every individual in the school demands that these rights questions face the light of open discussion and negotiated settlement.

*14*

# Teacher Organizations and the Future of Education

Teachers should have a much greater hand in running the schools than they now do. The ultimate goal, in my view, is for education to become institutionally autonomous, pursuing the humanistic and scholarly values to which it is committed, not necessarily putting down other institutions, but also not serving as a self-effacing lackey before the demands of other groups.

The behavior of organized teachers is absolutely critical to what happens to education. My reasons for this belief are both practical and theoretical. Practical because only organized teachers have the potential power to effect major changes. Theoretical because there are good reasons why only those closest to the learning situation can bring about the best atmosphere for learning. Whether teachers want the responsibility or not, they are the major guardians of the humanistic and learning values of the society as a whole.

## Visions of the Future

Dan Lortie (1975), a University of Chicago sociologist, has written an outstanding book on the sociology of the teaching profession. He has constructed three interesting scenarios of the future of teaching.**

* A version of this paper was presented to the Summer Leadership Conference, Michigan Education Association, at Central Michigan University, August 3, 1976.

**Scenario 1.** This involves the "erosion of tradition" within teaching. It goes like this. Pressure for change mounts from outside the schools. Businesses, government agencies, foundations, and universities continue to put pressure on the public schools for various specific changes that each wants for its own reasons. Governments offer incentives to schools to adopt particular innovations. Pressure for change becomes institutionalized.

New programs are created outside the schools, often based on approaches and techniques that teachers do not like. Schools are inundated with new programs and demands. They do not know how to respond or what to choose. Teachers do not have adequate information on which to decide. They resist defensively. Teachers are labeled by those outside the schools as reactionary and obstructionist and as being unworthy of public support.

**Scenario 2.** "Backlash in bargaining." School boards get their act together on bargaining. Teacher gains characteristic of the past decade become increasingly tough to obtain. In negotiation for salary increases school boards insist on measurable performance standards for teachers. Accountability schemes abound.

With the recognition of teacher power, the public ceases to accord teachers its ritual pity. Rather than being seen as innocent dupes, teachers are now seen as being jointly responsible for all the deficiencies of the educational system. They are blamed for test score declines and rising costs. The inconvenience of strikes arouses public anger. Tenure, automatic pay increases, and other aspects of the school system come under fire.

School boards, backed by state agencies, insist on firing procedures. The situation is exacerbated by the fact that there are more teachers than jobs. Teaching becomes less satisfying personally as public criticism mounts. The autonomy of the individual teacher is decreased as collective agreements impose increased restrictions on the individual teacher.

**Scenario 3.** Increased centralization of control. School districts become larger and fewer. The central office staff assumes more control. Things become more bureaucratized. As local property taxes are exhausted, the state pays a larger share of the costs. State agencies become far more aggressive in trying to control local education. Edicts, rules, and regulations flow from state capitols. Finally, only a few large districts remain and these are controlled by the state.

In this increasing bureaucratization, the teacher becomes more and more like a civil servant. Vertical authority emanating from the top becomes even more pronounced. Classroom behavior is regulated by rules of what can and cannot be done. Teachers try to counter the trend by bargaining at the state and national levels. Large bargaining coalitions are formed. School boards counter by forming their own massive coalitions. Bargaining is conducted at global levels. The individual teacher feels alienated from the government, the school district, and the teacher organization.

So ends Lortie's three visions of the future. I do not know which will occur, or in what combination, or whether any will occur at all. They are merely extrapolations from current trends, although reasonable extrapolations. One thing does seem clear: hard times, they are a-comin'.

## Hard Times Are Coming

It may be instructive to look at an item from the front page of the *Los Angeles Times,* dated July 2, 1976, and headlined "Jury Hits Teacher Tenure Law as Haven for the Unfit." According to the article the Los Angeles County grand jury urged that the state teacher tenure law be modified because it "has become a haven for the incompetent."

The committee chairman said, "Tenure has become a haven for the incompetent teacher. It should be altered to include a system of merit pay and periodic evaluation which provides incentives for quality teaching." The actual grand jury recommendation states that the tenure law should be modified to "facilitate removal of incompetent teachers who could not receive a successful evaluation on their teaching skills, and whose presence in the schoolroom hinders learning and in some cases, even retards progress in pupils."

According to the report, since teachers are united in strong professional organizations which represent them on every major issue, the tenure law is no longer necessary. The grand jury also encouraged all the school districts in Los Angeles County to "establish a review board and set uniform standards for evaluating teachers' performances at least once every three years as a condition of continued employment."

For good measure the grand jury recommended repeal of the Rodda Act, which regulates employee-employer relations for certificated employees, and which was passed by the California legislature in 1975. Among other things, the Rodda Act calls for selection of an exclusive bargaining agent within a school district. The grand jury wants the older Winton Act reinstated, and this would do away with exclusive bargaining and give back to the school board final say on school matters, as opposed to the binding arbitration of the Rodda Act.

The grand jury report says, "The committee feels that the fundamental problems of collective bargaining and strikes in the public sector, particularly in the schools, are incompatible with the rights of the electorate."

I think the meaning of the Los Angeles grand jury report is clear. There is a backlash against all public employee bargaining. Collective bargaining on salary issues is going to be tougher. Thousands of teachers are being laid off. Thousands have no jobs. The reason given for these drastic conditions is lack of money. That is a partial truth. The problem is not that there is no money. The problem is where the money is.

Here is an item from the *New York Times* financial section, dated May 23, 1976, and headlined, "All Systems Are Go for the Arms Makers." The article begins, "The outlook for the United States military production industry is more cheerful today than in years." Referring to the 1977 fiscal year, the article continues,

> "This new budget will include money for some of the most sophisticated and expensive weapons ever produced and could keep major contractors busy into the next decade."
> "What's more, the Pentagon is warned that profits of the weapons makers aren't high enough and is seeking ways to increase them."
> "The defense budget this year was up over $10 billion. . . . The Ford Administration makes clear that it sees its fiscal 1977 proposals for spending $101 billion as only the first step in a prolonged arms buildup."
> "This buildup will require real expenditures in arms and manpower to increase by 4 percent annually over the next five years, meaning a total Pentagon budget of $141 billion in fiscal 1981, up $40 billion from 1977. And, of course, major cost overruns are not unusual in arms buying."

The big increases are not for manpower or operating costs but for new equipment. In the 1977 budget alone spending was up thirty-six percent for airplanes, sixty percent for ships, thirty percent for missiles, and thirty-one percent for electronic equipment. Military research will increase sixteen percent to $11 billion a year.

Now if one takes another $40 billion a year out of the national income, one doesn't have to be good at either arithmetic or economics to see that there will be little left for anything else. Clearly, in making such plans the administration has already earmarked the funds. To say that the leftovers for social programs will be lean is an understatement. Such spending also means hard times at the state and local levels.

## Locus of the Problems

The problem is in the taxing arrangements. What taxpayers carrying a $140 billion defense establishment on their backs, and also accustomed to a steady stream of new consumer goods, will vote themselves new taxes? The property tax is the taxpayer's only chance to vote against higher taxes at all. Meanwhile the federal income tax creams off the top of national income and spends it on defense without any direct public participation.

How would the defense budget fare if the public could vote on each aircraft carrier or B1 bomber? How would the CIA budget fare if subjected to the two-thirds margin of plurality necessary for passage of educational referenda in some states? Defense is too important to be left to direct public participation.

Education is a subordinate institution subject to quadruple checks on its operation and autonomy. First, it is governed by a board of laymen onto which any particular interest group can put members, be they interested in selling school buses or harrassing an individual teacher. Secondly, it must periodically run the gauntlet of the property tax for its very existence. Third, extra monies must be supplicated from state legislators or the Congress, who in their munificence *may* deign to grant funds. Those funds increasingly have coarse strings attached, if not steel cables. In contrast, consider how Lockheed Aircraft, supposedly under federal supervision, could pay out millions of dollars in bribes.

Fourthly, any person or group can walk into any school and protest against a particular school policy or teacher and have a good chance of causing a stir. My most recent protest against business was in a pancake house where I discovered a half-inch chunk of glass in the pancake in my mouth. I complained and the management responded by giving me three free buttermilk pancakes—which, by the way, I did not eat. My only consolation came three months later when the cook shot the manager in the kitchen as a result of an argument.

Education has not only been a subordinate institution. Since the time when unmarried daughters living at home were recruited to be teachers, cost being a primary consideration, education has been an appropriately *humble* institution. It has been content to serve as a handmaiden to businesses and other institutions that needed trained workers to make their own enterprises more effective. Education has been sufficiently humble in its needs and its demands and its attitudes.

One of the trade-offs was that although the teacher was given meager resources in comparison with other professionals, the teacher was more or less left alone. Teachers were willing to settle for the personal gratification that came from interacting with kids. But that isolation is dissolving rapidly. If one inspects Lortie's three scenarios of the future, a common thread runs through all three: the erosion of remaining teacher autonomy. The world is closing in.

Why? My own explanation is that in societies where the economic institutions are dominant over all others, economic efficiency and productivity become the primary goals of the society. As the economy becomes more fully integrated, all the unnecessary waste from an economics point of view is squeezed from the other institutions. Anything that does not contribute directly to the productivity of the economy is defined as waste.

The values of other institutions are progressively smothered, be they humanistic as in education and medicine, or charismatic and traditional as in religion. Efficiency is impressed upon those institutions as their main objective and they are evaluated by their efficient contribution to the total economy. They become more business-like. That's why they must be changed. That's how they must be changed.

Such is the trend in the United States, the most advanced capitalist economy in the world. Such is the case in the Soviet Union, the most advanced socialist economy in the world. So it is in most advanced industrial nations. Even Britain, characteristically inefficient and traditional, has launched a "performance assessment" unit at the national level to improve education—their own brand of accountability to prod laggardly institutions like the educational. Whatever the explanation, the evidence is strong that teachers as a professional group and education as an institution are coming under increasingly severe pressure.

The politicians won't help—except insofar as pressure and incentives can be brought to bear on them. They are the ones who passed, with little significant opposition, a $101 billion defense bill. The school boards and administrators won't help much. They serve different interests. The parents —the parents *may* help if they are persuaded that teachers serve their interests too. They appear to me to be potential, natural, and necessary allies, under the right conditions.

But mainly, ultimately, teachers have to rely upon themselves. They have no protectors. That is perhaps the longest, hardest lesson to be learned in American education. In the long run, though, the prospects are encouraging. Over two million highly educated and articulate people are a formidable force—if highly organized. In spite of hard times, I see prospects for significant changes in the way American education is run.

It was out of hard times that Roosevelt's New Deal was born. The greatest reforms have often emerged when the current social arrangements were under severe duress. If teacher gains are to be hard-fought on the financial front, I would suggest other areas in which negotiation might be fruitful and toward which teachers might turn if they are to play a stronger role in improving education.

### Remedies—What Teachers May Have to Do

In terms of action, organized teachers will first want to take issue with priorities on government spending. This issue is nothing less than a fight over national priorities and values. Organized teachers will have to assert a priority on educational values at the local, state, and federal levels. There is no one else to do it. At the local level money issues will continue to revolve around the property tax, with its attendant difficulties.

At the state level the first problem is to get more resources from the state legislature. The second problem is to prevent state agencies from attaching strings to those funds, something they are very much wont to do. The reason is that state bureaucrats build their careers and empires on administered funding. The more strings there are, the more power they have. Their primary concern is their career. Anything that hits at their career attacks their soft underbelly. That is their vulnerability.

At the national level, the issue will be manifested in defense spending, for it has captured the federal budget. The great producer of government funds is the federal income tax and ultimately education must make significant claims upon it. The fact that a few billions now go into education compared with tens of billions going into defense is a reflection of our national priorities. Compared to other countries, we rank at the top in percent of national income spent on defense but well down the list in percent spent on education.

Contention for resources at all levels requires lobbying and political action: supporting politicians, getting close to the decision makers, making positions known, getting publicity, forming coalitions. Teachers are only now beginning to provide the kinds of resources necessary to make a difference in political terms. And the results are beginning to be felt.

In addition to things teachers want to do, there are some things that teachers are going to *have* to do, even though unpleasant. One of those is to agree to a stronger system to eliminate poor teachers. The outside pressure is just too fierce, the Los Angeles grand jury blast being one example.

In my first book on school evaluation I said that teacher evaluation was so fraught with difficulties that it was best left alone and that people should concentrate on evaluating programs. Slowly and reluctantly, I have come to the conclusion that teacher evaluation is necessary although no less fraught with difficulties. One of the difficulties is that what is a good teacher for one purpose and one student may not be good for another.

Nonetheless, the public has so lost confidence in public institutions that some kind of internal policing mechanism is necessary for maintaining public support. The older systems like accreditation visits to the school or the principal visiting the classroom a few times have lost their credibility. I think something will have to replace them. A highly publicized teacher evaluation plan might drain off some public enthusiasm for more dangerous accountability schemes and for attempts to do away with tenure.

Needless to say, cooperating in teacher evaluation schemes is perilous for the teacher organization. Several years ago a colleague and I presented to the leadership of one state association a plan for setting up and controlling part of a teacher evaluation system. The association leaders almost tipped their chairs over trying to back away from the table. It wasn't a very good plan but the problem is more basic.

A teacher evaluation plan places the association in something of a conflict of interest with its members. Ordinarily an association is expected to represent the interests of its members, not to police them. It may be, as the association leaders suggested, that such unpopular activities should be left to the administration.

It is important though that in the design and implementation of such a plan the teachers make sure the plan is a good one. For this reason I prefer the Connecticut teacher evaluation act to the Michigan one. The Michigan scheme has consisted of a rather mechanical testing program. The Connecticut scheme requires that local school boards negotiate with the local teacher organization in establishing an evaluation system and provides several years within which such a system can be worked out.

If I were designing such a plan, I would want to collect all the different kinds of information about the teacher being evaluated and have this information submitted to a private panel consisting of teachers, administrators, and parents. The ultimate recommendations would be those of the panel, based at least in part upon the opinion of the teacher's peers.

Such a peer review panel is not unlike that used in colleges for promotion and retention. One way of countering pressures coming from the administrators above and from critics from the outside is to assume more collegial authority inside. For example, my university has preempted the demands for program evaluation emanating from the state board of higher education by setting up an internal system to evaluate departments and programs, a system overseen by nine professors. If we are to be evaluated, we can at least decide how it is to be done.

I think that increasing collegial authority may be the way to go ultimately. It does have a price, however. It means the teacher's work will be more open to his or her colleagues and subject to their judgments. Traditionally the public school teacher has been isolated in the classroom and not subject to other adult interference, which is in fact considered by the teacher to be an intrusion. The changeover to a more collegial system could be traumatic for many teachers. I think more collegial control will come eventually, for the alternatives—vertical control and manipulation by external forces—are much worse.

## Decision Making—What Teachers Should Do

So much for what teachers may have to do. Now for some things that I think teacher organizations *should* do. The traditional posture of American labor unions has been to bargain for financial rewards and to let management run the business as it sees fit. If teacher organizations follow this practice, it will be a tragedy for education. It will mean that those who are in the position to know what is best for the students would abrogate their responsibility and let others further removed decide what is educationally proper. I find that an indefensible position.

It seems to me that teachers, both as individuals and in organization, must take strong stands on educational practices. Any other posture puts the teacher in the position of a doctor who merely serves as a conduit for the drug companies and much worse than the laborer who assumes no responsibility for the product. It is one thing not to care what a car looks like as it comes off the assembly line, but quite another not to care what happens to a child.

Of course, teachers do care and individually manifest that care daily in dozens of decisions they make. But what about decision making on the entire educational program at the school district level? How do matters now stand on collective teacher decision making versus decision making by administrators and others? A study was recently completed on how negotiated contracts limit the principal's authority.

In studying the problem Parker (1976) divided the principal's job into thirteen traditional task areas and examined twenty-five master contracts in Illinois to determine whether the principal's authority was greatly limited, moderately limited, slightly limited, or not limited at all by the written contract within each of the thirteen areas.

In none of the thirteen areas has the principal's authority been greatly limited. In only two areas—teacher evaluation and using regular teachers to substitute—has the principal's authority been even moderately limited. In eight more areas—academic assignments, extracurricular assignments, student discipline, curriculum, disciplining staff, determining organizational policy, school-community relations, and program evaluation—the principal's authority has been only slightly limited by the written contracts.

In three of the thirteen areas—hiring staff, determining financial needs of the school, and student activities—the principal's authority is not limited at all. Taking the thirteen task areas together and adding them up, it turns out that overall the principal's authority is only slightly limited by negotiated master contracts, as opposed to moderately or greatly limited.

This suggests that teachers are a very long way from collective decision making in the school, particularly on some of the most important issues. It is true that the principal's authority is often curtailed by implicit, unwritten understandings between himself and the teachers. It is true that the principal *sees* his authority as being limited by the mere fact that there are grievance procedures and a written contract. Nonetheless, these findings indicate that the principal's actual authority is not nearly as limited now as one might have guessed. As a group, teachers are not sharing in the important decisions, except as individual principals grant them a role.

These aspirations for decision making do seem to be legitimate teacher organization goals. A survey of teacher leadership conducted by Ward (1974) and published by the National Education Association suggested that the highest priority goal in instruction and professional development was for local organizations to participate with school boards in policy decisions in curriculum and instruction. This goal was followed closely in priority by state teacher organizations participating in the licensing and certification of teachers.

The next most important goals of the twenty-five ranked by the teacher leadership were for all teacher organizations to use their political power to establish legal and financial foundations for instructional improvement and for local teacher organizations to share in deciding how teachers and other instructional personnel are placed in schools. These are primary goals of teacher organizations and remain substantially unaccomplished. I am suggesting that as financial bargaining becomes more protracted, teacher organizations put relatively more emphasis on entry to decision-making processes. In the long run these are equally if not more important than financing, though of course both are critical if education is to secure any degree of institutional autonomy.

## Negotiated Innovation

Let me take the third of these four highest priority goals, establishing a foundation for instructional improvement, and suggest what it might look like when implemented and why it is necessary for teacher organizations to be involved in instructional improvement programs at all. Let us begin with the current national approach to educational improvement, which involves teachers in no significant way.

The current approach is the "research, development, diffusion" approach, sometimes nicknamed "the pipeline model." The basic idea is that a research and development process will produce a new educational program the way Detroit produces a new car, and this new curriculum or computer-assisted learning or new testing program or whatever it is, will be disseminated around the country to classroom teachers who will be only too happy to snap it up. Or in the cruder metaphor of the pipeline, the stuff is mixed up and pumped out to the consumers. (See Chapter 10)

Over the last ten years the federal government has spent several hundred million dollars on the approach, and much more than that if one counts all the other federal programs keyed to the overall plan. How effective has this approach been in improving education? According to most observers and studies, it has not been effective at all.

Why does this approach persist in spite of repeated and colossal failures? Conceptualizing educational improvement as a research, development, dissemination process with eventual adoption of the products by the schools places all the money and power in the hands of the few people who control the process. Everything is initiated by the government and the R and D agencies. That's where the money goes; that's where the power lies. A few people can control the flow of new ideas into the schools. The only role that teachers have is to sit passively and serve as a market for these products. Fortunately, they have generally refused to buy them.

Democratically, having a few experts control the educational change process is an undemocratic disaster. Educationally, it is no less of a catastrophe. Here are people who are far removed from the classroom creating materials and programs. The programs do not focus on the concerns of classroom teachers and are not attuned to the way schools function.

There is a fundamental flaw in the production of such materials. It is the idea that one can create materials that are equally useful all over. Anyone who has ever taught knows that that is not true. Even children in the same classroom respond differently to the same materials, and the teacher must continually adjust for each child until he or she finds what works. So-called "individualized" materials merely let some kids go faster and some slower. They are not "personalized" to the real personality of each child at all. That's what the teacher struggles to do. Teaching remains a variable and nonstandard activity. Yet the assumption that programs are highly transferable remains a central tenet of the R, D, and D approach because only by central production is control consolidated in a few people and production cheap.

Assuming that this is the situation and one still wants to improve instruction through innovation, how can one proceed? If one wants to maintain centralized control, it would be logical to reward individual teachers for innovating. This could be done through differential salary increases or promotions such as suggested in the Los Angeles County grand jury report. Those teachers who adopt an innovation prescribed by the school board or the government get so much money or are promoted to Teacher Level 4.

Another way it might work is for the Michigan state agency, as an example, to administer tests. A teacher's students, for whatever reason, do not do well on the thirty-five math objectives. The state says, "Here are special materials to use in achieving these objectives." The materials are keyed specifically to the objectives, and the teacher, anxious to look good, uses the materials. Of course, I doubt that the Michigan state department would ever harbor such ideas of interfering in the local schools.

Such an induced incentive approach would increase innovation. But I am opposed to it because it would increase morally *blind* innovation. Teachers would be innovating for the sake of their careers and personal interests without knowing whether it was better for the kids. The Michigan teacher might increase test scores but math instruction might well be worse. Innovation for the sake of innovation is not a good answer and reducing the judgment of the person who must implement the innovation is morally suspect. For a chilling illustration, consider the body count incentive in the Vietnam War.

As opposed to all these approaches I would suggest a more demo-cratic approach. I would suggest *negotiated* innovation. Those who wish to implement an innovation in a school should formally negotiate with the teachers in that school as to whether and how it should be done. Those to be affected by the innovation would bargain over the terms of the implementation.

How far would the innovation go? How could it be altered? What would teachers get out of it? What resources are available to implement? In the democratic negotiated approach the costs and rewards would be more equitably distributed rather than the costs going to the teachers and the rewards to the developers.

Negotiated innovation assumes also that the teachers are rational people who can look at an innovation and at local circumstances and determine whether there is a fit between the two. Innovation can be fitted to the local circumstances with each group bargaining for what they deem most important. Since they had a hand in shaping the innovation, and share in the rewards, teachers will probably do their best in the implementation.

Negotiated innovation puts teachers on an equal footing with the developers, instead of reducing them to the status of a passive, irrational group to be manipulated by various incentives. It forces the developers to address the real issues in the public schools rather than spin pipe dreams. Otherwise, the teachers will not cooperate. It establishes a two-way dialogue in the improvement of education. It just may be that teachers might have a few ideas about improving education themselves.

I am assuming that inquiry into educational processes is a good thing and that teachers will participate in such inquiry if they are accepted as partners rather than pawns. I have been talking about negotiated innovation at the local level but negotiation will have to proceed at the state and federal levels as well. It is ironic that the national teacher organizations have traditionally supported educational research and development and innovation funds and that only within the past year or so have the teacher leaders been invited to meetings even as a gesture of tokenism.

I am sometimes confronted by people who say, "How will you pay for such improvements?" Well, instructional improvement will cost money. The idea of improving an industry of fifty million people with a sum of $80 million is so absurd when you think of it that it is laughable. What if the government gave the steel industry, a far smaller operation than education, $80 million and said, "Go, modernize yourself." Preposterous.

One of the devices business has is the tax investment credit. The government allows each business a certain percent of its income tax-free to be used to buy new machinery and in general modernize itself. I would suggest a similar school innovation credit, say five percent of the school's total budget, to be spent for improving instruction however the district saw fit.

The district could pay for released time for teachers working on innovations, buy materials, or use the funds in a number of other ways. The government could not tell the district specifically how to spend the money. The funds could be stable over a period of years so the district could count on the money for long-term improvement. Innovation under such circumstances could be deeply planted and broadly based rather than ephemeral.

## What to Negotiate For—The Teacher Researcher

If teachers were able to negotiate instructional improvement, what kinds of things might they ask for? That would be up to local teachers who are faced with local problems. The possibilities are endless and depend on local circumstances. I would like to suggest a few possibilities in line with the themes of inquiry, more collegial authority, and greater teacher power over instruction.

The sociologist Lortie (1975) has suggested the role of the "teacher researcher." Although it hardly seems the time to initiate a new specialty, over the long run I think the role of teacher researcher would be of great benefit to the teaching profession. The teacher researcher would concentrate on classroom problems—unlike any other researcher working in education—and would see as his or her major audience the particular classroom teachers he or she is assigned to work with. Also unlike any other researchers working in education, his or her allegiance would be to the profession.

When someone gets an advanced research degree, he or she usually turns to research problems as defined by a discipline like educational psychology or to problems as defined by government officials or occasionally the administrators of a school district. These are almost never the problems as teachers see them. Teachers rightly see most research now being done as irrelevant.

For years teachers have been dominated intellectually by college professors, central-office staffs, and self-appointed free-lance school critics who like to snipe away at the public schools. The only defense teachers have had is to ignore the critics as best they can.

If education is ever to be institutionally autonomous, it must be intellectually autonomous. Teachers cannot depend on outside people to supply them with new ideas. Those people serve other interests. In the most pragmatic terms teachers must discover and nurture their own intellectual talents if they are to plan successfully and justify their actions in their society.

A group without intellectual autonomy, no matter what their political power, is a group without true autonomy. Both are necessary. The teacher researcher is not a panacea for this basic problem, it is but one step in breaking the monopoly of knowledge held by other people. There is more than enough academic talent among the two million teachers to do so.

In addition to the qualities of humanitarianism, idealism, and dedication traditionally valued by teachers, the teaching profession has also been characterized by tending to be very conservative in changing educational practice, individualistic in that teachers are confined to the classroom and do not share knowledge with other teachers, and present-oriented in looking for immediate feedback from the students, mainly because of the difficulty of judging the effects of teaching.

I have intimated that the profession may alter some of these latter values in adapting to new circumstances. The teacher researcher might provide trustworthy information and help the teacher decide on new approaches. The teacher researcher might help improve technical knowledge in teaching. Sharing knowledge among teachers and thus strengthening collegial bonds should be a major activity and a major outcome.

My assumption is that a tremendous amount of useful information about teaching exists in the heads of practicing teachers but that there is no current procedure to codify that knowledge about teaching and share it with other teachers far removed or those beginning in the profession. The teacher researcher could do this with case studies, teacher conferences, and so on.

In Britain John Elliot (1976) and his colleagues have been working on classroom problems with teachers for some time. The researchers train teachers still in the classrooms in research skills. The teachers define the problems and generate hypotheses and approaches they wish to try out in their classrooms. Over a year or two the researchers withdraw completely until the teachers are totally on their own in researching their own classroom problems and working with teachers in other schools doing the same. To an outsider, the results produced by the teachers are impressive. The teachers *say*, at least, that the process is fruitful for them.

I have deliberately left unanswered the question of who will pay for such a function. Leaders of teacher organizations are seriously split in the issue of whether teacher organizations should pay for instructional improvement. Certainly doctors and lawyers do not pay for most of the research that directly affects their professions. The price of not supporting such operations is an inevitable lessening of control. Much of the research in medicine is conducted by the drug companies, who undertake only research that will profit them. I leave the question open.

## A Final Scenario—Institutional Autonomy

I will end with a fourth scenario of the future. As pressure builds teachers become better organized internally and more sophisticated politically. They mount well-conceived and well-financed political campaigns at the state and federal levels. Legislators respond with more money for education and begin to see teachers as a formidable force.

Inside the schools, changes are quieter but equally significant. Through negotiation in district after district organized teachers enter the decision-making process on educational programs and personnel. They assume more authority and responsibility in training, hiring, and evaluation. Collegial authority among teachers becomes more pronounced as the isolation of the individual teacher in the classroom yields to cooperative team approaches to educational problems. Teachers present more of a united front to themselves and to others.

Government authorities and developers must bargain with teacher organizations when they wish to introduce innovations in the schools. Teacher organizations assume responsibility for assessing and implementing new programs. Increasingly, as national, state, or local government leaders wish to make critical decisions in resource allocation, they must consult teacher organizations. Education as an institution ceases to be the whipping boy for larger social ills or fall supine in doing the bidding of other institutions.

Education ceases to be subservient. It assumes an equal bargaining stance with other major institutions on important societal issues. Education achieves sovereignty in its own domain.

# 15

# Negotiating for Resources

## Collective Bargaining in Brandville

When it comes down to it, the ultimate strategy in negotiating for resources is collective bargaining. It pits the teachers in a district as a collectivity against whatever forces on the school board oppose them at a particular time. As we have indicated elsewhere, the school is one of the most porous of social institutions. It is open to whatever forces are able to mobilize themselves in the community and in fact is susceptible even to the ravings of a single person.

The school's operations are also extremely open to public purview. Because it teaches children who return home to their parents every day, the school's boundaries are transparent. Compare the schools to other social institutions such as the courts, the hospitals, the city government, and businesses, and you will see the extreme vulnerability the schools as an institution.

For this reason alone, it is imperative that the teachers present a unified front toward the rest of the community. Maintaining a stable learning environment and securing the resources necessary for a high quality educational enterprise, not to mention the legitimate self-interests of the teachers and students, depend on such collective action. In this chapter we take a close look at the formal instrument for collective action—the collective bargaining procedure.

Brandville was a fairly prosperous community of about 50,000 people in the mid-seventies, although like virtually all school districts it was victimized by severe money problems in the schools. The governor of the state was up for reelection and hence did not want to raise state taxes. In fact he had campaigned on a "no new taxes" platform. So there were no new state monies available.

The district had twice within the past year and a half turned down two educational referendums. The town had a high proportion of middle-class, white-collar workers who were traditionally sympathetic toward education, but they had been feeling the financial squeeze generated by the recession. Most were attached in some way to government-related jobs. The governor's austerity program had meant they were getting very small raises.

This financial stringency was felt in two ways. First, if they were getting small raises, why should the teachers do any better? As often happens, social discontent generated elsewhere was passed along to the schools. It's part of the common syndrome of "if my boss chews me out, I'll go home and kick the dog." Secondly, property taxes were indeed high. With no industrial base the middle-class homeowners had to foot most of the tax bill.

Of course there was no real financial impoverishment among most middle-class people. Most of them had at least two cars, were paying on fairly expensive homes, had campers, boats, etc. The amount of property tax paid for the schools was less than they would spend each year maintaining only one of their cars. But that's not how they saw it. Their material expectations were that they would have even more cars and boats, and bigger houses. The realization that such dreams might not come true began to creep into their consciousness and they did not like it.

So the public began to look for items in the school budget that they could cite as extravagances. Better to look there than in their own personal budgets, since looking at the school budget had fewer ramifications for them. And of course they found some extravagances—a few thousand wasted here, a few thousand there, enough to point to and say, "See, I told you they were wasting our hard-earned money." The fact that the teachers earned their money much the same way as most of the people in town was not an acceptable counterargument.

There were some things the schools might have lived without, such as air-conditioning and carpeting in some of the schools. For the most part these "extravagances" are nothing compared to those in private business. Those who say that the schools are not run like a business are correct. The schools are run much more stringently financially than are businesses. With few exceptions, the critics of the affluence of the schools have much more expensive life styles than do the teachers and children in the schools themselves.

## Preparing the Negotiations Package

The Brandville teachers began preparing for negotiations the October previous to the expiration of their current contract. The first step was to choose a negotiation committee. This committee consisted of a representative elected from each school so each school felt it had a say in the negotiations. The representatives are also important later on in communicating back to the teachers in the schools what the negotiation committee is thinking and doing. It is extremely important that the committee be representative of all the teachers.

In January the committee began working out their "package"—the initial set of demands they would present to the school board negotiators. The most crucial task in drawing up a package is to talk to the membership. The building representatives are the obvious people to find out what the membership is thinking. In looking for issues it's also highly desirable to talk to the grievance committee and to analyze past grievances. Not all grievances can or should be addressed in the negotiations but there may be recurrent problems that are worth consideration.

The most difficult and important thing is to find out what the membership really wants. This is not easy to do. One way to do this is to conduct a series of discussions at each school during the preparation period. This way visiting members of the negotiation committee can assess not only the issues the teachers are interested in but also how strongly they feel about particular issues. Do they feel strongly enough to strike over it? What are they willing to trade off for a particular issue when the going gets rough? This is vital information for the negotiators to have during the crucial phases of negotiation. The collective bargaining procedure does not allow for very many or very lengthy consultations with the membership in the final critical phases.

A second major consideration in preparing the negotiation package is not to set unrealistic goals. It is easy in the flush and excitement of talking to each other to set goals that have no chance of fulfillment. For example, one might set an impossibly high wage demand. There is also a temptation to pledge to the membership that you are going to achieve this demand "or else." This puts the negotiator in a difficult position.

First, a ridiculous demand will not be taken seriously by the other side. This gets the negotiations off to a bad start because they think you are going to be unreasonable. Second, they can and will leak this unrealistic demand to the press and public, which will result in an erosion of public support for the teachers. Third, when a good settlement is reached, it will still look bad to the membership if the negotiators have pledged themselves to an unrealistic goal. If the negotiation committee makes promises to the membership, the promises should be sufficiently general so the negotiators have plenty of flexibility and are not embarrassed by the actual settlement.

The opposite can also be the case with teachers. They often want to ask for precisely what they will get. As a group teachers are very reasonable people, often too reasonable, and they don't see why they should not be absolutely forthright in their demands. The reason is that bargaining simply doesn't work that way. Either formally or informally, collectively or individually, one is likely to get more if one asks for more. The adage that "the squeaking wheel gets the grease" is all too often true. At the same time one cannot remove oneself from the argument by making ridiculous demands.

So one must ask for somewhat more than one expects to get, knowing the other side will progressively raise its offer so that the two sides meet someplace between, although not in the exact middle of the demand and the offer. Situations differ dramatically but the general rule in private industry is that management usually initially offers about sixty percent of what the final settlement will be.

The initial package presented by the Brandville teachers asked for a fifteen percent wage increase. The teachers knew that they would not get that much increase considering the temper of the times but that it was a good position on wages to begin with. The school district was not in good financial shape with the failed referendums, and surrounding school districts were not getting such high increases. On the other hand, it was only a little more than the inflation rate and so was not a totally unreasonable demand.

It is extremely important that the negotiation demands be backed up by good arguments. Although the results of bargaining depend heavily on the political strength of the two parties and on economic circumstances, they also depend to a significant degree on the arguments one can muster. Negotiation is a form of argumentation. In fact, one's political support within the membership and with the public at large is dependent in part on how reasonable one's arguments are.

There are essentially three arguments on which wage demands can be based: ability to pay, comparable wages in other places, and the cost of living (Conners, no date). The district's ability to pay, what teachers in comparable places are making, and increases in the cost of living are the foundation upon which wage demands must be based. Mustering the arguments means finding the right comparisons to make. The Brandville teachers had the third one—the high inflation rate—going for them. Arguments for other types of demands are not so easily categorized but they are no less essential.

There is also the question of how many demands to present: ten or a hundred? Opinion is split on this. The membership will have more demands than the committee can handle. They will have to be screened. Some negotiators like to present a great number of demands so that they can be traded off for concessions on the part of the school board. The more experienced the negotiators on the other side, the less effective this tactic is. They know there are not dozens of issues on which the teachers are equally serious. They also know there are only a few on which the teachers will strike.

When negotiations reach the bind and push comes to shove, the teacher negotiators have to indicate to the other side which of the demands they are really serious about. They can't have them all.

In Brandville the negotiation committee did construct a long list of demands. Each of them had to be supported by facts and arguments. Partly as a result of that, the full negotiation package wasn't ready until the last day of school in the spring. It was too late to show the package to all the teachers and to get their reactions. This in turn caused problems in the fall negotiations since the teachers were not fully informed as to their own negotiating position. When friends and neighbors began pressuring them, they were not fully prepared to answer. This deficiency resulted in less internal cohesion and in less external public support then a better informed membership might have provided.

## The Negotiation Team

The entire negotiating committee representing all the varied teacher inter-ests is far too large a group for the actual negotiations. A negotiation team must be selected to do the negotiating. Usually the team is selected from the larger negotiation committee itself, as the commitee is in a posiion to know who is best informed on the issues and who would make good negotiators. How the team is to be selected should be clearly spelled out in the organizations bylaws.

The Brandville teachers elected a negotiation team of five members plus two alternates, in case the regular team members could not be there. A negotiation team should probably have at least five members. Not only does this provide better representation of different viewpoints on the team, it also provides a number of people who can communicate with the mem-bership later on. Communication with the membership is critical.

The team should probably also have representation from each school level. The Brandville team did not have any representative at the junior high school level and this led to problems later on with the junior high teachers. Of course it is not possible for every school to be represented except in very small districts. Selecting alternates also caused a problem. Since the alternates were sometimes present at meetings and sometimes not, they were never fully informed as to what was going on. This caused confusion. The negotiation team was finally expanded to seven full-time members to include the two alternates.

Brandville also had another selection problem. The teacher organi-zation was run by a group of young women who held most of the leader-ship posts. They also dominated the negotiation team. The coaches in the school district, who formed their own subgroup, agreed to support the teacher organization in the negotiations. But they balked at the team's being comprised mainly of young women. They were afraid the women wouldn't be tough enough. After some discussions they reluctantly agreed to have the women represent them.

The selection of the negotiation team is critical, because they, more than anyone else, will determine how successful the negotiations will be. In the critical phases of the negotiation they will make the decisions that the membership has to live with. While the membership will vote to accept or reject the settlement, what it looks like will be the result of the efforts of the team.

After its selection, the team must elect a chief spokesperson. Not everyone can talk at will during the meetings. The chances for contradiction and confusion are too great. All teams have a chief spokesperson to do the talking. Sometimes the specialization of roles is extended. The Brandville teachers had two "critical listeners" who had the role of making sure the chief spokesperson was hearing everything that was said and not misinterpreting the other side. They also had two "notetakers" who took down verbatim many of the comments of the other side, especially the informal proposals, in order to study them more carefully. One person also served as a "bookkeeper," keeping in order all the various proposals and documents.

The most important problem for the negotiation team is one of human relations. They must live through protracted and frustrating conflict without falling apart individually or as a group. Particularly in a strike situation the personal stress is heavy indeed. Some people, particularly teachers, don't like conflict situations and refuse to regard the negotiations as a conflict situation of "us" and "them," which it certainly is, and some refuse to participate fully in the process.

It is essential to the team that they be able to talk honestly and openly about their own emotions, their own actions, and those of the management. Personality differences are exacerbated under the intensely stressful conditions and it is important for the team to work them through with each other in private sessions. Much of team time is spent in one-to-one sessions with each other trying to work things out. It is a time for crying and shouting.

Management looks for weaknesses in the team and tries to exploit differences. They investigate team members to see what kind of people they are. Any internal differences and dissension that the team cannot iron out among themselves may result in a poor settlement. The Brandville team had one member who never disagreed in the conflict situation but who wanted to write a minority report later, which would have undermined the credibility of the team with the membership and the public and opened a major weakness for the other side to exploit. So the team must be extremely sensitive to its own interactions and feelings. Its own solidarity is critical.

The second most difficult problem for the team is communicating with members. After the negotiations begin, the membership can never be fully informed about what is happening. Negotiation is not a steady progression toward the settlement. It seesaws back and forth as offers and counteroffers are made and discussed. Most obvious progress is likely to come towards the end, in a flurry of activity. It's difficult for the membership, who are naturally anxious, to understand this.

The membership usually consists of several distinct groups (Conners, no date). There is an active, militant group that knows what is going on and is usually in charge of negotiations. There is another militant group that doesn't know what is going on much of the time. There are people who are terribly afraid of a strike at all times, no matter what. There is a group of teachers who are opposed to the teacher organization all the time. And there is a group of critics who like to second-guess all decisions.

Not all of these groups can be satisfied at one time, and some cannot be satisfied at any time. The negotiation team is going to come in for much criticism no matter what it does. The secrecy and rumors surrounding negotiation often make the criticism ill-founded. But there will be criticism, so negotiation team members had better be prepared for it. It makes internal team support all the more important.

Another good piece of advice is to have at the negotiation table only those members who are being held responsible for the outcome. Having observers who do not suffer the consequences of their remarks can lead to rather careless talk about the proceedings.

Overall the negotiation team should be comprised of those who are aggressive and flexible enough to be good bargainers, and who are willing to take the time to find out what the membership wants, to become familiar with every inch of the contract, and to be be able to work with the other members of the team. Above all, the team member should see the negotiations as a real commitment and not just a game.

## Negotiations

A few points should be made about negotiations in the atmosphere prevalent today. First, it is always true that collective bargaining depends on the willingness of both parties to negotiate and to live up to their agreement. If either party does not wish to negotiate an item, there is no room for bargaining.

Secondly, negotiations are much tougher today than they were only a few years ago. School boards have toughened up, even hiring professional negotiators to represent them in some cases.

The issues that school boards are likely to hang tough on are those that restrict their own power. Since professional control issues are likely to be pushed by the teacher organizations in tight money times, the scene is set for considerable conflict in the years ahead. In established contracts the conflict is likely to revolve around the obscure but critical issues of the contract language.

The Brandville teachers had had a good contract for many years, one of the best in the state. They had negotiated with the business manager, who was now the district superintendent. There was some feeling on the new school board that the superintendent had been too lenient with the teachers in the past and had given too much away.

In May and June the negotiation team met with the superintendent three times, with most of the discussion centered on a scheduling problem at the junior high school. After these meetings the school board suddenly announced that the superintendent would no longer negotiate for them. They were hiring a new negotiator, a lawyer from a big city law firm a few hundred miles away.

Taft, the lawyer, specialized in negotiating for school boards. In fact, he was simultaneously representing more than thirty school boards around the country. He was so busy he was very hard to get to see. The team anxiously awaited his arrival, knowing his firm's reputation as hard-liners in negotiations. Because of Taft's busy schedule, they were able to meet only three times before school started. While the teachers were able to use this fact to their advantage publicly, it made negotiations difficult.

Normally in early sessions both sides are uncomfortable and there is a lot of small talk as both groups try to wear off their nervousness. Both sides exchange demands in writing and begin to talk about the less important issues first. They try to size each other up. The team tries to assess the opposition's intentions and which demands the board negotiators are serious about—usually only one or two. The board negotiators try to size up the individual members of the team to see where they might make some inroads. Usually neither side wants a strike.

In the Brandville situation, however, it was already determined that Taft would take a hard line. Brandville teachers worked many years to build up their contract language. The first thing Taft did was to attack the contract wholesale. He suggested that the whole contract was up for grabs and suggested massive revisions in the contract language. From the first session with Taft, the negotiation team felt they had a strike situation on their hands.

It is not unusual for a relatively inexperienced team to face a skilled negotiator hired from outside. It is also a common tactic for the management to direct attention from the real issues by setting up smoke screens. By going on the attack the skilled management negotiator can gain the initiative. He can sow discord among the negotiation team members by asking each member for his or her views on a particular topic. He can pass judgment on each demand's merit, thereby setting himself up as the judge. He can praise and flatter each team member for his or her behavior or assume a parental role with the team. All these tactics give him ascendancy in the meetings. The antidote is to challenge him and to maintain the solidarity of the team. It is essential for the team to talk about these matters in private and to critique each other's behavior and susceptibility to the opposition's tactics.

It is also common for management to wait until late in negotiations to make their real offers. In the meantime they can try to crack the solidarity of the team and to assess the attitudes of the membership about what is going on. Usually they have good information about how the members feel. Sometimes the teachers can turn this kind of leakage to their advantage by making sure the school board members get the information the teachers want them to have.

By stalling around the board, negotiators can put extra pressure on the team, particularly if the team is inexperienced. The team gets upset over any lack of progress and begins to scale down their expectations of what they can get. Under this pressure a few team members will begin to wilt and to become a little too "reasonable" to the board's offers.

In typical negotiations there are two basic kinds of persuasion. One is the kind of reasonable argumentation that takes place in discussion. The other is the threat of a strike or some other action. The board negotiators must be convinced of the organization's strike capability without the team's bringing it up very often. The management negotiators do not like to be threatened, as indeed neither does the team. The action capability must be real but implied.

Neither do management negotiators like the team's attacking a particular administrator, questioning the motives of the school board, or using insulting language in the sessions. These actions raise the negotiators' backs and generally do not help. Another thing that damages the credibility of the team with the board negotiators is misinformation, either deliberate or accidental. One of the major sticking points in the Brandville negotiations was over a junior high scheduling problem which the team had learned of through a junior high teacher. The management negotiators kept insisting that the situation didn't exist. And in fact the team finally learned to their chagrin that it did not; they had been misinformed. This type of mistake really puts the team on the defensive. But such mistakes are inevitable. The team has to swallow hard and not be swamped by the mistake. A recess is a good idea at such moments.

Generally the strategy of negotiation is to make an offer that will get the other side to make the offer that you really want. The problem is how far to push them. Don't spend too much time on small problems. Let them know that you know the counterarguments to your own arguments. That reduces the effectiveness of the opposition. Watch the mannerisms of the opposition besides listening to their words for signs of intentions.

In Brandville, though, the attack on contract language was not just a stall or a bargaining tactic but a serious assault on the contract. Taft was insistent on revising such things as the hearing procedures for nontenured teachers. The issue became a power issue over whether the board could reduce the teaching force however it wanted to. The negotiation team was unprepared for this wholesale assault on their contract. The teachers responded by calling in more experienced help from their state and national organization.

## Teacher Strike!

Generally management will accept a strike rather than a settlement if the wage settlement is too far out of line with comparable settlements, if they feel the union is anxious to strike and there is no way around it, or if they feel their "right to manage" has been infringed upon. This case was closest to the latter. Although force reduction procedures were already written into the contract, the new board didn't want to accept them.

For their part teachers will seldom strike for money alone. There is usually another matter underlying the strike. In this case the teachers felt they could not give up on their contract. The stage was set for a strike.

The teachers realized they were in a serious situation. They declared an impasse and a mediator was called in. A mediator is sometimes helpful if there is a misunderstanding between the two parties or if there is much personal animosity in the negotiations. In this case the two sides were simply too far apart on the issues. The mediator was not terribly helpful.

The negotiations reached their climax the day before school was to start. In such crisis bargaining both sides are apt to make rash statements, and the board is likely to try bargaining past the team and attempting to reach the membership. The team should challenge the opposition on this. Also in such last-minute bargaining both sides should lay all their cards on the table and be clear about what an acceptable settlement is to them. This is when pressure is greatest on the management.

The school board in Brandville offered the teachers a contract extension. In fact, individual board members began to call up individual teachers to try to go around the team. A contract extension is a tough decision. It takes the board off the hook and it lets down the membership who have fired themselves up in preparation. It is very difficult to get them prepared again later in the year. A day or so extension may be useful but a longer one is probably not. The Brandville teachers refused the extension.

The board did two more things that fired up the teachers. They put an ad in the paper for substitute teachers in case of a strike and began to interview candidates. Then the night before school was to start the board negotiators and negotiations team were in separate rooms with the mediator as a go-between. The mediator returned to find the board room empty— the board had walked out. The team reported the walkout to the membership, who were waiting in a nearby building. Early the next morning the teachers took a strike vote. The strike was on.

The strike lasted eight school days during which the teachers were very cohesive. Support for the strike was nearly unanimous among the teachers, and this of course increased support in the community. The teachers were subject to external pressure from the community to end the strike and tried in turn to bring as much community pressure upon the school board. The teachers themselves did not know very much of what was going on and wanted the team to tell them.

The strike is the time of greatest pressure on the team. They cannot tell the membership everything because they would lose their flexibility to settle. There is always a strain between any negotiation team and any membership, but things really become strained during a strike. Members become suspicious of one another. This is not the time to let internal dissension show, for the opposition is looking for weaknesses.

Generally the organization should know when a strike is coming and be prepared. Yet even then a strike is always confusing to everyone. At first there is a holiday mood but the membership becomes progressively grimmer after that. Information control is a major problem. The team can only give the membership general information. The press always wants sensational stories and can usually find a member who will talk out of turn. The organization leadership must manage the strike while the team concentrates on bargaining.

The Brandville teachers tried to control rumors and gossip among the membership and the public by setting up a dial-a-message phone where anyone could call to hear the latest. They also set up a rumor center and urged their membership to call there to check things out. The team also found a leak in their own organization—someone who was trying to be helpful by informing some board members what the teachers were doing. They solved that problem by giving the person more work than could be handled.

Generally the Brandville teachers were very cohesive in their support of the strike—nearly unanimous. But by the third week of the strike they were beginning to weaken a bit. There were rumblings from the picket lines.

## Settlement

In a strike situation serious discussions often do not take place until the second week of the strike. Management sometimes feels it cannot give in too early. During the Brandville strike not much happened in the negotiations for a while. The negotiators met only twice during the entire strike. Waiting became a major problem.

After five days the board negotiator presented a proposal on maternity leave that was completely different from and irrelevant to the discussions that had taken place before. The team waited again while the strike went on.

In the second week, with considerable help from the state organization, the mediator arranged a secret meeting between the chief spokesperson of the team and the board negotiator. They met out of town and much of the bargaining was done by phone. Over a forty-eight-hour period the two bargained back and forth, with the board negotiator bargaining in between with the board itself. Nothing happened for thirty-six hours. Then during the last few hours everything fell into place.

Now the negotiation team had a decision to make. Should they take the settlement to the membership or should they push the board for more? This requires an intuitive judgment of whether the opposite side will go any further and how the membership will react. There is a danger the team may push beyond the settlement point. The team must decide.

The Brandville negotiation team decided that they had pushed far enough. They decided to present the board offer to the membership. Of course the team talked to influential individuals in the membership before the ratification meeting in order to secure their support. Whether the contract would be approved by the membership depended to a large degree on the opinions set by the informal power structure of the membership.

During the ratification meeting the members of the negotiation team were treated like heroes. They were given a standing ovation as they came down the center aisle. The contract was a good one—a nine percent raise and the contract language intact. Such a warm reception does not always greet negotiation teams, however. More often, the ratification meeting and especially its aftermath are times for second-guessing and expressions of dissatisfaction. The experienced negotiator becomes accustomed to such feedback.

Here at the end of this chapter, and this book, it is appropriate to ask if all the negotiations, the struggle, and the politics are worth it. Envision the ending of an old Sherlock Holmes movie as Holmes and Watson, having solved the case, ride in the back seat of an open car. Watson says, "Holmes, is it really worth it—all the maneuvering, the struggle for power, the poltitics?"

Holmes draws on his pipe for a moment. Then, still contemplating the passing landscape, he says slowly, "There may be a world, Watson, in which people succeed by their own merit. In which the weak are protected from the strong and where there is no need for power or politics. But that is not the world we live in. Until that time, old chap, we must strive through our own efforts to make this a better place as best we can." Slow fade-out.

## BOOKS TO READ

Conners, Terrence F. *Problems in Local Union Collective Bargaining.* United Auto Workers Education Department, Detroit, Michigan. No date.

There are not many books that deal with the nuts-and-bolts of collective bargaining. This is one of the best. Although it is written for shop stewards, it provides very practical advice on what to expect and how to behave in bargaining situations. It is well worth reading, particularly for those who have no previous bargaining experience.

BIBLIOGRAPHY

Anton, Jane, and Russell, Michael. "How to Get a Job." *Parade Magazine,* November 9, 1975, p. 14.

Ballantine, Hardin P.; Ballantine, Jeanne H.; and Cargan, Leonard. "Should Students Have Rights?" *Phi Delta Kappan,* October 1976, p. 207.

Beier, Ernst and J. D. Gill. "Non-Verbal Communication." Psychology Today Interview Cassette, Del Mar, California, 1974.

Berlo, David K.; Lemert, James E.; and Mertz, Robert J. "Dimensions for Evaluating the Acceptability of Message Sources." *Public Opinion Quarterly* 33 (1970), pp. 563–576.

Carlson, Richard O. *School Superintendents: Careers and Performance.* Columbus, Ohio: Charles E. Merrill Publishing Corporation, 1972.

Collins, Myrtle T., and Dwane R. Collins. *Survival Kit for Teachers (and Parents).* Santa Monica, California: Goodyear Publishing Company, Inc., 1975.

Committee on Rights of Minors: Illinois Commission on Children. "Draft For Improved Handling of Suspensions and Expulsions By a Legislative Proposal—An Illinois School Disciplinary Procedures Act (Subject to Revision)." Springfield, Illinois, February 1976.

Connors, Terrence F., *Problems in Local Union Collective Bargaining.* United Auto Workers Education Department, Detroit, Michigan. No date.

Davis, Carolyn R. "The Buckley Regulations: Rights and Restraint." *Educational Researcher* 4, February 1975, pp. 11–13.

Dececco, John P. and Richards, Arlene K. "Using Negotiation For Teaching Civil Liberties and Avoiding Liability." *Phi Delta Kappan,* September 1975, pp. 23–25.

DeFlaminis, John. "Teacher Responses to Classroom Misbehavior: Influence Methods in a Perilous Equilibrium." Paper presented at the American Educational Research Association Convention, San Francisco, April 1976.

Edwards, Dale. *The Behaviors of Acceptance.* Oaklawn, Illinois: Contemporary Curriculums, 1971.

Elliott, John and Clem Adelman. *Classroom Action Research.* Norwich, England: Centre for Applied Research in Education.

Endicott, Frank S. "Who Gets a Teaching Position in the Public School?" *ASCUS.* Madison, Wisconsin: Webcrafters, Inc. 1975, pp. 12–15.

Flygare, Thomas. *The Legal Rights of Students.* Bloomington, Indiana: The Phi Delta Kappa Educational Foundation, 1975.

Flygare, Thomas. *The Legal Rights of Teachers.* Bloomington, Indiana: The Phi Delta Kappa Educational Foundation, 1976.

Gibson, Ronald R.; Marshall, Robert D.; and Burd, John. "Preparing for and Getting That Teaching Job." *ASCUS.* Madison, Wisconsin: Webcrafters, Inc., 1975, pp. 6–8.

Glass, Gene V. "Teacher Effectiveness." In *Evaluating Education Performance,* edited by Herbert J. Walberg. Berkeley, California: McCutchan Publishing Corp., 1974.

Glasser, William. *Schools Without Failure.* New York: Harper and Row, 1969.

Gordon, Thomas. *P.E.T. Parent Effectiveness Training.* New York: Peter H. Weyden, Inc., 1970.

Gordon, Thomas. *T.E.T. Teacher Effectiveness Training.* New York: Peter H. Weyden, Inc., 1974.

Havelock, Ronald G. *Planning for Innovation.* Ann Arbor: Center for Research on Utilization of Scientific Knowledge, Institute for Social Research, University of Michigan, 1971.

Henning, Joel F. "Student Rights and Responsibilities and the Curriculum." *Phi Delta Kappan,* December 1974, pp. 248–250 and 256.

Hill, Jack D. "Teacher Selection." In *ASCUS.* Madison, Wisconsin: Webcrafters, Inc., 1975, pp. 26–27.

House, Ernest R. *The Politics of Educational Innovation.* Berkeley, California: McCutchan Publishing Corporation, 1974.

Karlins, Marvin and Abelson, Herbert I. *Persuasion.* New York: Springer Publishing Co., Inc., 1970.

Lapan, Stephen D. "The Development and Validation of an Instrument That Measures Student Perceptions of Teacher Credibility." Paper presented at the American Education Research Association Convention, San Francisco, April 1976.

Lapan, Stephen D. "The Development and Validation of an Instrument That Measures Student Perceptions of Teacher Credibility." Unpublished Doctoral Dissertation, The University of Connecticut, 1972.

Levine, Alan H. *The Rights of Students: The Basic ACLU Guide to a Public School Student's Rights.* New York: Avon Books, 1973.

Lichter, Paul. "Communicating with Parents: It Begins with Listening." *Teaching Exceptional Children,* Winter 1976, pp. 66–71.

Long, Nicholas J.; Morse, William C.; and Newman, Ruth G., eds. *Conflict in the Classroom: The Education of Emotionally Disturbed Children.* Belmont, California: Wadsworth, 1966.

Lortie, Dan C. *School-Teacher.* Chicago: University of Chicago Press, 1975.

Machiavelli, Niccolo. *The Prince.* New York: Washington Square Press, 1963.

McGivney, Joseph H. and Haught, James M., 1973. "The Politics of Education: A View from the Perspective of the Central Office Staff." *Educational Administration Quarterly* 8.3 (Autumn): 18–38.

Nichols, Ralph G. "Irritating Listening Habits of Supervisors." Undated mimeo.

Nichols, Ralph G. "Learn the Useful Art of Listening." Undated mimeo excerpted from *Changing Times,* December 1967.

Parker, Thomas A. "A Study of the Effect of Collective Bargaining Upon the Authority of the Principal in Secondary Schools in Illinois." Unpublished doctoral thesis, University of Illinois, 1976.

Phi Delta Kappa's Commission on Administrative Behavior Supportive of Human Rights. "A Sample Student Code," *Phi Delta Kappan,* December, 1974, pp. 236–242.

Rawls, John. *A Theory of Justice.* Cambridge, Massachusetts: Harvard University Press, 1971.

Rogers, Carl. *Client Centered Counseling.* Boston: Houghton Mifflin, 1951.

Rosnow, Ralph and Robinson, E., eds. *Experiments in Persuasion,* New York: Academic Press, 1967.

Rubin, David. *The Right of Teachers. The Basic ACLU Guide to a Teacher's Constitutional Rights.* New York: Avon Books, 1972.

Simon, Sidney B.; Howe, Leland W.; and Kirschenbaum, Howard. *Values*

*Clarification: A Handbook of Practical Strategies for Teachers and Students.* New York: Hart, 1972.

Tjosvold, Dean. "The Issue of Student Control: a Critical Review of the Literature." Paper presented at the American Educational Research Association Convention, San Francisco, April 1976.

Ward, Douglas, *Local Associations Eye Instruction and Professional Development.* National Education Association, 1974.

Whimby, Arthur. "You Can Learn to Raise Your I.Q. Score." *Psychology Today,* January 1976.

Wolcott, Harry F. *The Man in the Principal's Office.* New York: Holt, Rinehart and Winston, 1973.

.

# Index